Damned
from
Memory

Sparky McLaughlin

Damned from Memory, LLC / Swedesboro, N.J. USA

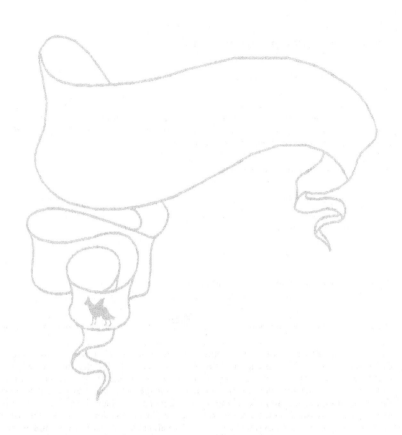

Damned from Memory

Printed in the United States of America

ISBN: 978-0-9884694-0-2

Learn more information at:

www.DamnedfromMemory.com

Damned from Memory: by Sparky McLaughlin

Published by: Damned from Memory, LLC.   P.O. Box 872, Swedesboro, N.J. 08085

For my Mom and Dad who passed on before knowing that I would be proven innocent and their faith in me when I told them, I hadn't done anything wrong. Of Course my Brother Frank and Sister Bonnie.

For My Wife who suffered as much, and at times, feared for her life, I will always be there to protect you.

For My Children Rob and Keara, and the rest of my family who stood by me and supported me all these years in my attempt to get to the truth.

For My Partners, Flash, Eggs, and Dennis. I have never known better men and would certainly withstand a firestorm, in defense of our reputations. We miss Dennis and his frankness in this age of deception.

For our Defenders of the Realm, Don Bailey, ESQ and Sam Stretton, ESQ. I have never nor will ever experience finer craftsman in support of the Constitution of the United States.

For my many K-9's: Casey, Blitz, Faolan, Brianna, Anya, and Finn, our protectors and extended family.

For my Compatriots in Arms, Ret. DEA S/A Mike Levine, Ret. DEA S/A Rick Horn, Ret. INS SS/A Joseph Occhipinti, Ret. CID S/A Tony Marceca, NYPD 34th Precinct's "Locomotion Squad."

For our investigative journalists and defenders through these many years, William Norman Grigg, Mike Rupert, Howard Altman, Jim Barry, Bill Conroy

For the greatest reactionary force in the streets of Philadelphia, The Philadelphia Police Highway Patrol, where your wings are "earned", not given.

For all the members of Region 9 and Region 2 that stood by us and did not walk away, especially "The Doctor", "Homey" and "Heat".

For all the citizens both individually and in groups that rallied to the unfounded allegations with tales of praise for our attempts in providing them a safer neighborhood.

And of course, Tommy

"It is not the critic who counts: not the man who points out how the strong man stumbles or where the doer of deeds could have done better.

The credit belongs to the man who is actually in the arena, whose face is marred by dust and sweat and blood, who strives valiantly, who errs and comes up short again and again, because there is no effort without error or shortcoming, but who knows the great enthusiasms, the great devotions, who spends himself for a worthy cause; who, at the best, knows, in the end, the triumph of high achievement, and who, at the worst, if he fails, at least he fails while daring greatly, so that his place shall never be with those cold and timid souls who knew neither victory nor defeat."

"Citizenship in a Republic"

Speech at the Sorbonne, Paris, April 23, 1910

Theodore Roosevelt

TABLE OF CONTENTS

Prologue

1995, Hope Street, Philadelphia: My partners and I are out hunting heroin dealers – hopefully a nice pinch. The tip comes in from an informant with a long *tail*, the length extending with each corroborated whisper that leads to an arrest. He is more right than wrong lately. Drug pinches are routine for me; I cannot remember a day without an arrest. Even the odd off-duty robbery arrests infiltrate my life to a point where the combination of on-duty and off duty arrests blurs together.

The neighborhood always looked the same: abandoned houses, cockroach covered walls moving in the dark, rats, no doors, no windows, and the *walking dead*, as we come to call the zombies who roam East division. Today feels different. We enter an abandoned house, some Agents are *hands free,* and some are carrying automatic MP5s. We make our way in through a dark empty hall to one huge room. The interior walls and ceilings are gone. Sunlight floods the place. I squint against the glare and the dust we kick up. There is a rainbow hanging high above the smell of death. No pot of gold here. The only sound comes from rats scratching on some aluminum sheets that board up the house.

The place is empty. Just one body lies dead in a maze of trash and rubble. The set of works from the community free give-away program stood shiny, new, and still stuck in his carotid artery. Same scene, same smells, but today is different for me. Everything is too bright, too sharp-edged. I start singing softly, "He's off to see the Wizard, the Wonderful Wizard of Oz" in a monotone, my partners stare at me. The irony gets to me. Here we are in what some call East, others the Land of Oz, the press terms it The Badlands, and I find myself once again singing, just above a whisper *Somewhere over the Rainbow* when all I ever see are death and destruction. The great and powerful Oz, which I recently equated with Al Gore and the Clinton Administration, once again fails to provide a solution to the drug war. They are somewhere in the bright sun, campaigning, shaking hands, probably enjoying a *Mama Juana*, a Dominican cocktail, with their supporters – all courtesy of the ten spot, this junkie and others like him spent to off himself.

All the connections are getting to me, running backward through my head. This guy, lying in his own vomit, probably stole from his own mother to buy the glassine packet of heroin supplied by the Dominican traffickers who write a fat check to Clinton and Gore who preach a War on Drugs. Traffickers in the Dominican Republic who are buying votes in the US and lining Bill and Hillary Clinton's and Vice President Al Gore's pockets supply the drugs dealt on Hope Street in Philadelphia. Gore accepted a check from them just the night before at Coogan's Bar in Washington Heights in the heart of the most notorious part of the Dominican drug trafficking area of New York City. The spoils of the War on Drugs are lining the pockets of the Clinton Administration.

I make the call to Homicide, and they will call the meat wagon. I will do my paperwork, and, like always, I will end my day asking myself, is this shit for real? Hope Street, of all places, in a house that looks like a twister hit it. No hope here.

For 19 years, until I was sidelined by forced withdrawal, I fought the Drug War on the streets of Philadelphia. I've never had a problem fighting the dealers and the addicts – it's the job I live for. What I have a problem with and what I am forced to withdraw from is fighting all the *good guys,* including my commanding officers, State officials, and Federal agents. I was a challenge to men and women in power who are supposed to be on the forefront of the War on Drugs.

As I find out the hard way, there are a whole lot of people in Federal, State, and Local Agencies who have agendas that fly in the face of law enforcement. My superiors gave my partners and me the moniker *Bastard Squad* because we won't back off of what we know is a major drug trafficking organization (DTO) that needs to be taken down, so now they isolate us from everyone else. No one is allowed to work with us; we are the bastard stepchildren. Word comes down that the CIA and the State Department are behind the orders; but I will tell you who the real bastards are. The way it plays out in the press is much different from the truth, but it's always that way, isn't it? Well, here is how it was reported.

In the fall of 1995, my partner, Charlie Micewski, aka the Flash, and I discovered that a Dominican Republic political party was raising campaign funds for Dominican Presidential candidate Pena Gomez by selling heroin and cocaine in Philadelphia and up and down the East coast. We worked with DEA agents in New York and attempted to seize half a million in campaign funds that we know came from drug deals. This campaign money was going to be given to the visiting Pena Gomez and his PRD delegation, and we knew when and where. We were to stop the entourage and confiscate the ill-gotten funds, but the State Department called the operation off. The U.S. State Department was backing Pena. I didn't give a shit.

Two weeks later, U.S. Attorneys and the local DA told the Office of Attorney General (OAG) they would no longer prosecute our cases. Over 80 accused drug dealers that we took off the street skated because of this decision.

My book takes the reader from my youth in Philadelphia through 34 years in law enforcement. I have no agenda, other than to tell the whole truth.

One of the agencies that most effectively blocked our efforts was the CIA. The CIA interference is documented. There's no conjecture here. I write the facts, including my firsthand knowledge, as they have been reported in every area of the media. The CIA ignored certain activities because these activities served their purposes. In the '80s and early '90s, the CIA helped keep the Haitian military and political leadership in power and in the process turned a blind eye to drug trafficking. They added positions to the CIA payroll for National Intelligence Service (SIN), which, ironically, was created to fight the cocaine trade. SIN officers, however, traffic drugs and aid some of the Haitian military and political leaders.

"We had problems in Haiti, where friends of ours -- that is, intelligence sources in the Haitian military -- had turned their facilities, their ranches and their farms over to drug traffickers. Instead of putting pressure on that rotten leadership of the Haitian military, we defended them. We held our noses, we looked the other way, and they and their criminal friends distributed, through a variety of networks, cocaine in the United States -- in Miami, in Philadelphia, New York and parts of Pennsylvania."- **(Jack Blum in testimony before Congress)**

My story follows Dominican traffickers, backed by Dominican politicians, who were backed by the U.S. State Department. It's a clear trail of drugs, money, and political deals.

Every agency has a mission and an agenda, and how each fulfills its mission often conflicts with other agencies' missions. My book explores these facts from a unique angle: I was one of the narcotic agents on the street who suffered the consequences. In trying to do the right thing every day, I was challenging people in high places who swore to uphold the law.

It just so happens that the losers in this game are citizens on the street, the kids who end up dying from crack and heroin, and the Narcs like me who risk their lives every day trying to make it all right.

***

Chapter 1

The Spark

My best friend's dad, Mr. Schraeder, spent his life as a Philadelphia Police Detective. Most people considered him "old school." He became my first role model in law enforcement, the kind of cop who cared about the junkie he took down in order to protect the citizens he served. He devoted his life to his job. He worked the street hard and did everything he could to keep the peace. I still have his obituary.

A retired lieutenant summed him up nicely, when he said, "Everyone wanted him along when they needed to hit a house or knock a door down or go after a holdup man. He was fearless, and he could never do enough for anybody. Once he made an arrest, he would turn around and do his best to rehabilitate the junkie. Many a time we went down to Dock Street and Larry would bum a bag of potatoes from a local market to make sure the [suspect's] family would have something to eat that night. He touched everyone with his humanity."

***

I got hooked on law enforcement early on. I wanted to know everything. When I used to go over Larry's house, we would go down to his basement and sneak through his father's files. We couldn't get enough of the details. He was a detective, and in those days, they handled everything, including narcotics. Larry's dad shot a drug dealer once after the guy was caught selling heroin out of his own baby's blanket – with the baby still in it. The dealer dropped the baby and ran to a rooftop with Larry's dad in pursuit. Mr. Schraeder shot the guy off the roof to the street below. Things are different now.

Mr. Schraeder was known to touch a drop or two of whiskey. One day after viewing files in the basement, I was going up the stairs, when *Whack*. Mr. Schraeder hit me in the head with a slapjack. A slapjack is a piece of iron surrounded by leather and sown into place so it cannot escape its sheath. It wasn't a hard shot, just a love tap. Mr. Schraeder said, "I hope I don't ever have to come get you boys and do that for real." Larry laughed. Mr. Schraeder hit Larry and said, "Don't think I forgot you."

My best friend Larry is a detective himself. At the beginning of his career, an occasional caller would ask, "Is this *the* Larry Schraeder?" His were big shoes to fill.

I'd been a cop my whole life. My career although based in Philadelphia had taken me through every part of the Delaware Valley and then some, chasing every kind of crook from petty thieves to international drug traffickers. I'd always taken law enforcement seriously, and I always will. It wasn't a paycheck that drove me every day; I was brought up to do the right thing. Too often fighting crime came before family and health, but never my reasoning. I was always two steps ahead of the criminal I was going to pinch, and I had the patience and determination to see the outcome and make it a reality.

This zeal for the job got me through special unit after special unit until I landed where I felt I found a home, surrounded by a crack team of Narcs that would make Philly sit up and take notice. Within two months of graduating from the Pennsylvania Attorney General's Bureau of Narcotics Investigation Academy, we were taking down two entire blocks in North Philly with over 400 members of *Philly's Phinest* in tow. In addition, we were aided by two helicopters, the National Guard, the Pennsylvania State Police, Immigration, Customs, DEA, Philadelphia Police Narcotics and K-9 Unit, Housing Police, the Philadelphia District Attorney's Office, and so forth. There were four of us: Dennis (aka Hoffa McKeefery), Eddie (aka Eggs Eggles), Charlie (aka Flash Micewski), and me, Sparky. Together we made so many arrests based on just one phone call Dennis' received, that a simple investigation blossomed into over 19 search warrants and eventually numerous life sentences and the dismantling of the Carlito Guitterez heroin and cocaine trafficking organization.

I learned from the best, and our inability to stop putting the pieces together collectively earned us the pejorative title of *The Bastard Squad* by our superiors and the unenviable status of *persona non gratis* by the local law enforcement community and officially by the Congreso Nacional de la República Dominicana (Dominican Republic National Congress).

There came a point in my career when my partners and I uncovered a Dominican Drug Trafficking Organization (DTO) doing business in Philadelphia. The members of the DTO had Federal protection – that's United States Federal protection. We were told to stop our investigation.

I said, "Yeah, right." I then circumvented every local, state, and federal agency that tried to stop me from doing my job.

***

Some might have considered my drive moronic, but there was no other way for me. I grew up in late '60s - early '70s in Philadelphia when violence was everywhere, and folks had to know where and when they could walk alone. Between the race riots, Vietnam War protests, assassinations, and the explosion in organized crime and drugs on the street, it seemed like everybody hated everyone else. It was all about turf: where you could walk in the neighborhood, which had rights, and to what gang you belonged. I grew up on Regent Street, southwest of center city below 58th Street and west of 30th Street Station and the River. We had a yard and a two-storied house. Hard working parents, who taught my siblings and me to be respectful of everybody, no matter their color or background, raised me. Sometimes as a kid, I worked as a laborer on side jobs next to black guys, and by the end of the day, we all ended up a pale grey color from the cement dust. I never understood the whole race issue because I was taught to ignore it.

There was a gang in my neighborhood called Dirty Annies, named after a store where the gang hung out. I wasn't sure if I was a wannabe or not, but an incident one day sealed the deal for me; I would not become a gang member. One of my classmates, Bubbles Morone, just a neighborhood kid, was stabbed to death by a black gang for no apparent reason; he was alone and helpless. The mob violence was pure, random hatred, and it made me angry.

A bunch of us went looking for revenge, on who I never knew, for we never learned who stabbed Bubbles. Shit, I didn't even really know him. He was in my grade at West Catholic, but other than that, I didn't know him. What was I thinking? I started heading home. I was alone, roaming the streets and searching for God knows what, when I was confronted by 400 young black guys coming down Cobbs Creek Parkway. They were picking up chains and any kind of makeshift weapon they could find. I ran to find the other guys and told them to get the hell out of the neighborhood, but I was too late. By the time I found them, the throng was closing in on us. We ran to a church at 58th and Chester Ave. This was it; I knew we were going to die.

The cops arrived. Two SEPTA buses pulled up, and the Boot Cops emptied out and formed a skirmish line between us and the crowd, which the news reported as over 500 by that point. The Boot Cops (the Highway Patrol) did not wade into the crowd or shout; they just stood their ground. We froze and watched as the cops did their stutter stepping, a half step at a time. The sound of their boots hitting the asphalt in front of them made the walls shake. They moved into a "V" type wedge and kept going forward, with the "V" getting larger and larger. The crowd parted like the Red Sea. No injuries, no nonsense but a lasting memory and a turning point in my life. I wanted that respect. Some say it may have been fear, but I believe it was the professionalism that the crowd couldn't deal with; they knew those guys weren't going to put up with any nonsense, no matter who you were. It was like watching an expeditionary force; they came, they saw, they removed the threat, they left. They won the battle by acting and moving as one, no emotion, just a job to do.

Ok, I was in. Where did I sign up?

***

Chapter 2

Special Units

I could not afford to live on any college campus, so when I got a score of 1146 on my SAT, my first consideration wasn't the best school; it was where could I get off the number 13 trolley and still come home every day.

The only logical choice in my mind at the time was Drexel University at in Philadelphia. The trolley stopped in the middle of the campus, and at the time, I could buy tokens wholesale, which made my commute even more cost effective.

In retrospect, although I was accepted into the five-year co-op business administration program, I could have used better counseling in making my choice. I left Drexel after my first year because I got lost in the crowd in that type of setting.

I needed some *Do, Re, Me* in the summer of 1975, so I applied and was accepted as a Skilled Distribution Worker or *SDW* as they liked to call those who dug ditches for the Philadelphia Gas Works. I took the Philadelphia Police Department civil service test and scored a 98.5 out of a possible 100. However, because of federally mandated court rulings, certain minorities, women applicants, and veterans were given preferential treatment and were awarded 10 extra percentage points on the same test. This action by the Philadelphia Police set me back on the waiting list, and I wasn't called until late June of 1977. Then I was set to start the Police Academy the first week in July. I asked for two weeks' vacation from the Philadelphia Gas Works and gave my two weeks' notice at the same time. My son Robert was born days earlier, so I could not afford to miss a paycheck.

***

"Stay alert, Stay alive, Read directive 45"

I bet that every graduate of the Philadelphia Police Academy Class 241 has taken or will take that phrase with them to the grave. It was the directive concerning Driver Safety, taught by Sergeant Thomas. It was the last thing I remember en route to my first assignment at the 17th Police District at 20th and Federal Street in South Philadelphia.

Our entire Academy Class, Number 241 along with Class 240, was assigned to replace seasoned veterans, some of whom were recently indicted for federal corruption charges. The sweeping FBI probe stated that "widespread corruption" permeated the entire district. That was all the top police Brass had to hear. Whether the rumor was accurate or not, the Brass was going to make sweeping changes, even if the transfers meant sending all rookies to the district without anyone to show them the ropes.

Captain Jack Carini, increasingly frustrated, kept coming to roll calls and vowing that the next officer who *car-stopped* him in his unmarked Ford on his way through the district would be walking a beat under the Schuylkill River. The press had a field day lately with the corruption probe, and soon the district was full of rookies who stopped everything that moved. A car-stop occurs when a police officer pulls over a vehicle for an obvious infraction of the vehicle code or if an officer in the line of official duty was responding to a crime in progress. The first car on the scene put out what is called *flash information,* and the officer stops anyone who fits the description given by the flash information. Flash Information has become generalized. The information could be something as *there are 2 b/m's approx. 23, dark skin blue jeans, with black hoodies that were last seen escaping south on 17th from the scene in a black Ford. No further description at this time.*

With nothing but rookies in a district, every black Ford within a certain radius of the crime scene was stopped, and quite often, it was the Captain, even though he was white.

***

The call about a child being trapped in a burning house came in over police radio. As was the procedure in Philadelphia, the police were dispatched as soon as or before *fireboard.* Fireboard was the term in Philadelphia that identified every piece of Fire Department equipment and manpower by the Philly PD. The first officer to arrive was Nick Manini, who raced to the second floor but was beat back by smoke. Being in 179 car, I was next to arrive and saw flames and smoke pouring out of the second floor of a two story brick building. As I ran inside and up to the second floor, I immediately started crawling on the floor with my handkerchief around my nose and yelling for anyone who could hear my voice. The fire was overwhelming. I could feel my shoes melting, and someone pulling at my leg to come back. I crawled back and down the steps. Four of us had attempted to find this child who was reportedly lost in the fire.

The good news was that the child, unbeknownst to her mother, had slipped out and gone to a neighbor's house before the fire started. She had no injuries, but she was unaccounted for at the time the distraught mother arrived on the scene.

The firefighters treated us on the scene for smoke inhalation, and we found out later that Captain Carini had put the four of us in for heroism commendations. The heroism commendation was one of the top awards the department gave out, and I was going to receive it at a ceremony attended by the Mayor, the Police Commissioner, and the press. This was a photo op. We were to be prepared to have our photo taken by many people and to be happy about it, and that was an order. I did not understand the commendation at the time, for we did not save anybody, but I found later that we were being used as political pawns.

This formerly beleaguered and corruption riddled police district received so much bad press, it needed a shot in the political arm, and we were the injection into the front pages.

***

K-9 UNIT

I had definite reasons for getting into the K-9 unit. One day, when I was still in my younger years (just three years) on the force and still assigned to the 17th police district, my partner, Lionel Barris, an African American male, thirty five, and I responded to a foot beat chasing a shooting suspect toward us. Heavy ice and snow covered the ground. We both got out of the RPC (Radio Patrol Car) and started chasing the B/M, a kid, 17-19. The driver should never leave; instead, he should drive ahead, cut off the suspect, and trap him between the two police officers so that it was easier to catch him. Well, three blocks later we arrived at 2321 Mountain Street; I will never forget the address. The kid banged on the door just as we caught him and started yelling, "Dad, Dad, help...the cops are dragging me away," as we were arresting him. As we started down the steps, out came this guy built like a brick shithouse and arms like cantaloupes. He got in on the fray and said, "You ain't taking my son away."

Big fight, we weren't winning, but we weren't losing either; however, because we did not carry handsets in those days, no re-enforcements were coming over the horizon.

On his own, my partner decided, to leave me. He said, "I'll go get help," and disappeared.

There I was, fighting a guy by myself, and I can't shoot him. The situation was not that far along in the force continuum; he was just resisting, but he was pretty damn good at it. Again, I wasn't winning or losing. Minutes seemed like hours until I heard sirens. Two Boot Cops from the Highway Patrol were the first to arrive on the scene where we were fighting on the steps. The Highway Patrol in Philadelphia was like John Wayne and the Calvary; you breathed a sigh of relief.

A melee ensued, and we won, but I did not see my partner Barris for some time until I wound up at the Detective division a little bit later. The old school detectives took me inside, and after I told them what happened, they took me in to the Inspector. He wanted to know if I wanted to take "Barris" *to the front* (prefer charges) for cowardice. I never considered it. I was still trying to put back pieces of my shirt that were ripped and bloodstained.

Later, on my way home, I realized how bad this incident could have been. You see, we didn't pick partners. There was a federally mandated racial mixing of partners to get some grant money. I never considered race; it was the officer inside the blue shirt, who either had it or not. My next partner was handpicked by me, another black male named *Smitty,* who liked to work. In the meantime, I put in for a transfer to the K-9 unit.

Sgt. Rob Stilson grabbed me outside the operations room one morning after roll call and told me my transfer to the K-9 unit came through. I was to report to the Academy on Monday April 1, 1980.

The first day of K-9 training is designated as *Cherry Day*. Cherry Day is when you get into what is known in K-9 circles as the *Philadelphia Wrap*, and get to extend your suit coat-covered, wrapped arm to one of Philadelphia's Phinest Land Sharks. Thus the moniker Cherry Day. The picture of a K-9 decoy with an oversized sleeve taking on a working line German shepherd and walking away unscathed was not an appropriate portrait painted on this April Fool's day at 8501 State Road.

The Philadelphia Wrap is a leather gauntlet tied like a corset around one's forearm, covered with burlap. It is used with a Goodwill suit jacket worn over the decoy to simulate a street situation.

The 750 pounds of pressure per square inch of a German shepherd's bite is enough to bring down the cop with the biggest mouth or the district hot shot. Standing two feet away from a barking, snarling apprehension-trained German shepherd that was going to clamp down on your arm as hard as he could was a life altering experience. Then there was the *re-bite*. The K-9 trainers did not tell me that little tidbit until Max was already on my arm and growling like a crocodile about to take me under. The K-9 handler says, "Freeze," and I heard, "Get 'em." The re-bite is when the K-9 adjusts his grip for a better hold; in other words, he sinks his teeth in further. The re-bite is when the tallest of men come crashing down to their knees.

I got the word the next day that I had successfully passed Cherry Day and would be staying on in K-9. There were two conditions; one concerned everyone. While going through K-9 initial training, which is sixteen weeks long, no one went IOD, (injured on duty). It is an unwritten rule. For those that want to go out injured or IOD for every little, or not so little, bite or puncture, it looked bad for the K-9 unit to the Brass and would also look bad to the workmen's compensation attorneys. It was also the K-9 trainer's way of saying that you just weren't up to snuff, for the position, if you didn't make the grade.

Not much bothered me. I was the decoy one day at an abandoned sanitarium where we ran the dogs in the building. I hid with the trainer, and when the dog found us, we banged on the closet door to get the K-9 barking. The handler hooked the K-9 up and escorted us out of the building. Occasionally on my way out, I turned and teased the K-9 to keep him excited and on guard. Unless I was specifically going to take a *hit,* I would not be *wrapped,* moreover, often in just a tee shirt and jeans. Wrapped means wearing a protective sleeve, to protect the person taking the hit, or in common terms, the canine bite. Well on two occasions, two different handlers, while escorting me down the steps, could not hold onto their K-9s. They fell and accidently released their dogs.

The K-9s did their jobs and came running to apprehend me. The only thing to do was to stick my arm as far into their mouths and hold their heads on my arm until their handlers could reach them to hook them up. The dogs hadn't learn to fully *recall* as of yet, for they had just started training, so I ended up with some nice punctures.

I did not report the accidental bites officially because the handlers would get in trouble. Being berated and screamed at by the trainers was punishment enough for their mistakes, that and cleaning up the kennels and other just as unpleasant tasks. Seasoned cops keep quiet about such things.

Second, as for me, there was one spot left in this class, and it was mine, if I didn't screw up. A trainer, Ed Tillman, came up to me and said, "Listen, there's only one dog left back there; the other trainer washed him out because he was gun shy, but I looked into his background. He came from an attorney who lives out in the suburbs. I don't think the dog was ever exposed to noise in the right way. This dog was pureblood and met the standard except for one crooked left ear."

I said, "I'll take him."

Ed replied, "I'll work with you on lunches. Eat quickly, and we'll spend the rest of your lunch hour bringing him out of the shyness."

Casey turned out to be the best apprehension K-9 ever, despite noise, debris, water...you name it. Our first building search, and his first test, came from a request outside Philadelphia.

Lower Merion Township PD called the *Roundhouse* (Philadelphia Police Headquarters) switchboard on a Sunday morning looking for a Police K-9 for a building search where they knew they had at least one perpetrator still inside.

I was on the elevated train station platform when the call came over the Police radio that I was going to be picked up by a wagon crew and transported to a steel warehouse inside of Lower Merion Township. I shit myself. Not only was this going to be my first building search, but also I was on the line with another department and representing the entire Philadelphia Police department.

Upon arrival, I went through everything in my head and started asking all the right questions concerning the perimeter being secure, any known hazards, any areas that the suspect was heard to be, inside the building.

Shit, I sounded professional, even though my stomach was doing the final scene in *Titanic*. Casey, my K-9, was pumped too. Somehow, he knew he was in the limelight and was more than ready. We went to the entrance, and I made my announcement: "This is the Police, I have an attack trained K-9. If you don't come out, I will release the K-9."

After making two subsequent announcements and receiving no response, it was time to send Casey to do what he was trained to do. Casey was uncanny in his organized hunt, his nose to the ground. Almost immediately, he went to a 12-foot pile of steel plates and I-beams. I could not see anyone and called him off. Casey ran throughout the warehouse but kept going back to that pile of steel. I took Casey outside to give him water, for the warehouse was a football field long, and just as wide.

We went back inside the warehouse. Casey started immediately to the same pile of steel plates. Casey had this unusual way of zeroing in on the suspect, and that's what he was doing. He was panting heavily, his breathing getting heavier and heavier. He was going faster and faster... now he was trotting.

My mind wandered to Bill Cosby's *Wonderfulness Album* in which he does the skit "The Chicken Heart that Ate New York." I could just see the suspect in his hide, as he listened to the sound of Casey's breathing, getting heavier and heavier, closer and closer; the suspect's heart, of course, must have been racing and popping out of his chest as he listened, much like the description that Bill Cosby gives… "Thump Thump, THUMP…THUMP, THUMP… THUMP."

Just as Casey seemed like he was about to strike, he put on the brakes, took a giant snootful of air, which sounded like something getting sucked through a vacuum hose, and a millisecond later he was totally silent tilting his head upward. He let out a blood curdling series of barks and growls that surely must have had the suspect smearing in his pants, whatever substance he just involuntarily secreted. However, unlike Bill Cosby's character, the suspect's excreted smear had to be a classic reaction to the fight or flight response. However, in his case, he could not flee or fight for fear of exposure, so chemicals like adrenaline and cortisol, that released into his bloodstream, needed a way out.

Casey looked at me and looked back at the steel plates, and if he were human, he would have said, "Yo, snap out of it. I found him, now get off your ass and get up there and get him; even you must smell him by now." I started climbing up the plates, and as I got to the top, I found the suspect wedged in between an I-beam, where he could not be seen. I did smell him however. The *Land Shark* made him shit his pants. I commanded him to come out. Casey started barking even louder, jumping up in the air as the suspect started to slide out of his refuge. However, upon his getting his footing, he apparently thought he could make another escape. I physically stopped him, and a short fight ensued. I say short, because I still do not know how he got up there, but Casey flew out of what seemed like thin air. I did not even hear him coming at first, except there was the sound of toenails across steel, and he clamped down on the suspects leg and started humping him away from me. The screams of the suspect had the Lower Merion Police, who were outside the building, broadcasting over the radio, asking if we needed any help. I told them, "Just a first aid kit. Apprehension made by Casey Badge #K329."

I learned the hard way to trust again, but trust I did, in a four footed partner that I learned would never run the other way. Casey and I became inseparable on the job and off. It took the Philadelphia Sentinel newspaper and a load of political pressure to end our partnership on the job.

I was injured while going after a couple of strong-arm robbery suspects; Casey went after one, I grabbed the other, but twisted my ankle in the process. During my recovery, I was sent to the K-9 unit on restricted duty, when I started reading about alleged "Unprovoked Philadelphia Police K-9 attacks." My name was never mentioned. I read the stuff for several months, going nuts over how the press was maligning these guys, and the Police Department was not allowing them to say anything. All along, I was thinking I'm glad I'm not involved, but I really feel bad for those guys. The people who were being written about in the paper were taken off the street and just languished at the Police K-9 unit kennel, hiding from the press, at the orders of the top Brass.

When I was released to go back to full duty, I was called into Sergeant Walsh's office, and told that I was also off the street. I went off. I had only thirteen *hits* or canine apprehensions in over seventy-seven part one arrests in four years with no complaints, and no one sued me. I now became one of *Malimows Maulers*. Malimow was the name of the Sentinel reporter writing the articles. His reporting was so one sided I made up a new slogan. "In Philadelphia not only is Justice Blind, it's been run over by a truck driven by Bill Malimow."

What they did to us was a crime. Our rights were violated every day. When the press came up to the academy, they ordered us to hide in trucks, filled with the donated suit jackets that we used to put over our hit sleeves. It was 85 to 90 degrees, and we were in metal trucks with the doors closed. We baked. We were off the street for a long period, about six months, and never interviewed by anyone, not even internally, until the FBI, who never interviewed anyone either, finally cleared us.

Cops have a sick sense of humor, and we got those invisible dog leashes and drove the K-9 supervisors crazy. We heard that the press was coming up to the Academy, and one of the cops would have the *invisible dog,* attack one of the other K-9 cops who would roll around on the ground outside the supervisor's window, right before the press arrived. We drove them crazy. I made jackets up that said Malimow's Maulers, we all wore them in front of the Brass to and from work, and there wasn't anything they could do about our choice of off-duty clothing. They would not let us talk, so we protested in our own way.

The Police Officer who was on permanent limited duty, pumped gas just outside of our office, and he was prone to fall asleep in his chair. One day when he did, we got jumper cables, attached them to his chair (metal), hooked them to a battery (negative at first), and then slammed the door so he would wake up just as one of the guys was pretending to connect the positive charge; I think he's still running. That was how bad it was, and that is how angry we were when we found out by reading the Sentinel one morning that we were kicked out of the K-9 unit. The Police K-9 supervisors have the decency to tell us personally the day before we were expelled. I became the voice of *Malimow's Maulers* and, called the Mayor, the Managing Director, and finally the Police Commissioner, demanding a meeting to explain why we had just got the shaft.

Commissioner Samuel Gregorian agreed to meet with us, and the next day I found myself in the Roundhouse outside the Commissioner's office in a conference room. Gregorian started the meeting by saying that we did not do anything wrong and that the decision to take us off the street was out of his hands. He added that if anyone tried to quote him, he would deny taking us off the street for political reasons. The Commissioner further stated that he did not have a problem with us going back into K-9 but with another dog and attending another 16-week training program. I went off on him.

"Commissioner, with all due respect, what if we do what you say and we're on the street one day, but now we're bums, we don't want to make arrests, we just want a gas card like the rest of these do-nothings. Moreover, say a heinous crime was committed in front of us as we walked around a corner, and we have no choice but to deploy the K-9 to do what he is trained to do, apprehend the bad guy. Say the papers get a hold of the fact that it's one of us and that starts making a splash that we're out here again. Are you going to guarantee that we won't be taken out of K-9 again?"

The answer came as one word, "No."

"Well, why would I ever want to go back into K-9 in this department? I do have one request respectfully," I said, speaking for all of us. "Can we have some input into where we go from here?"

I was on a roll and felt I had nothing to lose.

Gregorian in a monotone spoke softly: "Ok, that seems fair. Pick three units or districts, and I personally will schedule interviews and if the commanding officers of any of those units accept you, you are transferred immediately."

I made the best of a bad situation and was on my way to the Philadelphia Highway Patrol; I just needed to get past Captain Edward Stagler.

***

Highway Patrol

The interview was etched in stone, one time only, Bustleton and Bowler, Blouse Coat and Sam Browne Holster and as for the holster, it had better be spit-shined.

As I entered the driveway at Highway Patrol, the row of *Wheels* lined up against the wall was one awesome sight. The glint coming off the chrome froze me in the driveway until I heard, "Hey kid, don't be lookin' at them there motorcycles; you ain't been properly introduced."

I found out later that this fireplug of a man, who was called No-Neck for obvious reasons, was one of the baddest asses I ever had, or would ever have, the pleasure to know.

I found my way to the Captain's office and his clerk, Eddie Mazzola, had me waiting in the vestibule. Butterflies, the size of Mothra from the old Japanese Sci-Fi movies, invaded my stomach.

"Officer McLaughlin, Captain Stagler will see you now."

Oh, shit! Here we go!

Saluting, I replied, "Good morning Sir, Officer McLaughlin reporting for an Interview.

"Interview, what's this about an interview. I didn't schedule an interview."

"Sir, the Commissioner's office apparently scheduled the interview. I was just told to be here at this time for you to interview me as to my qualifications to become a member of Highway Patrol."

"Says who... I pick all my own people."

Great, now I really had him pissed off, I might as well go for broke.

"Sir, I'm one of the guys who were in the K-9 Unit and was removed recently because of bad press. We were given an opportunity to pick three places and if accepted by the Commanding Officer, we will be transferred."

"Great, I have an elite unit and they send me a fuck up."

"Who do you think you're talking to?" he had gotten my Irish up.

"Excuse me?"

"Sir, with all due respect, I hope that comment wasn't directed at me because if you're relying on what you have read in the papers regarding the K-9 situation, first, you have it all wrong, Second, never believe what you read in the papers, and third and foremost, nowhere except in a summary of the number of bites my K-9 was credited with, will you see my name in any paper.

"Well why are you in trouble?"

"I'm not in trouble; I'm just out there every day doing my job and not just collecting a paycheck and a gas card. I didn't do anything wrong. The papers just compared us with K-9 officers that are assigned stationery security details, and others that don't do shit."

"Good answer. You will hear from someone one way or the other soon. You're dismissed"

***

August 17, 1984, was a great day for being at the shore in Sea Isle, New Jersey. It is traditional that my family goes to the shore close to my mother and father's wedding anniversary, which is August10, 1940. I just returned to my shore house and checked my home answering machine. There was a message to call Highway Patrol immediately.

"This is Police Officer McLaughlin; I got a message to call in."

"Hold for the Captain."

"Welcome aboard McLaughlin. Be here ready to go tomorrow 8:00 a.m. I 'm taking a chance here, so don't disappoint me."

"Ahhh, Sir, I didn't know when or if you'd be calling so I took my son on vacation."

"Starting already, huh, Mac? OK be here Monday, that is, if you can fit it in to your schedule."

"Thank you, sir. I'll be there."

***

His name was Bobby Dennehey, but he called himself Jesus; so I was now partnered in Highway Patrol in the Line Squad with God the Son. I kept getting weird looks from other boot cops. I figured it concerned trust, who I was, and how I got into this special unit. I found out later the looks were more about how long I was going to last with Jesus. Bobby gave new meaning to the word crazy, but in a good way. As we stopped in various districts along our way, I heard stories of Bobby putting live chickens in other officers lockers, dressed up in full Police holster, fake gun, and hat, with a badge.

This follows the fact that Jesus was assigned to work the K-9 vehicle while his normal RPC (radio patrol car) was down for mechanical repairs. Bobby didn't take too kindly to the smell of the K-9 vehicle, so in retaliation, he went to the Italian Market, bought a live chicken, dressed it up in full Police regalia, and started walking his beat at Broad and Ellsworth at St. Rita's with the chicken on a leash.

The problem was that the Commissioner at the time was Frank L. Rizzo, who lived in South Philadelphia off Broad Street, drove northbound every day, and made it a point to check every beat along the way while en route to City Hall.

The call came quickly over the citywide J-Band channel of Police Radio one morning, I was told it went something like this:

"Car 1 to 17 Command."

"17 Command, go ahead, Sir."

"Car 1, you have a 302 (certifiably insane person) in uniform walking a live uniformed chicken at Broad and Ellsworth. Get that lunatic and his chicken into Headquarters immediately and report to me ASAP in-person."

"17 Command, understood."

"Car 1."

"Yes Sir."

"FYI, at least they both are wearing their hats, which is an improvement as of late, but I need to know how he gets the chicken to salute."

Jesus (allegedly) went down to internal affairs to be interviewed, took out all his nut shit, and put it on the Inspector's desk. His nut shit included his identification as a reverend in the Sun Yung Moon church. He told the Inspector so many different stories that he ended up getting only a day or two suspension and a transfer to the 35th district.

This occurred, of course, before he was transferred to the Highway Patrol.

So here I was with a legend, patrolling Philadelphia in an unmarked car, responsible only to make arrests and respond to major events.

It was cold as hell as we pulled up across from the Third World Asian bar at 49th and Catherine. Jesus, of course, was driving when he spotted a black male in an army jacket that just didn't seem right to him. His word for every suspect was Zippy, so it was not unusual for him to get my attention by saying, "check Zippy out."

My radar went up, for Jesus was rarely wrong. As we slowly drove alongside the three males standing outside the lounge, Zippy bolted, with me throwing open the door in foot pursuit, heart racing, eyes scanning, looking for hands and what was attached to them, as Zippy turned into an alley. As I hit the alley, I was faced with blue steel pointed in my direction and what in my heart, I heard, was the pounding of the hammer hitting the cylinder of a bullet casing. Instinctively, I dove to the side and didn't hear an explosion. I bolted upright to see Zippy frozen for a millisecond, dumbfounded that he misfired. That millisecond was all I needed to catch up and snatch Zippy as he was trying to go through a window of an abandoned house. I was able to disarm him and recover the weapon, but he managed to kick loose and escape through the window of the abandoned house.

Bobby moved to the other end to cut the suspect off and met me in the alley. He already called an Assist Officer, which was a radio call that means a cop needs help. Now there were Boot Cops everywhere. Boot Cop is the vernacular in the City of Philadelphia for the Highway Patrol because we wear boots and britches, technically, because we ride motorcycles as well.

In the tough neighborhoods and all the surrounding areas, we were just known as Boot Cops.

The area was blanketed and the only place that the suspect could not possibly be was back in the bar, or so we thought.

Jesus said, "Come on, let's check the bar."

Inside, we found the suspect, heart pounding, in a booth. He had traded jackets with a female; however, the sleeves on the jacket only reached past his elbow. Bobby handcuffed him, ever so gently, and we took him to West Detective Division for processing.

The weapon showed that there was one bullet, which the hammer struck, but misfired. Zippy was charged with Attempted Murder, weapons charges, etc., and I later found out that my Sergeant put me in for a Bravery commendation. What meant more to me at the time was that when we got back to headquarters at Highway, Jesus told other Line Squad members that I was "all right."

Another night, we were patrolling East Division when we heard gunshots. This was a normal occurrence in East division, but these were closer, followed by screeching tires. We were now trolling for armed predators. We intercepted a late model Olds at a high rate of speed and were off in pursuit. I grabbed the radio, but Bobby yelled, "Don't put it out yet!"

"Why!"

"They'll stop us. It's against policy, but these guys are strapped, and we gotta snatch'em."

"Watch Zippy on your side, he's reachin' under."

"Got it."

"Hold on, I gotta ram them."

"OK, you realize we're doing a buck ten."

"Oh, OK Nancy, I'll put a seatbelt on."

"Thanks, Jesus, I know you're all powerful and all that shit, but I don't want to see you ascend right now. I may need a back-up when I pinch these guys."

"Details, details...OK ...Hold on... ramming speeeeed."

We whacked the rear of the vehicle on Hunting Park Avenue, sending them into a spin and a stop, with a resulting minor crash against a light pole.

We skidded to a stop, ran over, and saw that two of the males had weapons in their hands and were starting to raise them in our direction. We both drew down from a defensive position. Jesus shot the driver and the other passenger in the front, gave up. The male in the back wanted to do a "John Wayne" as he was getting out of the car, but Bobby swung him into me. I hit him with a good right. I guess it was a lucky punch because the suspect fell like a downed tree in the forest, except he made noise, kind of like a splat, with blood squirting everywhere. We recovered three semi-automatics, and the guns all showed signs of just being fired recently.

The Sergeant put us in for another Bravery Commendation, but again later I got a better comment from Bobby to the rest of the Line Squad. "The kid can hit."

"Ahhh shit, we have some damage on the car" Bobby sighed.

"Well, we got a good pinch, we won't get jammed."

"Stay Alert..."

"Don't finish it...I get it...No reportable accidents...OK what do we do?"

"We take it to where I take Mr. Benz; it's always ready in a day, no extra charge."

Mr. Benz was Bobby's classic Mercedes Benz that we took to be serviced. We worked two tours of duty – 6 p.m. to 2 a.m., and one tour of day work from 8 a.m. to 4 p.m. It seemed like every day work, I followed Bobby to his house where he always announced as we walked into his house, "I keep my mother in a closet." I initially had to agree because I always heard her voice from somewhere in the house, but I never saw her.

We picked up his Mercedes Benz and took it to a mechanic in South Philly. I never knew what was being repaired, but by the way Bobby drove, it could be anything.

Partners get on each other's nerves from time-to-time and little quirks sometimes become bigger issues. Such was the case between us. I ended up partnered with P/O Joe Reardon. Joe and I were a good match most of our partnership, and we made many commendable arrests, one of which specifically comes to mind.

A call came over Police radio of a truck just stolen; Green NJ Lic/GRJ-279, last seen headed northbound on Seventh Street from Tioga. We were on Seventh, headed southbound. I was filling out our log when I looked up and across from us, at the stop sign, was the vehicle that was just reported stolen.

"Joe, that truck was just stolen. Turn around and come up along its side."

Joe stopped beside the truck, but in front of it, just a tad too much.

I told the driver that he just rolled the stop sign, and I needed to see his driver's license and registration. While the driver feigned reaching for his registration in the glove compartment, I stepped up on the truck's running board and tried to reach in to take the keys. The driver looked back and hit the gas slamming me against the open car door, which buckled under the pressure and blunt force of my weight. The suspect dragged me, hanging on the outside of the truck onto Roosevelt Blvd. It was a six-lane highway, and the suspect repeatedly slammed me against the guardrail.

Enough! The driver was trying to kill me, and I needed to stop him even if I needed to use deadly force to do it. The things that go through your mind when you're about to shoot someone for the first time are not exactly what should be taking precedent.

"Am I far enough along the Force Continuum?"

"Will I get suspended or fired if I made the wrong decision?"

"How do I explain this to Internal Affairs?"

"Is Internal Affairs out to get all Policemen?"

The only question that suddenly took over was *"Is this guy trying to kill me?"*

The answer was "Yes" but still I hesitated; I needed to give him a chance.

I found myself saying aloud, "I'm going to shoot you, if you don't stop, I'm not kidding."

"All right already," I was saying to myself, *"Shoot him. But where? If I shoot him in the head he'll crash and I'll still get hurt. Worse, if I shoot him in the stomach, he'll crash, and the truck will roll over on me, and I'll get hurt.*

Oh shit, here comes a tractor-trailer, and he's going to put me in front of it. I got it; I'll shoot him in the ass. He'll jam his foot at least...well maybe. Here goes."

I reached in, put the muzzle of my revolver against his hip, and pulled the trigger. The shot went off with a loud bang. The suspect yelled "OOWWW," and stopped the truck.

The suspect started to get out the other side. After my initial shock that he was still mobile, I reached in and put him in a headlock.

"Joe, *Officer Involved Shooting,*" I yelled back to Joe who was trailing, with lights and siren.

"Get your ass up here and cuff this guy. He's trying to get away."

Joe ran up, cuffed the scumbag, and turned to me as the troops were arriving.

"Spark, are you hurt?"

"I don't know." I found myself saying.

"You *gotta* be. Did you see the doorjamb of Highway 41? You crushed it."

Although the entire incident only took what seemed like minutes, it felt like hours. The adrenaline that was still overflowing blocked my pain receptors. I didn't feel a thing.

It did however wear off; and I found myself sitting down on the ground, wobbling to my feet only as Sergeant Blount approached me, to give him my weapon, as is the procedure in any officer involved shooting.

The Sergeant saw me wobble and the next thing I knew I was that I was shouldered by several Highway Patrolmen who took me to a waiting Highway Patrol Vehicle, and I was off to the hospital.

The hospital became a sea of Brass, half telling me I was not allowed to say anything except to Internal Affairs, and the other half on the phone to other Brass Hats, and the media. The detectives, of course, were already there, and asked short pertinent questions. I was told it was a good shooting.

I finally exhaled.

The Sergeant put me in for another Bravery Commendation, but again I took another step in the eyes of the

Highway Patrol... my first shooting. Upon my return to work, I was greeted with signs on my locker that read "Ride'em Cowboy." There were even a few cowboy hats sent my way because of the stories in the press about my rodeo style arrest.

I was now a Boot Cop.

***

Bureau of Narcotics Investigation

Attorney General Ernie Preate created a Bureau of Narcotics Investigation Task Force in Philadelphia, first headquartered at Old Swedes Church at Delaware and Washington Avenue. Ernie pulled some of the top talent from the Major Investigation Unit of the Narcotics Division of the Philadelphia Police Department by advertising higher salaries to start, and better health benefits. Many of the top talent jumped camp. This was a bold move; for the Attorney General's office was traditionally a Republican held Office. They were infiltrating a Democratically run District Attorney's area of responsibility, along with a primarily Democratic voter database, and publicly held offices.

Edward "Eggs" Eggles, Dennis McKeefery, John D'Amato, their Sergeant Thomas Litcello, and their Lieutenant John Sanderson are five of the top Narcotics officers that were the first to leave the highly respected Major Investigations Unit (MIU) of the Narcotics Division, which was located at 4th and Girard Avenue in Philadelphia in the East Division of the Police Department.

***

November 22, 1989

Agent Eddy Booten, a former Philadelphia Police Detective, now a BNI Narcotics Agent, inadvertently stumbles onto a group of Hispanic males whom he thought suspicious. He observed them for a while and saw that they were picking up what he believed to be a delivery of cocaine at 11102 ½ S. Front St. in Philadelphia. Agt. Booten went back to his headquarters to get other BNI Agents for back up and further surveillance. Unbeknownst to Agt. Booten, Agents Bartin and Wensley are in the midst of a meeting with the Philadelphia District Attorney's office (Bartin and Wensley are detailed to the District Attorney's Office) over impending arrest warrants from a non-consensual wiretap investigation that they undertook. Agt. Booten and other agents stop a group of Hispanic males, pursuant to probable cause and recover an amount of cocaine, Agents went back to 11102 ½ South Front St. and covered the front and back of the property, waiting for the search warrant application to be approved and to secure a search of the premises. Agents while in the back of the property heard glass break and saw a Hispanic male try to escape. They apprehended him. Knowing that the agents were seen, the command structure made a decision to secure the property and await the search warrant. The search warrant was obtained through the Philadelphia District Attorney's office and served, and approximately seven kilos of cocaine and $52,000.00 were confiscated.

The Philadelphia District Attorney's office was working a long-term investigation that included many buys, video surveillances, and non-consensual communication interceptions. BNI agents (not Agt. Booten) were working alongside the District Attorney's office. The DA'S office later accused the Attorney General's Bureau of Narcotics Investigation of interfering with their investigation although the DA's office didn't have probable cause. They did not have any knowledge of the address of 11102 ½ South Front St. or what role this address played in their investigation. Sgt. Jerry Roberts of the Philadelphia District Attorney's Dangerous Drugs Offender Unit made all the accusations from the DA's office.

The relationship between the Philadelphia's DA's Office and the Pennsylvania BNI was like oil and vinegar; the agencies would mix from time to time, but would always separate, on some issue. I would eventually find out, the mixture was terminal for my personal career.

March 16, 1991

The Office of Attorney General opened up a Task Force at 7801 Essington Avenue, comprised of Philadelphia Police, Pennsylvania State Police and Office of the Attorney General Bureau of Narcotics Agents. Agent Micewski (who at the time was still Sgt. Micewski) was assigned from the Philadelphia Police Highway Patrol along with four Highway Patrolmen.

At the same time that I heard about this detail, there were some bad rumors on the street concerning my partner, Joe Reardon. I worked solo on numerous occasions, especially on day work, or when Joe was having practice for the Highway Patrol Drill Team, which was quite often. Paid and unpaid Informants approached me and asked what was up with my partner.

"Albert, what do you mean, what's up with my partner?"

"You know when he be stoppin' somebody and telling them to take all the money out of their pockets and hold it in their hands?"

"Yeah, I never touch anybody's money either, unless I'm locking them up for drugs and putting it in inventory for evidence."

"Well, he does that alright, but did you ever see him not lock somebody up and throw their money down the cellar window of an abandoned house?"

"Yeah, he's done that, but Albert, you know the *Yo Bro* alarm system? The dealers have the lookouts on all the corners or on bicycles yelling that the Police were coming. When you stop one of these guys, you can't really arrest them, so Joe threw their money down a cellar window of an abandoned house; so what? They get a little dirty, but they get their money, and they're not sounding the alarm for a half hour or so."

"He ain't throwin' all the money down the cellar."

I flew out of my car and lifted Albert up by the collar, pushing him against the wall.

"Sarge, SARGE, do you think I would say that to you knowing you the way I do. I know you would kick my ass, if I even mouthed off against another cop, let alone YOUR partner? I may be a junkie, but do you think I'm crazy?"

I had known Albert for a long time. Shit, I arrested him several times for possession of heroin. He was a stone junkie; he sold *works* (syringes) to make the money to buy a bag of heroin or he would clean out an abandoned house and run a line to someone else's house to steal electricity, so that he could have some light and set up a shooting gallery. He ran the house and sets up the *gimmicks* (bottle caps, glass pipes, rubber armbands) for the other junkies to come and shoot that black pearl into their veins. Albert would get two dollars for the works and a dollar for the gimmicks and anything else that the street hustler might need. Occasionally, there might also be a need for two junkies who just happened to be suddenly in need of releasing some sexual fluids. The upstairs mattresses, strategically placed in each room, were also for rent, if you didn't mind the occasional "can I get me some of that?" from the straggler who happened upon the renter and his woman. The junkies would be in the middle of some long forgotten position of their youth, bare ass naked, screwing to what they thought were only the cockroaches and flea circuses.

I slowly let Albert down, not releasing him, but letting my mind wander to the last time I saw Joe throw money down a cellar window. Joe had this habit of throwing car keys away and other things, such as writing NDMF on a person's driver's license right before he threw their car keys away, if their license was suspended.

I asked him the first time what the initials were for, and his response kind of made sense in a twisted sort of way.

"NDMF? Spark, you know when you stop somebody and not only are they the worst driver you have ever seen, their license is suspended, and they still give you *mouth*, tell you, you work for them, tell you, they will have your job, etc."

"Yeah..."

"Well, after I give them as many tickets as I can, I want the next cop to know what their dealing with as soon as they get this son of a bitch's license. NDMF means exactly what it says, that this guy is a No Driving Mother Fucker. This way if I can send this message enough times, more cops out there will start doing the same thing, and we will stop wasting our time with these assholes."

"Oh...Ahh...Ok Joe."

Albert struck a nerve. I didn't want to believe it, but I too thought that Joe was doing some funny things with the money from people that we just *ped-stopped* (stopped for investigation). He would purposely walk away from the Police car to an abandoned house and would talk down to the person telling them they were going to have to get dirty to get this money back. I never actually saw him take any money and told him that I thought he was going overboard with this bit, but I thought he stopped. Now, Albert told me he was taking money when I wasn't around.

***

I was working as a 'Santa's Helper' at the Fraternal Order of Police Lodge five when Bobby Durst approached me and asked how I was doing. Bobby was one of the first granny cops in the Philadelphia Police Department. He was famous as a Stakeout Police Officer for his many Officer Involved Shootings, that he earned the notorious nickname of Dr. Death. He would dress up as an old drunken man, a grandmother, or his personal favorite, an insurance salesman and go wandering around the darkest holes of center city, waiting to be mugged. He would flash a wad of bills, some nefarious denizen of darkness, would follow him into the alley, and after Bobby's famous "give me back my money" cry, if the suspect was brandishing a firearm, they would never walk out again.

"Hi Doctor, how's business?"

"Planting the bad ones six feet under," with a sheepish grin he whispered as he came closer. "Hey, Mac, keep this under your hat for now but I'm putting together a Delta Force for the Bureau of Narcotics Investigation. Interested?

"What do you mean?"

"Just like Stakeout but a team that will travel around the state doing high risk entries."

"Bobby, I don't have the background, unless you're going to use K-9 alongside it."

"That's what I was thinking, A Special Operations Team equipped with a K-9 team, a paramedic team, the whole nine yards."

"That will be an answer to a prayer. I'm having a little conflict of interest right now, and I need to leave Highway, but I don't know where to go."

"Ok let me get this up and running. You want in, right?"

"Right!"

Ok, I had a place to go without having to worry whether or not Joe was or wasn't doing something that crossed the line. I told Albert the same as I told everyone else. If you have a complaint against any Police Officer that you go to Third and Race Street to the Internal Affairs Unit and they had to take your complaint. I told Albert that I couldn't take his complaint anyway and that he would have to do it, but I did offer to take him down to IA, if he didn't have a ride.

***

I was working the 6 p.m. to 2 a.m. shift with Joe, when in the 2900 block of North Leithgow Street we came upon a car that was running with no occupant and the doors locked. This car was at a known drug location, so we ran it through Police Radio for any wants or warrants. Police Radio came back stating that the vehicle was previously reported stolen. Normally we just disable the car by flattening a tire and call the owner who arranges to have the car towed. The old procedure of having a Police tow truck come out and tow the stolen car was phased out because of some civil lawsuits surrounding the pickup and garaging of these stolen cars. Joe, however, had some mechanical experience, and he had a *slim-jim,* a device to open the vehicle door, should a person ever lock his or her keys in the car. A person opens the door by inserting the tool inside the car window and the rubber gasket. The device is a thin piece of steel with several curved pieces that are manipulated so that the locking mechanism is eventually caught and unlocked by either pulling or pushing down on the cars locking mechanism. Joe opened the driver's door, got in, and eventually drove to the 25th district.

I followed in Highway 41 and met Joe in the East Detective Division. However, before going up to the detectives, a Hispanic male came to the downstairs window at the 25th District and stated he was the person who stole the car and stated that there was $3,000 in the vehicle, when it was brought to the district.

I was across the room and immediately looked at Joe and gave Joe what we call the stank eye. Joe shook his head "No." I was relieved. The male was obstinate. He wanted to be arrested. Joe wouldn't look at him. The detective handling the case looked at both of us and said:

"Maybe you'd better go check."

And check I did; I took that car apart. I could not find a dime. Joe swore there was nothing.

I was done, either way. I needed to leave the unit, or one night I would be taking Joe across the street to the Super Fresh parking lot where we always had after work midnight barbecues and I would be having a *come to God meeting* with Joe, and only one of us would be able to digest any food that night. The Highway unit had a tradition of settling any disputes in the parking lot, man to man.

***

"Captain Jobs, when a spot opens up, I am respectfully requesting to be considered to be assigned to the BNI Task force on Essington Ave."

"OK, what brought this on?"

"Well, since Joe's always doing things with the drill team and being picked for details with other drill team members, I think it was time I looked at what I can do, to broaden my resume."

"Ok, Sparky, that's a good reason. You're next in line."

I'm not a rat, and I do not speculate on anything or anyone's character without factual evidence that I see firsthand or know that the source was reliable and impeccable in its or his or her own right. I have seen too many times that rumor and innuendo will destroy a good man's reputation, and I would have no part of it, but I was not waiting around to witness the tearing down of what was a good partner, if I could help it.

***

January 21, 1992

"Eyes right, dress right dress, ready front, attention to roll. Reardon, see me after roll call. You'll be teaming up with a new partner. Sparky pack your bags, report to BNI tomorrow 08:00 to Sgt. Micewski. Call 215-937-1500 before you go. Make sure that's the time he wants you there. They work crazy hours there, and good luck, you'll need it. You're working with a legend, Tommy Bolman, the orneriest, hungriest, son of a bitch there ever was. Don't plan on ever going home; when I say hungry, I mean for overtime. He's one *pinchin'* bastard."

Sgt. Edmonton was on a roll.

I made it, hell, I could walk to work, instead of driving the thirty miles or so it took me to get to Bustleton and Bowler every day. It was only a mile and a half from my house to 7801 Essington Ave, which was at the end of the auto mall where the BNI Task force made headlines all over the city.

I showed up bright and early Tuesday and found that the building wasn't open, or it seemed that way. Apparently, there were security measures in place that I was not privy to, and I needed a special identification card to gain entry, for this was a secure building. I went around the back of the building and not only was I not early, but it seemed like I was bringing up the rear, for the parking area was filled with officers and agents from all different agencies preparing to assault what seemed like a third world country.

I saw a marked Highway Patrol unit, H-49, made my way over, and found a flat topped, silver haired Tommy Bolman who growled:

"You're late."

"I'm late?"

"Yeah, Slick, what do I stutter?" the hash marks on his sleeve were just as long as the grin coming from the main deck, under that flattop haircut.

"Marines or just plain Swabbie," I retorted

"Marine, the Swabbies are just a taxi service."

"OK, Gyrine, where's Sgt. Micewski?"

"Probably calling Highway seeing why you're AWOL."

"Hey, aren't you the comedian? When is the last time you saw your shoes?"

Tommy Bolman was another fireplug of a man, 5'7", 230lbs or so. He could be Archie Bunkers twin brother, at least, in attitude, but he could shoot the eyes out of a fly at 50 yards. He could also smell a pinch, I found out as the months went by. We became good partners and had each other's back through every situation, as it should've been.

I found Sgt. Micewski in his office as he was getting dressed in his raid gear. He did not have to wear a uniform here, and he opted to go plain clothes more often than not.

"Sparky, this raid was a last minute thing, and I didn't have your pager number yet, so I didn't have a chance to get a hold of you. Since you managed to get here early anyway, see if you can find Tommy Bolman, you can't miss him, he's..."

"Sarge" I interrupted "I met Mr. Happy already."

"OK. First, unless there's Brass around, which is hardly ever, my name's Charlie or Flash. Knock off the Sergeant shit. Second, Tommy's not Mr. Happy, that title is reserved for Agent Booten, but you'll meet him later. For now, get your gear, jump in with Bolman. We have information on a couple of kilos coming in, and we're going to do a couple of search warrants. If we get time today, we'll go over the admin stuff when we can. For now, here's a key to your office and a temporary pass to the electronic door until you get your State ID. Welcome to BNI."

I hit the ground running and from that day until I was hired by The Office of the Attorney General, we never stopped.

***

Chapter 3

Drug Raid – Carlito Guitterez Organization

"Number One Narcotics Agent in the State of Pennsylvania, can I help you? You want an appointment for a driving test?"

A slow grin spread across Dennis' face.

"Sure, when would you like to come in? Saturday at ten? Let me see if that's a good date...Eggs," Dennis winked covering the phone, "we got a live one. If she looks the way she sounds, she be loving us very much. Get on the three-way."

Dennis (Hoffa) McKeefery and Edward (Eggs) Eggles were partners since they worked at the Philadelphia Police Department. Known as "'Fric and Frac" and joined the Bureau of Narcotics investigation within a year of each other. If you couldn't find one, you certainly wouldn't find the other. They were inseparable.

They always positioned themselves strategically in the center of the office so they could break the balls of every man, woman, and child who entered headquarters. No one escaped unscathed. Dennis would start in harassing you, and Eggs, even if he was just arriving on the scene, would pick it up, never missing a beat.

They were not politicians, and everyone in local law enforcement knew it. They knew the technical end of the job and had the real experience to back it up. Many guys are book trained, but when it came to a real situation; everybody consulted Dennis on heroin and union issues and Eggs on meth and legal issues. Not that we didn't have Deputy Attorney Generals assigned, but they weren't always available, no matter what they said at the monthly staff meetings.

"You know...we have to interview you first before you can take the actual physical driving test." Eggs sat back, putting his feet up on the desk.

"Yeah, and all of our interviews are held off-site at Hastings Bar & Grill. We try to do it at lunchtime so as not to disrupt the other straight-laced driving examiners who ride along with the applicant. We try to make the applicant at ease before the test." Dennis picked up without missing a beat.

"We always find that a few beers and a sandwich take the butterflies right out of your stom...Hello, Hello! Ah shit, another one got away, Eggs."

Dennis's desk phone number was 937-1515 and the Pennsylvania driving test center number was 937-1551. Dennis got so many wrong numbers that this charade was part of his daily routine. The lines changed only slightly. In addition, applicants arrived all hours of the day to find themselves alone in a parking lot of white lines and construction cones.

"Den, before we get interrupted again by another episode of Days of Our Lives, can you answer my question?" I asked.

Suddenly, Manny walked in. Dennis started riding him...

"Where have you been?

"Huh?"

"Regional Director Sanderson's been paging you all day and he's even got the head of Special Ops, Von Kook looking for you."

"For what?"

"I don't know. Something concerning missing money."

"Whaaaat?"

"Look at him Eggs. He's so easy."

"C'mon, man, don't even play like that."

Manny Rodriguez, aka Pineapple, came to our squad on loan from the Philadelphia Housing Authority, who shared the building with us. We requested him as a translator because my Spanish was conversational only and not good enough to take a lengthy written statement, just consents to search. Dennis first came across Manny in the lunchroom where he was frantically looking for me. He had a Hispanic male on the phone who was trying to give him information in reference to a large stash of drugs on Third Street. Dennis was on the phone screaming.

"Listen, you rice 'n beans *eatin* son-of-a-bitch, I can't understand a word you're *'sayin*."

Immediately, a voice came from the lunchroom.

"No arroz y pollo."

"Who said that?"

Dennis was laughing; not the least embarrassed that he'd been overheard. Dennis wasn't prejudiced; he just grew up in a world of stereotypes, often referring to himself in his younger days as a drunken *Mic*.

"I did. I like rice and chicken better," said Manny.

"Get your ass on the phone and tell me what the hell this guy is trying to say."

The conversation translated, P/O Manny Rodriguez was on his way to becoming a member of the Red Team. We called ourselves the Red Team because the Crystal Palace, aka the 16th Floor Executive Offices of the Attorney General, sent our Region too many red vehicles. With the cars we confiscated and put back into service, we ended up following traffickers with a plethora of red undercover vehicles.

Dennis told Manny,

"You work with us now. Go find yourself a desk."

"But, but..."

"Do you think I stutter? Hey *Kookaboo* (Dennis' other nickname for D'Amato depending on what came out of Dennis' mouth first), get Creaton on the phone."

Manny never looked back. Pineapple was our secret weapon in the never-ending saga of the war on drugs. We tried not to expose him; he was never on location when we stopped somebody or were serving a warrant. He was our eyes and ears, but the only time a suspect saw him was in court. Manny cleaned up well, so you'd never recognize him again on the street.

***

The caller gave up the stash location as being in the 2800 block of North 3rd Street. He said that the package of heroin and ounces of cocaine were stored in the abandoned building right next to the drug dealer Terrible's house. Terrible got the order at Third and Birch, went into the 2800 block of North 3rd Street, up the alley in between his house, and into an abandoned house. The abandoned house was boarded up with plywood on hinges that opened out for quick entry. When he got an order, he went up a stepladder, opened the plywood, rolled in, grabbed the product - heroin or cocaine - and went back out in the alley, to meet the customer in the 2900 block of North 3rd Street.

He didn't trust a street worker, so as a Lieutenant in the Carlito Guitterez Organization, he did hands-on deliveries.

The pecking orders of the organizations are a science unto their own. Carlito Guitterez owns the 2900 Block of North 3rd Street. Dominican Traffickers, who had their own hierarchy, supplied his drugs. In the Carlito Guitterez organization, there were different areas of impact in the 2900 block. You had 3rd and Birch, which had "Chevrolet" stamped heroin on blue bags with the "Chevrolet" logo in red on a blue glassine paper packet. In the side street, Stella, which intersects 3rd, there was "Black Rabbit" heroin with an image of a black rabbit head stamped on a blue glassine paper packet. In different areas in the block, at any given time, other hustlers tried to move in. They were also working for street bosses, for a couple of rival owners, who Carlito Guitterez and his son Fernando kept at bay by paying protection to an enforcer, Ismael Rosado. Ismael told Carlito that for one thousand dollars a week he would take care of everything. In other words, he was the enforcer for the organization. There were mini-organizations trying to entrench themselves along the street, each with a couple of workers and a street boss, for this area was prime territory. The blocks are long and the drugs are prevalent. It's a regular pharmacy for addicts. Ismael earned his one thousand dollars, at least twice which we knew of.

"Good Morning to you. Good morning to you. We're all in our places with smiles on our faces."

"Good morning, Marcus," I said wearily, "and stop being so goddamn cheery at 5:00 a.m. Bob, how do you put up with his rotten demeanor?"

"Sorry, Spark, I had my Walkman™ in. Did you say something?"

"Disregard!"

"This is your INS emergency response team; we're en route to East. Are we still stopping at Double D's?"

"Yeah, Stan. Is Lumpy with you?"

"Spark, there's something on the seat next to me. I guess you can call it a lump. It just belched or farted. I can't tell which."

"Flash, are you out here yet?"

"Yeah, did anybody tell Mr. Silks we are doing the early thing?"

"The LT's inside, drinking a cup of coffee and talking to some woman in a booth."

"Chal, Chal! You know he has to do the fireside chat *thaang* whenever he sees the opportunity. The brother got that early morning roll of tarpaper to contend with!"

"Good morning, Dennis."

"Mornin,' Spark. Everyone accounted for?"

"Everybody but Eggs and the Pineapple. I haven't heard from them yet."

"And, if you ever, EVER wake me up at this hour, you won't hear from me," Eggs piped in.

"Yo, Eggs, did Manny get a radio from you?"

"Get a radio from me! That little rice 'n beans eatin' son-of-a-bitch stole my radio. I had to steal one from country row."

"Well, the other squad won't miss it. They are up in Air One, out in the sticks in Chester County looking for heat plumes from meth labs, or road kill, whichever comes first. You know how those country boys are. If it's dead, they'll eat it. If it's not, they'll kill it, then eat it."

"Pineapple, you out there? Does anybody remember his pager number?"

"Yeah, I got it, Spark. It's 984-beans."

"Nah, that's too many numbers, Flash. Manny, if you can hear me, you better stop talking to those senoritas and turn that radio up."

"Spark, Sergeant Flash, is anybody out there?"

"Yeah, like you didn't hear us, you little pineapple, rice 'n beans eatin' *pendejo*!" I was a little annoyed.

"Yo! Why I gotta be all that?"

"Because you're always eatin' rice 'n beans."

"Yeah, but *pendejo*?"

"Doesn't that mean upstanding citizen? Or is that *maricon*? I get the two confused."

"We have a hearing at Front and West, and it's Judge Conroy. Are we stopping the van?" Marcus asked.

"Nah, we have something brewing on Third Street. We're just grabbing addresses and we'll get a hold of Sixes on the way back from New York at 3:00 p.m."

***

The sign said La Familia Services, but what got the attention of the Bureau of Narcotics Investigation Task Force is that every Dominican drug trafficker that we stopped or arrested had a card for a van service that promised door-to-door delivery, Philadelphia to New York, round trip.

We stopped Sixes for a routine traffic violation and found out he was an illegal alien from the Dominican Republic. After explaining to him the advantages of working for us as a confidential informant instead of being deported, he became one of our most valuable assets.

Through Sixes, we found that most of the heroin and cocaine traffickers in Philadelphia's infamous Badlands used this van service on a daily basis to transport drugs and money to and from New York. Also popular with the Dominican Trafficking Organizations or DTOs, who all but control the Badlands, are Jose's Express and Geraldo's. Both services were stopped repeatedly by BNI and the N.J. State Police.

"You gonna stay around and try to get something else?"

"Marcus, have you ever known us to go in without a prisoner or two, *especialmente* if we start out at this godforsaken hour?" Charlie chimed in.

"Sorry, Sarge, I lost my head."

"I ain't your Sergeant anymore; knock that shit off."

"Once a Highway Patrol Sergeant, always a Highway Patrol Sergeant!"

"Ah, isn't that cute. You are making me sick! Bob, smack him!" Eggs retorted.

"Mr. Silks, do you hear this shit? I have never seen so much ass kissin' in my whole career, and he doesn't even work for him anymore," Dennis screamed over channel two.

"Dennis, you callin' me?" was the answer from Lt. Jimmy Cotts.

"Oh, sorry LT; did we wake you up?"

"No, I'm watchin this little mommy over here. I can't figure out if she's wearin a skirt or a handkerchief!"

"Mr. Silks, your location please...LT, where you at? LT?... LT?..."

"Eddie, he ain't answering. Where's he at, Eggs?" Dennis was beside himself.

"I saw him sittin' at American and Lehigh, and I'll be there in...holy shit! Den, Den you gotta' get up here. Ya gotta see this Honey...She be lovin' us very, very much."

"All units American and Lehigh." Dennis blurted out. "INS emergency response team, en route." Stan added. "What's going on? I was out of the car taking a personal when Marcus drove by me lights and siren," Charlie interrupted the radio traffic.

"Zip it up Chal, the LT's on the prowl."

"901 to 928; 901 to 928."

"Alright, does anybody know their car numbers?"

***

John D'Amato who took over the squad when Tommy Litcello went on disability because of a heart attack, tried in vain to get our squad to use car numbers on our car to car radios also known as 150's. We weren't buying it. We were on our own dedicated frequency and we all used nicknames and a vernacular that was distinct to our needs and rapid fire. We also had our own system. If we say we were at one place we would be at two streets north of that location or two streets east of that location. We did this on occasion to see if anyone was listening in or trying to identify one of us. Shamefully we also did this to *Johnny D,* aka *Von Kook* once in a while, to keep him off our trail.

John was one of the best cops out there, of course, former Highway Patrol. He was shot three times because of a contract placed on him by the *Black Mafia* in Philadelphia. He earned his *regulation 32* disability, which means he couldn't do the job description of a Policeman. Yet here we were, enforcing the Pennsylvania Drug Device and Cosmetic Act of 1972. However we were classified as Narcotic Agents, which are Law Enforcement Officers not Policemen, therefore John D'Amato and several others could have their pension and Special Operations too. The Special Operations Group, nicknamed the *Ninja Turtles*, was his baby. John thought every move we made needed to be planned way in advance.

Drug Traffickers don't *roll* like that though, especially Dominican Drug Traffickers. We learned early on the hard way when we intercepted a courier *re-upping* a corner and sent him to headquarters. While we prepared search and seizure warrants for stash locations, time was not standing still. The warrants have to be reviewed by the Deputy Attorney General and signed by a Judge or Bail Commissioner, and normally two to three hours go by; this wasn't the movies, this was the Philadelphia *Injustice* System at its finest.

The owners of the Dominican corners would time the couriers from the time they left the stash house. They had 20 minutes tops, to get to the corner where the drugs are being sold or dropped off. If the couriers weren't on time, the phone calls would start, if there wasn't a response or not the right response, the drugs from the stash house would be moved. If the occupants saw what they believed were Police outside, the drugs would be destroyed, usually by flushing down the toilet.

We had to secure properties and await the search warrants to make sure that no evidence was destroyed. We had the Confidential Informants that could explain to a Judge ex-parte (in his chambers), if need be, but we also had the expertise necessary to lay out the known exigent circumstances in the application for the search warrants and none were turned down.

Von Kook or *Kook a Boo* as Dennis titled *Johnny D* was as I said, a planner. We were always going from job to job, at a moment's notice, depending on what was jumping at the time. If one of us had a bead on something, the rest of us made our way over to that area, made that buy, or buy-bust, or whatever we needed to do. If it included prisoners, we called for a Philly Police Wagon, sending the prisoners to Headquarters to have the preliminary paperwork processed by other Agents. One of us always broke off, to fill out the fact sheet for the charging DA.

Von Kook couldn't keep up with us. We told him we were trying to raise him. as he called us over the *air*. No one got hurt. We had Lt. Cotts from the Philly PD with us. John was still free to train the *Ninja Turtles* and have them called out for statewide SOG (Special Operations Group) Tactical Entries where the threat level might be perceived to be a little higher. Since Philadelphia rose to the notorious rank of one of the top murder capitals of the nation, I serious doubt that the threat level was higher anywhere, but as I said, John was a great raid planner.

***

"Chal, go to channel two; *Von Kook* is trying to raise us on channel one. We can always say we didn't hear him. Meet us at American and Lehigh."

"Everything all right, Spark?" Flash asked again.

"Von Kook is heading up with the *Ninja Turtles* and he wants a *meet,* but we have to keep an eye on the area to make sure that *Terrible* doesn't wander off without our *early morning roll call."*

We wanted him to answer *present* or at least let one of us get an *eyeball* on him going to or from the property, when we hit it with the search warrant.

"Yeah, the LT got a *Mommasita* stopped and Dennis and Eggs says she *be lovin'* them very much."

"Shit! I thought it was an *Assist.*"

"Nah, it's just the LT giving us all a lesson in the art of the fireside chat."

***

Charlie 'Flash' Micewski was my Sergeant when I first came to BNI as a task force member detailed from Highway Patrol. I only knew him to say hello when we were in Highway. He was in a different squad, and also on the drill team. He made Sergeant and being the rookie again, was saddled with being the supervisor for the uniform interdiction teams detailed to the Attorney General's office. The job started to grow on him. After being spit and polished for so many years, he liked donning plain clothes from time to time. By the time I was assigned to BNI, the only time I saw his uniform, was in old pictures.

Once when we were driving back to headquarters from court, I was driving the marked Highway 46 and Charlie was riding shotgun, in plainclothes. We drove Eastbound on Market Street from 13th approaching 12th. Flash was sipping a coffee he just bought. I saw a black SUV going across 12th Street in front of us with a black male hanging on the outside of the passenger door. I told Flash to dump his coffee and "get ready." He didn't understand, but he was reaching for his gun as he dumped his coffee. I flew around the bus in front of us as the SUV crashed into the southeast corner of 12th and Market. There were two black males on the outside of the car and one was seen jumping out of the driver's seat. We jumped out and not knowing exactly what was going on we drew down on everyone, commanding for hands to be shown and to freeze. I had one male on the ground under my knee with my weapon drawn on the other, as Flash had the other male, spread eagle on the ground.

It was 12 noon and the lunch crowd was getting an eye and earful. I recognized a court officer in the crowd and had him go to my vehicle and call for a backup, but to first turn off my damn siren. I couldn't hear myself think. I threw my second set of handcuffs to Flash. I kept two sets on me, one in my vest in my leather coat, the other hung visible on my Sam Browne rig. I handcuffed my *prisoner*, who was yelling that it was his car and that the other guy just hijacked him and his buddy. I ordered him while he was still in the sights of my nickel plated .357, over to me and put him on the ground until backup arrived and we had two complainants and one hijacker. We just made a sight arrest for hijacking.

But it got better. When we went to Central Detectives to process the job, the Emergency Patrol Wagon crew or EPW, who transports prisoners, took the prisoner out of the back and was walking him through the parking lot when we all heard a voice from the second floor of Central Detectives.

"That's the guy who just robbed me."

Another complainant positively identified the prisoner as the person who just robbed him an hour before the hijacking occurred. It was a two for one day. Charlie and I were awarded Policemen of the Month by the Fraternal Order of Police Lodge 5.

We became pretty good friends and decided to leave the Police Department together to enter the Attorney General's office. We started the Pennsylvania Attorney General Narcotic Agent academy together, on February 6th, 1995.

After graduating from the Academy, we became partners. We wanted to set the world on fire, or at least our little part of it. We proved successful and received numerous accolades from our peers as to the quantity and quality of the arrests that were coming in on a weekly basis. Our superiors noticed us too, but for a different reason. We were bringing assets into the region. Assets kept our Regional Director, AKA "God," and his bosses very happy. Even in this regime, "God" answered to other deities.

***

"OK, now that everyone had their morning tent post adjusted, can we go off to see the *Lizard King*, the *Terrible Lizard of Oz*."

I wanted to pinch *Terrible*, and Jim Morrison and the Doors came across the car radio and I couldn't help the metaphor jumping into my head as I cranked up *Break on through to the Other Side*. Anyone in our *game* needed to keep track on the music industry and its influence on the illegal narcotics trade, and Val Kilmer in the character of Morrison on the big screen, dancing around the desert referring to the *Lizard King,* was an image that came to mind when I saw junkies floating around in stupors. We were going to break through a door to serve a search warrant for heroin. The song was a good sign, it was time to go and go now. This was just one of the preemptory strikes that led to the taking back of an entire city block in Philadelphia. It was the beginning of the end, for dismantling the Carlito Guitterez Organization in the *Badlands* of North Philadelphia. And it was the Bureau of Narcotics Investigation and the *Bastard Squad* that would be credited.

Actually we hadn't been labeled with the pejorative term the *Bastard Squad* yet, we were still the *Red Team* and East Division wasn't named the *Badlands* until after I went down to BNI as a Task Force Officer. We set up shop in an abandoned factory and were filming the 2900 block of Third Street from a fifth and seventh floor window. We entered the block long building from the 2800 block of North American Street in the South East corner of the building and walked up five floors, some of which were missing steps, with our cameras and equipment. After walking across the entire length of the building, setting up the cameras, we sent in undercover cops and agents to make buys, off the various dealers in the block.

All of these dealers worked for the Carlito Guitterez Organization. They sold heroin, and cocaine, mostly blue tape and black tape, which wasn't just a piece of tape that secured the plastic bag that the cocaine came in. It also denoted in what area, you bought your drugs. The Philadelphia Police Narcotics Unit Strike Force, not the one assigned to us, took a Philadelphia Sentinel Reporter up to the same place where we were surveiling the 2900 Block of Third Street. This reporter and Mallo's squad initiated the term *Badlands* to describe this area without checking the DECS system (Drug Enforcement Coordinating System] for conflicting investigations. Mallo's Philadelphia Police squad screwed our investigation by revealing our spot to a Sentinel reporter. The reporter put the photo on the front page of the newspaper showing the drug sales on the 2900 block of Third Street. Here's the kicker: The only place the photo could possibly have been taken was from that abandoned factory. That abandoned factory was set on fire and destroyed the next day. The Philadelphia Sentinel's coverage possibly led to the torching of a neighborhood.

***

Terrible was walking down toward the 2900 block of North Third Street. Pineapple was the eyeball on location and gave the play-by-play on our approach. I was traveling eastbound on Cambria and *reached out and touched* Terrible. As he *tripped* to the ground I recovered one .45 cal. Smith & Wesson semi-automatic with one up the pipe, ready for action.

Tripping was always in the mind of the Police report writer. When you approach a target and you can see what you know, or can surmise, was the outline of a weapon in the small of his back, you are going to trip, force, knock or any other verb...insert favorite here...that *target* to the ground and disarm him or her so the *target* doesn't know what *hit 'em*. My favorite verb was *trip*. It was a feel good kind of word; people trip every day. It's one of those words that public defenders glaze right over when they're reading discovery. No harm, no foul, and I go home at the end of the day.

The Special Operations Team secured *Terrible's* house and found 26 handguns, shotguns and assault weapons – a gun within reach of any spot in the place. It was amazing. Von Kook got on his soapbox, but he deserved it on this one.

"Do you see what I mean, you guys just don't understand. Any one of these places we hit can be a disaster for you or your families. Should you take one little move that you make on entry, for granted. Just look at this place, everywhere you can possibly reach there's a weapon fully loaded. This place looks like a goddamn armory. Look at this *weaponry*."

Eggs couldn't help himself: "What kind of tree is that, John? Is that like a Douglas Fir, or an Alberta Spruce? Is it Christmas season already?"

"Eggles you Son of a Bitch", and Kook a Boo was off to the races out the door of the house chasing Eggs up the street, toward Cambria, reaching down, grabbing stones and throwing them at the Eggman. As Eggs ran, he was yelling: "It's Weaponry, W-E-A-P-O-N-R-Y, it's a science, not a tree."

The older members of the community who gathered to watch the excitement had a look on their faces that was one of bewilderment and confusion, and rightly so. Two grown men with guns, in full raid gear, one chasing the other...locos.

This was a running joke with *Johnny D.* John got excited and carried away, when talking about a Police related subject and crucified the English language sometimes, but only because of his passion for the job. However no one escaped our harassment.

One year while putting up the Christmas tree outside his office, I got the idea of getting pictures of all different types of guns and hanging them on the tree. We all gathered around the tree when he came into work and watched him as he stood there puzzled as to why pictures of automatic weapons and machine guns were taking the place of traditional ornaments. We started humming the melody to "O Tannebaum", and after a short intro, as he was staring at us, Eggs put his thumb and index finger in front of us like a conductor, and we broke into, "O Weapontry, O Weapontry, how lovely are your *cartridges*, O Weapon..." We started backing away, and here we all were, running around the office, like little kids being chased by the schoolteacher, all of us laughing so hard we were crying.

***

The abandoned house next door was secured as well. It's funny. After Dennis sent the K-9 team in to search the abandoned property, the team came out empty handed. I knew the handler and she didn't keep up with her in-service training. The handler said her K-9 didn't indicate anywhere and that there weren't any drugs inside. Dennis was beside himself. Everyone went inside and searched everywhere except me. I had the prisoner outside and Charlie and I were keeping one eye on him and the other on the events unfolding in front of us. Everyone came out of the property empty handed. I asked Dennis if he minded if I went in and searched. He begged me to, as he knew I was a scavenger.

I went in, and after watching my K-9 for so many years, I just surveyed the room. I went over to the cellar stairs and saw a shelf above the stairway that had a little 1" x 12" built up so that it was like a cubbyhole. Apparently since it was a little high, no one stuck their hand over the side. I stuck my hand in and grabbed an 18" x 18" yellow page wrapped *package*.

That *package* turned out to be 15 *racks* of heroin. A *rack* of heroin is 12 to 15 *bundles*, which is 11 to 12 glassine wax paper packets, usually stamped with a corner logo or imprint. The mark denotes who was selling that particular heroin. $27,000.00 isn't bad per package for a days' work, and more, if it's a banner day, should the corner need to be *re-upped*. The packets are wrapped in a rubber band. The significance of the 11 or 12 bags to a *bundle* was that 10 dollars of the proceeds of the sales of the bags, go back to the owner. One sale of a bag goes to the actual seller of the *bundle* and the sale of one bag goes to the street Lieutenant.

These *bundles* are stacked together in groups of 12 to 15, which constitute a *rack*, the quantity of the *bundles* being left up to the individual owner. These *racks* are usually wrapped together in

Yellow Pages paper and taped together; much like one would tape a birthday present.

15 to 20 of these *racks* are put together again and wrapped with Yellow Page paper to form the *package*. The *package* is delivered to the Drug Traffickers corner from the out of area, *stash house*. The corner re-ups throughout the day until the *package* is depleted and the Street Lieutenant calls the owner for a new *package* to be delivered.

I brought the *package* out to Dennis, knowing without opening it, what I found, and Dennis yelled:

"You son of a bitch, how the hell...oh never mind, good job Sparkster."

All the other officers and agents ran back in the house and start searching again.

"Dennis, I'm not done, when they come out. Let me go back in and see what else I find."

Dennis marched over to the abandoned house, steps in the doorway and orders:

"Alright, Everybody out, I gotta get my scrounge back in there. Hey, I'm not bullshittin', YO!! OUT...NOW."

I went back in and as before, I surveyed the house, which wasn't an ordinary abandoned house. All of the trash looked neatly swept into a pile in each of the rooms and each pile was tightly compacted. That didn't fit with me either. If someone went to the trouble of sweeping all the trash together, why didn't they pick it up and get rid of it.

"Hmm..."

I was now adjusting the focus of my eight cell Streamlight© to the trash pile.

There it was, hiding in plain sight. It was so full of 1/4 ounces of cocaine that it was solid white in its appearance, even though it was actually a clear plastic container. It was pushed together with all of the other trash and unless you were really looking for it, or actually knew what you were looking for, you would pass it up anywhere, even out in the public.

I wanted to let Dennis find this one; it would make his day.

"Ah, Dennis, do you want to come in here and pick up all this *coke?*"

"Do I what? You're *shittin* me. I was just there myself. You got to be *kiddin* me."

"OK if you don't want it, I'll just have to dump it."

I could hear Dennis running and laughing as I disappeared into the house.

"Stop, STOP."

He was almost choking with laughter. As he got to the door, I had the container opened in my hand and all you could see in the dim light was the white powder. I spilled the contents as Dennis entered the room.

"NO!!! What are you crazy?"

"Relax, they're quarter ounces," I said as the baggies hit the floor.

"Would I do that to you?"

"You fuck, you trying to give me a heart attack? OK, how many we got?"

"Quick *eye count* looks to be 28 bags, or around 7 ounces."

"Heroin and cocaine and *weight* at that, this guy's toast."

Dennis grinned.

"*Tag 'em and Bag 'em*, let's get some pizza."

"Marcus, six half pepperoni, half plain, Dennis is buying."

 Flash went over the air.

"I'm whattt...?"

"Dennis, shaddup." Eggs retorted.

"Don't embarrass me any further, you're supposed to be a Narc and you got that ex Boot Cop finding dope you couldn't find, I'm ashamed of you."

"I lost my headdd, Eggs, I don't know what I was thinking."

"Hey Eggman, Highway is in your blood, once you earn Highway, its emblazoned forever in your heart, mind, and soul," Marcus interjected.

"Yeah, and on the metal plate *youse* guys have in your dome."

"OK girls, are we finished? *Wheels up!* Let's go eat, and put this one to bed."

Von Kook ended the good-natured ribbing with Highway's traditional end of assignment slogan; it was time to go to headquarters.

***

The Big One

May 27, 1995

We put on quite a show for North Philadelphia–the usual hot spot–2900 block of North Third Street. Four hundred cops descending on the neighborhood after a grand jury indicted 34 residents with doing over $4 million a year in cocaine and heroin business. Seven of the dealers were already in custody, we were serving search and seizure warrants on 19 more properties, seven of which will be demolished, this same day, with arrest warrants in tow, for more traffickers as we rounded them up.

Dennis orchestrated the play by play as the *eyeball,* from high atop an undisclosed location while Von Kook flew overhead in one of two black camouflaged National Guard Special Ops helicopters. The massive, never seen before, multi-agency force descended upon the one square city block. This juggernaut caused such a panic among the heroin hawkers that they were scrambling to get into what Dennis was describing as a clown car from the circus. Some Hispanic males were piling in, driving, and getting blocked off at every direction, and backing up out of the side streets, piling out, with others piling back in, trying to drive back the way they came. They finally gave up as they were swarmed by a sea of black and blue armed Law Enforcement with numerous alphabet soups emblazoned in gold across their varied jackets and bulletproof vests.

In a matter of less than one minute an entire city block was neutralized in the most coordinated effort this City had ever seen to bring back some sense of civility to what was once a clean block. A neighborhood, that if you got past the 4th grade without witnessing some violent act, you had to be blind, deaf and dumb. Death and violence was a way of life for these people and their innocent children playing on this block amid the heroin, crack, and cocaine, users and abusers. They needed a break, from those that lived off the profits of others addictions.

If you do not know North Philly, the blocks feel small, intimate, except for the two or three major throughways that light up like Christmas trees when a major crime in progress was underway. The strobe lights from the responding radio patrol cars, turned the night sky into urban northern lights. The steps, porches, and stoops of the row houses jut out onto the sidewalk, creating an outdoor space just right for doing business. Four hundred Police Officers streaming in were like too much sausage, stuffed into a casing. We filled every space and moved into the buildings and backyards.

We came out with 14 prisoners, including the alleged "Drug Lord" as the papers called him. They were right. Carlito Guitterez was the *Boss* as the sweatshirt he was wearing intimated, but he would not be wearing designer clothes from Hugo Boss™, just federal prison greens. At 54, he ran the *puntos* (drug corners), but not anymore. He was facing twenty to life in prison.

Guitterez did quite a business for himself and ruled with an iron fist. He bought the stuff in New Jersey and brought it back to one of four houses on the block where it was processed and packaged. The books revealed some eighty thousand dollar weeks in 1992. We arrested Ismeal Rosado for shooting two competitors who dared to sell another brand on Guitterez's turf.

In the past couple of years, we took in over 435 drug suspects but most of them went back on the street due to the *swinging door* justice system in Philadelphia. The courts always came up with one excuse or another when one of the criminals we pinched was arrested again for some violent felony.

The May '95 raid was meant to impact a community and send a message. The *Red Team* would stop at nothing. We would tap every resource to have our investigations come to a successful conclusion. We gave people back the right to watch their children walk across the street without being afraid. As the papers reported, the neighbors were supportive, saying that it was about time. It took something this big to show them, we were out there every day trying to fight the war. What these supportive neighbors couldn't see were the roadblocks the government put in front of the Police.

We tried to skim the scum off the street, but we needed the people to take the politics out of the courtroom.

The DEA report said that as much as one-third of all cocaine coming into the U.S. was coming from Dominican Trafficking Organizations (DTOs). The DEA's National Drug Intelligence Center estimates 20–25 percent of all cocaine and heroin revenues inside the U.S. was controlled by Dominicans with smuggling centered in NYC and Philadelphia. In the '90s it was believed that around $180 billion was transacted by Dominican drug traffickers. That's a pretty hefty opponent–even for us.

***

Chapter 4

Callahan

The Latinos knew me as *Callahan*. They knew my real name and their pronunciation of "McLaughlin" was recognizable. However, I believe it was my nickel-plated .357 old-fashioned *wheel gun* I carried that got me this nickname. When the corner boys asked why I never carried a Glock, I said with a smile:

"One shot, one hit; I'm not out here for target practice."

The corner boys christened me *Callahan*, which stuck with me from the 1980's until present day, on the other side of the thin blue line, west of Fifth Street.

October 20, 1995

That day I was in *East* in North Philly, traveling with BNI agent, Charles Micewski, Special Agent Stan Breward of the Immigration and Naturalization Service and the rest of the *Red Team*.

It was early enough to be hunting for breakfast, but instead we were *huntin' dominions* as our task force member, Marcus, referred to the Dominican drug traffickers. As we neared one corner we saw an Olds 88. It was huge, bulky and there was plenty of room for hidden compartments—the car of choice for drug smugglers. There were two men inside. I got on the *horn* to Pineapple, who was less than a block away.

Pineapple was our nickname for Manny Rodriguez, a cop with the Philly Housing Authority. He was bilingual, and could pick up plenty among the various Latino groups. I could get by in Spanish, even with the paperwork, but I liked having someone there, who knew the lingo backward and forward. I knew what I needed for the street—Spanish Miranda warnings and *consents to search*.

"Hey, Pineapple," I said into the mike, "park your car on Somerset right before American. Walk around to the tire shop, and see what those two Hispanic males are talking about. They just got out of a dark blue Olds 88 in front of the tire shop."

"OK, Sparky."

Pineapple's voice crackled through the speaker.

As we watched Pineapple walk by them, I told Stan:

"Look at those guys staring at us. They know something's up."

"Yeah," he agreed. "We'll see what Pineapple picks up."

Pineapple's voice came over the radio a minute later.

"Sparky, they're real nervous."

"Why?"

"They're hoping you won't stop them because one guy's illegal."

"Gotcha!" Stan said.

We waited just long enough so any connections these suspects might make with Pineapple would disappear. We always waited for him to get away from the scene. Manny Rodriguez was our secret weapon: an officer with big ears, big eyes, and a look and demeanor nobody noticed—a rare combination in the B adlands. Suspects never saw Manny until they got to court, and they only saw a Police Officer in a suit and tie who looked entirely different. If a suspect we arrested passed by Pineapple the next day on the street, he wouldn't recognize him. Pineapple was like a walking camera-and-mike.

Finally Stan and I got out of our car, crossed to the Olds. As we closed in, the Dominicans slumped a little, trying to feign indifference.

"Hola, amigos," I said. "¿Usted tiene identificación?"

Neither of them said a word.

I looked at Stan. "Stannn, they don't want to play," I said, glancing from him to them.

"Because you spoke to them in Spanish," Breward replied. "It won't get their attention." He turned to them, and started speaking sternly. "Hi, I'm from Immigration and Naturalization and you're on an airplane in the next 24 hours if you don't give me some ID."

They started scrambling. The driver came up with a card, handing it to me. As I looked at it, Breward said, "See Spark, you just gotta say the magic word, 'airplane'."

"It's magic, all right," I said, handing the card to Stan. The guy's name was Daniel Croussano, and the card was an alien registration ID. That means he was legit. The other guy was a different story. Jose Primivito Miriano-Ortega was here illegally. The fact he was with a suspected drug trafficker Croussano, did not help him. Miriano-Ortega doesn't have any papers helping him either. In no time he would be flying back where he came from.

A pile of papers sat on the car seat. The page on top said, "Triunfo '96." I picked them up and started reading, but my Spanish was not quite up to it.

Stan peered over my shoulder. "What's that?"

"I'm not sure. It looks like some kind of political campaign stuff. You ever hear of the Revolutionary Dominican Party?" I handed the papers to him, and he took a look.

"I think so," he said.

"Let's put these guys in the car, and get Pineapple on the radio. I wanted him to talk to them and figure out what's in these papers."

"Pineapple, talk to this guy over the radio. Ask him what these papers are all about. All I can make out are bits and pieces. It says something about the Revolutionary Dominican Party."

"Hey, what are those papers all about?"

"Knock it off, smart ass."

Pineapple got serious on the radio, and Stan read something from the document, and talked to him in both Spanish and English. In a minute, they were all speaking Spanish. I was getting bits and pieces. As Croussano answered questions, Stan studied the sheets, occasionally reading more aloud, listening to Manny and the suspects.

Finally, Stan turned to me. "It's some kind of fundraising plan, all about a political party back in the DR. This was what this revolutionary thing was. They were running a candidate named Pena-Gomez for president of the Dominican Republic. They're financing it from here."

"Here?"

"From guys like our friend, Croussano."

"They're soliciting drug money, from dealers on the streets, for a guy running for president?" I asked ..."What am I saying, of course they are."

"Why do you say from drug dealers?"

"Because the one strategy states: it prohibits the personal illusions of any one type, as well as the public debates on value judgments and their targeting those between 18 and 35, but it never says anything concerning the refusal of any money from undocumented sources. Remember, this guy Daniel is Carmen Croussano's brother. We just pinched her."

"Political drug dealers on our street, amigo. I guess they're like Willie Sutton, going where the money is."

"What's the world coming to?" I exclaimed.

Croussano looked at Stan then at me. "You read Spanish?" he asked.

"Poquito", I answered, meaning 'a little'.

He gestured to the radio. A minute later he was chattering at Pineapple. Pineapple replied:

"He's saying you can have copies of Triunfo '96, Sparky. He's suggesting we pass them around to all our Dominican friends."

"I'll bet we can."

Daniel smiled at me. I smiled. We cuffed his friend, who did not pass go and will not collect two hundred dollars. His airline ticket was being prepared as we spoke. We were playing just another game of Monopoly, seeing who owns which corners. I took the papers, and rode off into the sunset. As we drove away, I rifled through the papers, commenting:

"Looks like good reading material for the *porcelain library* and a night deposit in the *round file*."

I was wrong. In the next weeks and months I would find out I was wrong about a lot of things.

On the first day I was amazed and intrigued. The politics of a far off island nation depended on dope deals in Philly. This seemed a little ridiculous, but it was hardly impossible. Stan was right about it was like Willie Sutton's classic explanation of why he robbed banks; *that's where the money is.*

Like any ghetto of any big city, North Philly contains the paradox of block-after-block of grinding poverty, and huge wads of cash changing hands. The cash was drug money, and there was no reason why those profits couldn't finance a political campaign. Money is money, power is power, and the two usually find each other. Nevertheless, money and power do not always respect the law. That was where I came in. But my job was here on these streets. When things go international, there was no choice but to let the *suits* above know, even though our crew could probably handle it better and quicker, given free reign.

During the day, as we processed our illegal alien, I did not see where a link between Dominican politics and Philly drug dealers was going to change much for me either way. I busted the street dealers, and the feds go after the international cartels. This document was evidence, but again, it could just as well be light reading for the porcelain library while it made its way around the stalls of the men's room. I opted to put it into a case file for now, as part of an initial investigation. If the crimes reach south of the border, someone else will be responsible. We would cooperate in any way possible, but our main role was on the street, stopping Olds 88s, taking contraband into evidence, and halting drug sales at their point of origin, following backward to the source. We are simply making life difficult for an illegal alien. We could have the alien on a plane within 24 hours, and he would have to plot his return on one of the mule trains through Mexico, or Puerto Rico, or whatever route was popular this month. The papers were just one more link in a chain of evidence, but my link in the chain was right here.

While I assumed someone else would deal with the Dominican Republic, I did have a job in front of me. If drug dealers were recruited as fundraisers for a political party, most likely one of our C/I's was aware of the Party and could infiltrate. Croussano's invitation to hand out copies shows he was not alone and he was a cocky son of a bitch. This was an ongoing operation. Later, I told Pineapple to contact the G-Man and Sixes, two of our Dominican Confidential Informants, about Croussano, and learn more things that fed my suspicions.

"There has to be more," I told my partner, Charlie Micewski. This *pendejo* is hiding something.

"It makes sense," he said, "but we need proof, and I'll get it. I'll wire the G-Man."

"Those papers show a plan for getting money from crack dealers here," I said. "Not quite proving the link, but it is evidence. Croussanos's a link too. A couple of weeks ago we busted his sister, Carmen. She had 86 grams of coke, and over 4,000 crack vials."

"Is she sending money home to the *Party*?" Micewski asks.

"I'm not sure but her brother's a *remitter*, let's go back over the documents from the seizure in that case," I said.

He agreed. What we did not know, was the people who should be on our side, did not want us to look.

***

Evidence mounted in the days and weeks following the initial stop. In the immediate aftermath of the bust, we got a complete translation of the PRD document. This was a chore necessitating a lot of patience, time and *fine wine*.

I placed a call to the "Demon Princess" who, depending upon what time of day it was, lived up to her pseudonym.

"Jo, did I ever tell you how beautiful you are?"

"WHAT do you want?"

You sweet talker, you! "Do we have the capability to fax a document into the computer and transfer it into the translator?"

"WE?"

"Well ah…You?"

"Yes."

"Alright, I'm going to fax this over. It's pretty long. Once you receive it, could you put it in the other program and start translating?"

"This will cost you wine."

"Red or white?"

"Yes."

We went through a lot of wine over the next year.

***

Though it does not specifically state narcotics should be sold to finance a presidential campaign, it does target 300,000 Dominican voters living in the U.S. Most of these voters are concentrated in northeast cities. Funds raised are by means of profits made from business activities. It does not specify the activities, but the only venture producing cash quickly among Dominicans was drug dealing.

On October 23rd, one of our analysts, retired CIA employee, Wilson Primkin, called his former agency and spoke to Agent Victoria Baylor, giving her a heads up on what we found. She gave him an address where he could send the "Triunfo '96" document. In the next few days, Primkin and I got the translation to our Regional Director, John Sanderson. He sent it to the Deputy Director, Tim Miller.

We all knew we were onto something big, and we understood the Feds would see it from a broader view. But on the street we were finding things confirming the plan. On November 2 another Olds turned up in the hands of Dominican nationals. It had over $5000 bucks in one secret compartment. On November 6, we find Daniel Croussano's brother Ramon, with an ounce of coke and almost $3,000 in cash. November 13th Sanderson met with the FBI. They will not touch the PRD investigation unless it involved overt terrorism. On the same day, an informant told us one reason the PRD wanted to get to power in the DR was to pave the way for an easier route for narcotics to travel. They wanted to be able to sell more drugs to our addicts, increasing their profits. After all, if drugs could finance their campaign, why not use the same strategy to finance a government?

December 7th, Primkin called the CIA's David Torrence. He told him someone from *The Company* should look at this. "We're getting more information every day." Torrence said the CIA wants to know all about it. "We'll send an Agent over right away." I was not there when the first memo was dropped off but the rumor was, we got a visit from a CIA Agent who I heard has nice legs according to the *Eggman*, Eddie Eggles. On her next visit I saw for myself he was not lying.

CIA Agent Baylor walked through our door on January 31st, 1996 sporting a pair of purposefully distracting legs. *God,* (our name for Sanderson) boomed over the intercom.

"Sparky, conference room now!"

A second bellow, "Agent McLaughlin!" When 'God' calls you by your real name, the veins are popping out of his forehead; it sometimes takes two hours to reset them back into the crevices of his lunar surface supported by a neck. I flung open the door stating flatly,

"Sorry John I was going to the *shitter*."

My eyes were next affixed to those legs, enveloped by fishnet stockings making me flash back to the cold war spy movies. *God's* laser look of death, magnified by those glasses never staying on his nose, told me I stepped in shit again.

"This is Agent Victoria Baylor from the CIA and she wants the first memo returned. Agent Baylor says we shouldn't have received it."

I already knew the Chief of Station, Larry Weightley, goofed by admitting in the memo, the United States was backing Pena Gomez for the Presidency of the Dominican Republic. It was like re-visiting the revelation concerning Samper of Columbia backed by the Cartels and the embarrassment this caused the Clinton Administration. The frying pan had not gone cold, and yet, here we were again.

I flashbacked to cold war cartoon images of Boris and Natasha, heavy on the Natasha character.

As I greeted Agent Baylor with the usual compliments, I could see *God* in my peripheral vision silently mouthing the words:

"Copy that motherfucker."

It was then I realized, we just opened the proverbial can of worms, into a sinkhole full of piranha.

***

Chapter 5

CIA

"Ok, Red Alert, DEFCON 3 is in effect."

In the military DEFCON 3 refers to an increase to force readiness above normal. Radio call signs used by American forces change to currently classified call signs. *God* put us at DEFCON 3. Damn that Wilson Primkin.

Wilson was our intelligence analyst. He had a prior history with the CIA but we were never sure what the history entailed. He talked in riddles, never *confirming* nor *denying*. I got curious one day and did his ancestry and found all his port entries and exits as well as his Fathers'. He was indeed a world traveler and the port data seem to back up his stories. A wisp of a man, he resembled an English gentleman's *bumbershoot*. Straight and narrow when closed, but when he opened up, he covered a lot of area and experience. Neither *confirm nor deny;* those words are still etched on my brain to this day. I cannot help wondering if he was secretly shielding something or someone.

I look for the *'Doctor'*. *Doc* was our resident *B* tech. A *B* tech in our agency is a Narcotics Agent who undergoes intensive training in electronic eavesdropping and physical installation of the equipment to facilitate interceptions. We did it by the book in our agency; however, there are those agencies *C*arefully *I*ntercepting *A*ll others without regard for the legal process. The great thing about *B* techs was they not only know everything about installations, they also know everything about detection, and jamming anyone else who may be transmitting radio frequencies.

I wanted *Doc* to outfit me discreetly with an RF detector, to let me know if Natasha (Agent Baylor) was transmitting our conversations to any electronic surveillance platform nearby. I found the *'Doctor'* in the Tech Room fitting the tiniest of cameras into a…well, never mind. He fixed me up, but he has a sick sense of humor. He informed me later, too late, the device will make a loud obnoxious noise (the kind you do not want to make in church) if Agent Baylor was transmitting any signal. I think he was pulling my leg, wrong appendage; it's my finger he intended to pull.

I thought the device I wore would just vibrate, not quack like a sick duck. However, as I was walking back in the conference room another Agent, who was consensualized on a different investigation, was checking his transmitter as he passed by me. Sure enough, my RF detector went off.

"Brraacck." What a noise! It was too late. I was already a foot back in the room, my face beet red. "Please excuse me, the Boss caught me in the men's room when I was paged; I must have eaten a bad burrito for lunch." I just kept talking. "Here's the original of the January 17th 1996 memo from Chief of Station, Larry Heightley. Please excuse me. I'll need 15 minutes to get my files together, some are in my car, Charlie has some, and I have to call Stan from INS to see what I can disclose ...you know, getting all my ducks in a row." *Oh shit I said ducks, they're gonna think I did it on purpose. I better apologize.* "Ah I didn't mean anything by the duck shit; something just went screwy with my pager." *Oh shit, I just said shit.* They just stared.

I darted out of the room. Besides being crimson, I needed to make sure, all my notes on this case were in a secure place. I wanted to go over the timeline real quick before going back in the conference room. This was a new development. Where's my decoder ring? There must be some kind of a special cryptic message or some other odd reason; they cannot be this anal. Why would the CIA want the first memo back? They must know John would have made a copy of it. I was not going to leave any stone unturned.

My case file was under my desk but it was not in the exact spot where I usually kept it. The folder, although intact, was in a single knot instead of a double knot, which was my own idiosyncrasy. I always double knot because I was afraid I would lose some hastily written scrap having a tag or an address written on it from a surveillance that I saw in passing, en route to another job. Someone tampered with my files.

I started reviewing the timeline. My mind was racing. *Why would the CIA want the memo back? They already screwed up by giving it to us... it backs up our investigation. Did they really think we would give back the original memo? Now I know the memo isn't brought up by Diplomatic pouch, it is sent by telex, so by 'wire', in fact the 'original' is still just a copy. What is so damn important in the 'original' memo necessitating it be returned.* I only proceed on logic and evidence and this situation had neither.

October 23rd, 1995

Wilson Primkin contacts the local office of the CIA using the dialing 1-800-533-2841; the call is taken by Agent Victoria Baylor. She stated the information concerning the Revolutionary Dominican Party and the soliciting of the illegal proceeds from narcotics sales to fund Jose Francisco Pena Gomez's upcoming election can be sent to P.O. Box 729 Narbeth, Pa. Another CIA Agent David Torrence is willing to go to OAG/BNI office today to discuss the PRD.
I can see now Baylor and Primkin must know each other. Wilson already had her contact number from a prior experience, according to his handwritten notes.

October 26th, 1995

Wilson Primkin sends a memo to Regional Director John Sanderson outlining the scope of the documents received from Daniel Croussano on October 20, 1995. Agt. McLaughlin & P/O Rodriguez complete the translation of Triumph '96 and have the documents available.

October 31st, 1995

Regional Director John Sanderson forwards to Richard P. Diller, Deputy Bureau Director a memo delineating a request for the Intelligence Unit to get involved with this investigation (PRD) in as much as the PRD is getting most of their funds through the sale of illegal narcotics. God further states, it appears the PRD has an agenda to overthrow the Dominican Republic's Government. I'm almost positive Wilson dictated this memo from his cold war days to Carol Maynor, the Regional Director's Secretary and John just gave it his OK and it is passed on, because *there is nothing like saying someone's overthrowing a Government to make bureaucrats sit up and take notice.*

I remember this next entry clearly. It is the day Sixes, one of our most important informants, crossed our path for the first time. We found Sixes (our unofficial name for him) not by chance but by good Police work and being in the right place at the right time.

November 2nd, 1995

Another registered Confidential Informant 'Lucho' who frequents the 'La Princesa' restaurant on the corner of Hope and Lehigh Avenue, overhears Sixes bragging how la policia could not catch him. He also brags about having the best way of hiding heroin even if stopped by the Narcs. Lucho tires of this Dominican and he needs some green, so he places the call to the Red Team.

We learn from 'Lucho', Sixes owns the drug sales in the 2800 block of N. Hope Street. The stamp on the heroin is 'Octopus'. This is a tough block to surveil because there are so many abandoned houses, which offer limitless escape routes for the pharmacological sales men. These dealers make their living darting in and out of vehicle traffic to sell to the walk up, or drive by junkie, in the classic 'stop and cop'. It made North Philadelphia the capital of the Heroin Highway in our area of the East Coast.

We make undercover buys, but catching these people or identifying them is like grasping wisps of air. One minute they are here, the next they vanish into the abandoned houses with uniformed Police in foot pursuit only to find the dealer is jumping across rooftops, exiting out the back and up into another block with a change of clothes and on to sell another day. The workers in this block went so far as to station a half rabid pit bull on the second landing of one of the abandoned houses-chained in such a way the dealers know exactly what steps to take running up the stairs to avoid the canine, climb over the banister, past the landing between the third and fourth floors, and when the Police would noose the dog after a botched pursuit, the dealers would find a replacement the next day.

Lucho is a tried and tested informant. As the information warrants, we watch several days for a copper colored Olds 98 driven by a Hispanic male who drops off a 'package' every day. We need to see someone open the package to reveal what we know is heroin related. On the third day, we get a break; the package is opened in view of the BlackHawk® electronic surveillance platform and what we see on film is not Halloween candy. The street dealer is unwrapping the package, letting his fingers do the walking through racks of 'Yellow Page'® paper which I know are used to wrap bundles of heroin. We took off a couple of buyers we know bought heroin out of this particular package.

With the connection in place, we plan to take Sixes down the next day.

We were in the 2800 block of N. Hope Street and just got back in our vehicles when Sixes drives down the block behind us. He knew we were cops. There was nowhere to go and feeling confident, he continued down the street. He would probably back out if he knew Stan Breward from INS was with us.

Stan carried the weapon of choice against Dominican Narcotics Traffickers, the United States Code. TITLE 8, CHAPTER 12, SUBCHAPTER II, Part II, § 1182 under (a) Classes of aliens ineligible for visas or admission (A) In general (2) Criminal and related grounds (C) Controlled substance traffickers any alien who the consular officer or the Attorney General knows or has reason to believe—(i) is or has been an illicit trafficker in any controlled substance or in any listed chemical (as defined in section 802 of title 21), or is or has been a knowing aider, abettor, assister, conspirator, or colluder with others in the illicit trafficking in any such controlled or listed substance or chemical, or endeavored to do so; or (ii) is the spouse, son, or daughter of an alien inadmissible under clause (i), has, within the previous 5 years, obtained any financial or other benefit from the illicit activity of that alien, and knew or reasonably should have known that the financial or other benefit is the product of such illicit activity, is inadmissible.

Put simply, anyone Stan thinks might be illegal, he can detain, just 'because'. This was kryptonite to every Dominican trafficker; Stan Breward and Walt Meddow were two of the best Special Agents INS will ever produce as far as we are concerned.

  Sixes immediately fails the INS test to impress series of questions. Sixes and his Olds 98 are sent southbound on I-95. The search and seizure warrant gets extra juice by the always-reliable nose of K-9 Hans my former Philadelphia Police K-9 trainer's canine which is available to me on short notice. Eddie does not mind and Hans can find the proverbial needle in ten haystacks, he is good and deadly accurate.

  We let Sixes watch. Hans did a perimeter check on the car and indicates by crawling under the car on the driver's side, jumping up on the hood on the passenger side, and tries to eat through the windshield where the wiper sits in the well. Once the warrant is signed, it is open season. We open the car door and Hans immediately hits on the glove compartment and the driver's side running boards. I open the glove box but nothing is there so I use a pry bar and see some sort of a strap attached to the glove box. Enough!! I rip apart the glove box and find a motorized strap allowing the entire glove box to lower out of place. It reveals a huge space behind the glove box filled with numerous racks and bulk heroin in the form, we call Fingers. The Fingers look like pieces of chalk. However, they are actually compressed processed heroin, called and sold by the name of Fingers. We are not finished yet. My partner, Flash pries open the running board on the driver's side and finds stacks of U.S. Currency. We have Sixes by the short hairs. It is time to lay it on the line.

  "You're history, you are going to do several years in prison, and when your time is up, if your still alive, you'll be deported, and, if you somehow manage to get back in this country, you'll get caught again, do another five years automatically...and any other time you have coming to you, or you can take door number two. Pineapple, tell him what he's just won...in Spanish."

  "A New Car!!!."

  "Damn it Pineapple I'm gonna knock your lights out."

  "Ah...he speaks English Spark."

  "Why the hell doesn't he say something?"

  "I don't know; why are you yelling at me, he's right there ...and he understands you."

  "Well, you got anything to say" Now I am in his face.

  "Callahan, the second door, you didn't splain."

  "Splain, huh...oh, so you know me do you?"

"Yeah Callahan, you're loco."

Sixes, who got the moniker through sheer repetition and his own sense of security, opted to work down his sentence, being closely monitored by both BNI and INS. As is the case with a great many ethnic Spanish surnames, Sixes has two hyphenated last names but he also uses both his first and middle name interchangeably. His first name is the same as another C/I. Sixes puts in a code of a certain pre-arranged quantity of the number six when he leaves his phone number on one of our pagers, thus the nickname. He has to give us good verifiable jobs ensuring an investigation, in accordance with all existing statues and laws and in return, we will give a recommendation to his sentencing Judge. This recommendation needs authorization by the Deputy Attorney General, but it usually works out. There will be numerous assets coming into Philadelphia Region 9 keeping the "Crystal Palace" knee deep in headlines and hard cash. First course of business for Sixes is to show us how the secret compartments work, which he does, making this piece of information worth its weight in gold.

November 2nd, 1995

Sixes is 'on' that day. We get information from Sixes targeting an 84 Olds Pa.Lic/AWA2627 in the 2900 block of N. Ella Street used to store drugs and money by Dominicans. We are lucky enough to spot the vehicle double parked. We wait for the driver to return and after a consent search and 'hit' by K-9 Hans, we find a secret compartment on the driver's side rear armrest with $5,910.00 in US Currency. Also found on the driver is a membership card for the Revolutionary Dominican Party. Case # 9052873-95TA.

November 6th, 1995

Sixes calls again and gives information regarding 42710 N. Bodine Street. A surveillance is initiated and Rafael Morales and Ramon Croussano, both Dominican PRD Members, leave the location in a Grey Honda Pa. License ADK5820. I call for the marked Highway team to stop the vehicle, which they do in the 3800 block of North 2nd Street. The passenger fits the description

Sixes provides and during the pat down, I feel what I believe to be a knotted plastic baggie consistent with the shape and size of an ounce of cocaine. Based on the prior information received from Sixes and the pat down, I retrieve the plastic bag, which later field tests positive for the presence of cocaine, just over an ounce.

I apply for a search and seizure warrant for the location the two males just left and find drug tally work, empty vials used to package crack cocaine, plastic bags used to sell cocaine, a grater and a strainer along with an electronic scale. In what is identified as Ramon Croussano's bedroom I confiscated $2,950.00 U.S. Currency.

While on location at the residence, the phone rings.

"Pineapple, Grab the phone," Charlie barks.

"Yeah, see if you can get any more bodies to join the party," Dennis quips.

"I ain't typing any more warrants, my one finger is worn to the bone; this is a long one." I said, as I looked lovingly at the Eggman.

"Oh no way, Spartacus, 'Don Cheech's' Wheel of Misfortune is out of business.

Wow, the Wheel of Misfortune. I remember when Eggs first made the Wheel.

It is a particularly busy week; we are grabbing Dominican traffickers left and right, working till all hours of the morning, starting at 5:00 a.m. every day. Tommy Litcello, our Three, which is a first line Supervisor, recruits a C/I, 'Beto', and he is hot this week. Ed Eggles is Tommy's typist and warrant guy. First, because Eddie is good at what he does and knows his shit, second, he could type. I feel bad for Eggs, but not too bad; better him than me. I can't type worth a lick.

Eddie, during a breather while typing out three warrants, put his head down and seemed to be coloring. He makes a homemade compass, draws a series of circles, and now is using a ruler and colored pens, coloring in something, on what looks like a pie. He won't let us see, but is moving along like Santa's elf and grins from time to time. He gets some paper clips and punches holes through the cardboard and attaches the paper clips to some rubber bands and some paper. He uses some markers and when he is done, he sits back and admires his work for a minute, as he spins what appears to be a makeshift hand. He turns the project around to reveal what looks like a carnival wheel with little spokes and a lever hitting each spoke when spun, like the old baseball cards in a bicycle wheel.

This game of chance has four names on it; Eggs, Flash, Dennis and Sparky. Eggs name takes up three quarters of the wheels' spaces while the rest of the Red Team's names only take up one quarter. The sign reads "Tommy's Wheel of Misfortune."

I'm first. "OK Eggs, I'll bite, what the hell is that?"

"This, my friend, is the goddamn way Tommy picks the next guy who is typing the next warrant. It must be, because you sons of bitches are doing one to my four."

The Eggman still has the shittiest grin, which will have you laughing till you choke. Eggs puts the sign down, lights up a cigarette and continued typing.

***

"Spark, a culo named Pedro is on his way to drop off money for the Rock."

"Oh so he thinks he's gonna pick up some crack huh?"

"Nooo, Rock in this case is 'Pena'; 'Pena Gomez'," Manny grins.

"Boys," Dennis sits down next to one of the handcuffed prisoners on the couch putting his arms around their shoulders and talks to them like they understand him, "I'm going to make myself comfortable, seems like we just hit a homerun. Wake me when we're going to snatch this mutt."

We send the marked units away and soon we see a male coming up the walk yelling "Chicilito."

"En la cocina." Pineapple yells from the kitchen without showing himself. When Pedro Pagan walks in the house, the look on his face speaks a thousand words.

The Ninja Turtles, our affectionate term for the Special Operations Group, are in defensive cover positions with guns drawn and ready for bear. Pagan drops to the floor in the assumed position tossing a banded wad of bills in the process. He goes down putting his hands behind his back; he obviously saw this drill before and he has his part down pat.

Pedro, Rafael, and Ramon are all taken to BNI headquarters where Philadelphia Police K-9 Shep hits for the indication of narcotics present, on the U.S. currency, which totals $2950 and $500 separately. Shep is another Ed Hillman trained K-9 who once ripped the pants right off me in a training exercise, he is hard to fool on any level.

***

November 13th, 1995

Regional Director John Sanderson meets with Special Agents Thomas Crowd and Jack Sweaton of the FBI in reference to the PRD and the FBI state, in the absence of any evidence of terrorist activities within the continental U.S., the FBI will not undertake a major investigation of the PRD.

New information received from Sixes, tells us if the PRD and Pena Gomez win the Presidency of the Dominican Republic the flow of Narcotics will flow much easier into the United States. The G-Man, is a member of the local chapter of the PRD and is now going to be our man on the inside.

December 7th, 1995

Wilson Primkin makes a phone call to CIA Agent Dave Torrence and states he is requesting a representative of the CIA come to OAG/BNI to discuss the PRD as BNI is getting new information every day. CIA Agent Dave Torrence states their Dominican Republic station's interest has escalated because of corroborating information and the CIA will send a field representative to BNI's office on Dec. 11th, 1995.

CIA Agent Victoria Baylor relays to Torrence she will talk only over a secure phone, so Torrence instead instructs her to go in person to BNI.

December 8th, 1995

I receive information from the G-Man there is going to be a contract hit, carried out on a suspected snitch by members of the local PRD. Unbeknownst to G-Man the suspected target is our other informant Sixes. The word on the street is that everyone knows the task force took Sixes in, however he is out on the street, so he is a rat according to rumors. We give Sixes fake court papers with court appearance dates; the rumors on the street however, will have people believing what they want.

I needed to act fast. I use my undercover Blue Pathfinder, as I know I will have an advantage of height and attempt to pull alongside a silver Ford whose passenger is taking a black semi-automatic out of the glove compartment according to our eye on the street. As I pull up, I can see the gun in the passenger's waistband as the vehicle speeds off, only to be blocked at the end of the street by P/O Joe Banks in Highway-49. Both occupants flee. The passenger, who is later identified as Jose Chichardo, is apprehended and the weapon, a .9mm Semi-Automatic, with the serial number obliterated is recovered. The weapon is untraceable and there is one round in the chamber. We only have these guys for weapons offenses but we also have Stan Breward INS Super-Agent. These illegal aliens are hit with Immigration detainers before I am done the weapons charge paperwork. Stan will make sure they get lost in the shuffle and get deported. Catastrophe averted.

December 11th, 1995

CIA Agent Victoria Baylor comes to OAG/BNI and is given a copy of the strategy plan of the PRD. Agent Baylor states the CIA station in the Dominican Republic wants to open up a liaison.

December 12th, 1995

I receive information from Sixes regarding a blue Subaru station wagon Pa.Lic/AYB6824 he followed to 50410 N. Whitaker Ave. (Daniel Croussano's house - the PRD Treasurer) and again our secret weapon, the Pineapple, deploys and observes Hispanic males taking full trash bags from 22522 N. Howard St. Because the bags are not Hefty®, Hefty®, Hefty®, when one snags on a car fender it rips a bit, and green capped plastic vials fall out. This is a known drug paraphernalia selling location. These bags are filled with green plastic empty vials, the kind used to put rocks of crack in, to sell on the street. At the Whitaker avenue location the males from the Subaru are joined by a third male who drives up in a blue Olds Pa. Lic/ AXA2604. A male later identified as DeJesus opens up the secret compartment behind the glove box and takes out two bundles of green crack vials, alleged crack cocaine. The vehicle is stopped and confiscated from where the males reached inside the secret compartment is $22,169.00 of heroin, $2,240 of cocaine, and $6,760 of crack cocaine and 3 illegal Dominican males, all members of the PRD.

Daniel Croussano, Secretary Treasurer of the Philadelphia Chapter of the PRD at 416 E. Allegheny Ave, Philadelphia, Pa, is also the owner of 50410 N. Whitaker Ave and as such he is requested and does give his consent to search his premises for any proceeds of illegal activity. Documents from inside Croussano's house found pursuant to consent to search show numerous members of the PRD to have criminal records. Case # 9058810-95TA. Of note is one Carmen Croussano who is living in Daniel Croussano's front bedroom. We arrested Daniel's sister Carmen, previously on October 31st, 1994 and confiscated pursuant to a search and seizure warrant was 3500 crack vials with a street value of $17,500.00. This is BNI Case # 9061710-94T.

December 18th, 1995

After going through all of the documents seized inside of Daniel Croussano's house, the various pieces of the money laundering trails are coming together. The seemingly insignificant business cards for Dominicanos Echoes, with Daniel Croussano named as Marketing Executive, are quickly identified as the nexus. It is the address listed on the card jumping out at us – 14000 E. Wyoming Avenue. The neighborhood Dominican Newspaper is being published out of The Jose Express Building @ 14000 E. Wyoming Ave. in Philadelphia, Pa. 19120. Pay dirt!

The Red Team is familiar with Jose's Express. Along with M & J Transportation, Jose's Express is a subsidiary of Geraldo's Transportation, Inc., which according to numerous Dominican Informants we cultivate and cases we work prove the theory behind the information. The van services are used primarily by Dominican Trafficking Organizations to transport money and *drugs to and from Rhode Island, Connecticut, Massachusetts, New York, New Jersey, Maryland, Virginia and Florida and of course our own Keystone State, Pennsylvania with Philadelphia being the hotspot.*

For a discounted fee of $25.00 U.S. Currency, a drug courier can call the toll-free number with a pick up location. With no questions asked, a sixteen passenger, unmarked van will pull up at a designated time. The courier will fork over his dinero and sit back and be delivered to the area of Amsterdam and 164th Street in the Washington Heights section of New York City. This is where the Dominican Wild Cowboys, made famous in the Wild Cowboys book by Robert Jackall, reign supreme in the drug market and where a kilo of heroin can be obtained at $85,000.00 (a bargain as compared to $95,000 on the street in Philadelphia).

We have plenty of history with this operation. In August of 1994, we start investigating Jose's Express in Philadelphia. On the 11th, we interdict the van based on a C/I's information and arrest a Dominican Male, Jose Pena and confiscate $10,000.00 and 5 grams of heroin. On September 13 t h, we grab Richard Miranda Cruz with $24,000.00, on his way to New York, and Ana De La Cruz, on the 21st, on her way back with $6,000. When we ask both, whose money it is? They reply, "You didn't find it on me," even though it was under their seats. Again, on November 15th Rafael Hidalgo was en route to the Big Apple with $6,473.00 with money he says he never saw before. The State thanks Rafael for his donation.

These facts and the additional documents confiscated from Daniel Croussano the money remitter, have us taking over the large conference room and bringing in God and Wilson Primkin for an impromptu meeting. I spread everything out on the tables and with Eggs, Dennis, and Flash's help, we lay out a plan to map out all of the drug corners in East Division and run down each organization. We are ready to draw the big picture - how they intersect, how they transport and conceal their drugs and currency, and how it all ties in with the attempt to put Pena Gomez in the Presidential Palace on May 16th, 1996. But we only have six months to connect all the dots.

Wilson lights up like the twinkle in a child's eye on Christmas morning who sees the first shiny toy he actually wanted.

He takes a long look at all the documents spread out across the tables, beset with photographs, scattered here and there.

"John, we have to go OCDETF on this one, don't you think?"

"Wilson, I can't just go poof, 'it's an OCDETF case' - you know it. But I'll be damned if ever I saw a case needing designation, and receive federal money, it's this one."

"Matt Sackett from DEA Group 2 is pretty good in getting our cases adopted federally here, so I would say to contact him first." Eggs chimes in.

"OK Sparky, open up another case on the van service and make sure you put a history of all the times we stopped both vans before, and cross reference what you can, and bring in Customs, Postal, etc... run the gamut. I'm not promising, but to do this properly is going to take time and resources, and resources cost money, money means we need OCDETF."

The OCDETF (Organized Crime Drug Enforcement Task Forces) is established in the '80s for multi-level attacks on major drug trafficking. For a case to be designated OCDETF – it has to be very large scale, national, or international – because it brings in all the agencies including the DEA, FBI, Immigration, ATF, IRS, US Coast Guard and the list goes on. It also means there exist the resources to fight large operations.

"Marie, I'm taking out a new case number, 90597-95TA. Title it Valerio, Geraldo, #593 Walk Hill St, Jamaica Plains, Mass."

"Is this an arrest Spark?" The secretary inquires.

"Give me six months to get back to you, and I'll let you know, if I'm still sane, it is an arrest and then some."

December 21st, 1995

Highway Patrol Officer Joe Banks assigned to the Task Force, stops the Geraldo's van service, the driver, who in front of Officer Banks opens his wallet revealing a PRD membership card showing the service has a license from the Interstate Commerce Commission to transport people as a service. I prepped Joe as I already checked, and the company's license expired and they needed limousine tags. The driver, Joaquin E. Sanchez is also an illegal Dominican Alien.

We have bigger fish to fry. We have arranged for Sixes to take a ride to New York up and back. His mission is to certify the information we received regarding the van transporting drugs and money as a routine practice for the funding of the PRD campaign to elect Pena Gomez of the Dominican Republic.

Joe saw me in his peripheral vision up the road dangling my radio by the antennae out the window. He knew what to do.

"Highway 49 to Command Center."

"Control, go ahead H-49er."

"Control I have a van full of passengers who have paid their fare on a 'shopping trip' to New York; however it seems they have an expired ICC license and the driver has some identity problems with the INS as well, I have my hands full. Control, what do you want me to do with all these people? Do I have to take them all in?"

Joaquin starts to sweat and is ready to do just anything to get out of his current situation.

"Highway 49, this is Control. If the driver can substantiate where he picked up all those passengers and where he is dropping off each passenger, we can account for each person if need to, and if he has some form of ID you can kick him loose and have him take care of all his paperwork issues with the ICC and the INS and you can just issue a warning unless he is giving you a hard time; the decision is yours."

Joaquin is already going into the van and producing every passengers' name and address and their pickup and final destination and it is in Joe's hand within seconds.

Joe and I are speaking out in the open, but it is still a code. Joe told me we could detain everyone and ask for identification because the driver is illegal. We knew the bus license isn't valid and Joe played the good cop and as usual he played it well. Joe told me Joaquin is ripe for the pickin' and would give him whatever he wanted. It is Joe's choice of words and the inflection in his voice giving me my lines. Seasoned Cops are always acting on the stage, playing off of each other, knowing each other's moves, even if they just met, as long as they have time and experience on the job. In turn, I am now in the role of the

Director. I make him out to be the hero and still get what we want, real time Intelligence.

"OK Control, he seems like a decent hardworking guy, I'll let him go with a warning."

We just received names and addresses of five pickup spots and the source of supply for those five spots in New York. One of the pickup spots is Saldivars at 2nd and Lehigh, which is one of the Dominican meeting, spots in our area of responsibility where the traffickers discuss pricing and distribution of narcotics. Several of the other pick-up spots are known drug traffickers' houses. Our intelligence gathering is in full swing.

January 3rd, 1996

Sixes is sent to New York on Jose's Express and on his return the van driver asks him if he is bringing back any material to Philadelphia. (Material is a word often used by Dominican traffickers to denote wholesale narcotics whether it be heroin, cocaine or methamphetamine.) The van departed from 164th Street and Amsterdam and stopped to pick up two Dominican males who just exited an apartment house on the corner. Sixes strikes up a conversation and finds they are bringing back two kilos of heroin and three kilos of cocaine. The van stops in Philadelphia at Front and Wishart Street and one of the males gets off and goes into Daniel Croussano's store on the corner. The other male tells the driver to take him to 51130 N. 5th St. We hit this address before on 11-13-1995 and took over 700 Crack Vials and over $2000.00.

All the reports are now pouring in from the Department of transportation in Maryland, Rhode Island, and New York. The Massachusetts State Police are on board and sending us information on the PRD in Massachusetts.

January 12th, 1996

CIA agent Victoria Baylor calls John Sanderson and states they have been in touch with the Santo Domingo Station and they are very interested in the political aspects of our Revolutionary

Dominican Party and the Pena Gomez election and they will call on the 16th and set up an appointment to send an Agent to BNI.

Between January 13th & January 16th, 1996

DEA Agent Matt Sackett from Philadelphia DEA Group 3 give information to Agt. McLaughlin from a DEA HIDTA (High Intensity Drug Traffic Area) group out of Boston who send detailed information from a C/I who states Bernardo Diaz is the head of the PRD in Worcester, Mass. Worcester Police state the PRD is the hub for large scale narcotics distributors in the New England area. PRD meetings are held once a week and the pricing controls on the narcotics distributed are discussed, among other topics as a course of business. Bernardo Diaz has numerous drug distribution convictions in New York. At one time during the late '80s Diaz is considered to be one of the upper echelon Dominican Distributors of cocaine and heroin in the City of Worcester, Mass. A check with S/A Stan Breward shows an active warrant still in the system for Diaz's Deportation. DEA Case # CC-95-00714.

In the file there is also a Telex from DEA Boston to DEA Washington confirming all of the above information.

January 17th, 1996

CIA Agent Victoria Baylor calls on Wilson Primkin and states she is having an Intelligence official from their Caribbean desk meet with BNI, location to be determined later, for security reasons, to give us a briefing on the PRD. However, before they do, the CIA wants to run a preliminary check on those attending this meeting. The CIA wants the Name, DOB, SSN and where each person is born. The CIA also provides a confidential memo from Larry Heightley, Chief of Station which in part states: PENA is widely seen as the "U.S. Embassy's Candidate" in the 1994 elections."

Personal Information is provided to the CIA on the people attending the meeting with the CIA in the Caribbean.

January 19th, 1996

Arrested Francisco Rodriguez Dominican National (PRD Member) for 125 grams of cocaine case # 90013-96TA

January 23rd, 1996

A C/I (G-Man), gives the same information as a different C/I (Sixes), as to the PRD; if they get into power, they will facilitate the flow of narcotics into the U.S. The C/I goes into the local PRD HQS at 416 E. Allegheny Ave. Bernardo Diaz who speaks at the meeting tells the members PENA-GOMEZ himself sent a message to members to be careful getting caught with drugs on their person or in their cars between now and the May election since it may hurt the party and cause it to be investigated. He did not however urge them to stop selling drugs. A discussion also ensues on the difficulty some members would have in raising $2500.00 In the case of the drug traffickers there is no problem mentioned.

Another discussion is of a plan to ship old cars used for the party in the Dominican Republic. These cars also conceal five to six handguns inside the engines in case of problems surrounding the elections. Bernardo Diaz stresses the need for secrecy because if the current President of the Dominican Republic finds out, referring to the shipments, he will seize the vehicles. Diaz states PENA-GOMEZ will collect the funds at the Grand Reunion, which is will be held at the end of February. Diaz reminds the members, if PENA wins, he will facilitate the flow of drugs into the U.S.

DAG Rick Batton is unreliable so Regional Director John Sanderson orders Agt. McLaughlin to start keeping a diary of when we page Batton and he doesn't respond. Patton never responds to pages, (three search warrants are ready). Batton finally responds to a page on the 24th.

January 25th, 1996

Wilson Primkin calls CIA Agent Victoria Baylor and tells her of the important information received by the G-Man (C/I) and urges the CIA to get a representative up here to our Headquarters in Philadelphia to give direction ASAP.

January 26th, 1996

Agt. McLaughlin and P/O Rodriguez attend a hearing at the Criminal Justice center for the arrest on case #905880-95TA and Daniel Croussano (who collects monies for the PRD) is at the hearing for the defendants. Daniel Croussano approaches me and hands me a business card stating he is the marketing executive for Echoes Dominicanos a Spanish Newspaper, which is being published out of the JOSE EXPRESS office. (Case # 905970-95TA) at 14000 E. Wyoming Ave.

January 29th, 1996

John Sanderson sends a memo to CIA Chief of Station Larry Heightley telling the CIA of the information which is gathered from the C/I (G-Man) at the local meeting of the PRD. John Sanderson suggests that appropriate action be taken in light of the revelation President Samper of Colombia knowingly used drug money in his political campaign.

January 30th, 1996

Wilson Primkin contacts the CIA with two questions Wilson writes in his notes: "Does PENA Gomez have Diplomatic Immunity? The CIA Reported he is not accredited to the State Department as an official of the Government and therefore he does not have Diplomatic Immunity. However, these Banana Republics' issue diplomatic passports freely to citizens and he would probably wave it around and raise hell if he is carrying one.

If, with probable cause Pena-Gomez is stopped while in this country, what would the political ramifications be? CIA replies he is a VIP - he only lost the last election through fraud and is probably going to be the next president of the Dominican Republic. If he is stopped and the charge does not stick it would probably adversely affect U.S.-DR Relations. He said if we are considering stopping him we had better clear it with the State Department first. We would have to do this through DEA."

***

I gathered up my files and ran back toward Doc, who gave me the most innocent look as he re-activated my RF detector repeatedly, making me sound like duck season was in full swing.

Homey, one of the *Ninja Turtles*, jumped out of the armory with an automatic shotgun cradled in his arms.

"Duck Season?" he has an old Hunter's cap on doing his best impression of Elmer Fud and although he scared the shit out of me plastering me against the wall, I responded without missing a beat.

"No, Wabbit Season you big ugly Fudder Rucker, now get outta my way, God's pissed."

"Yo, Spark, Why I gotta be all that? Spark! Spark!!" I threw the device on Doc's desk as I ran by on my way to the conference room. God wasn't amused or at least feigned displeasure well, in front of Natasha who pushed back from the table and her one leg was crossed over the other flipping the top leg impatiently, not unlike a trampoline.

"Where the hell have you been, and don't tell me any crap about burritos again."

"How do feel about tacos...just kidding John." I saw his veins popping a glorious shade of purple. I overstepped my bounds.

"My apologies, Ms. Natasha... I mean Baylor." Jesus I gotta watch myself. "Normally, I have my items close at hand and organized, but this case has so many tangents going off in so many directions and there's our potential political faux pas."

Victoria's eyebrow twitched. She sat upright. I got the reaction I was looking for. I gathered some hint of - you know what WE KNOW, but we wish you didn't.

John slid the memo from Chief of Station Larry Heightley dated today, January 31st to Natasha.

"What do you mean by our faux pas?" Victoria was in full Natasha mode.

"Come on now Victoria, President Clinton is being soft on Colombia announcing a "national interest waiver" exempting Samper and Colombia from being designated as a major drug-producing and drug-transit country so the United States still gives a country aid, whose President's campaign was financed by the Cali and Medellin cartels, and here we are again."

"I'm sorry, what's your name again agent?"

"Sparky, S-P-A-R-K-Y."

"Sparky, enough!! Keep your comments to yourself. Let's stick with what we know and where we go from here." John was getting pissed now.

"Well Sir, a quick look through this document from Mr. Larry Heightley and one part specifically stands out and I'll quote:

"...the Dominican Drug Control Directorate (DNCD) has photographs of PENA in the company of known Narcotics Traffickers."

"Seems to me like since Pena was the U.S. Embassy's candidate in the 1994 election and Natasha here wants the memo back, and here we are again backing the same guy in 1996, I'd say somebody in Washington has their foot stuck in their mouth once again. All I'm trying to do is let somebody know we're backing the wrong horse and instead of making the same mistake twice, let's grab him, lock him up and throw away the key, take all his money and screw the politics."

Victoria was giving me the same look Sister Purifica gave me in the fourth grade when I told her about the Superball® that had gotten away from the guys in the first aisle, flown through the open window, hit the blackboard, ricocheted off her desk, hit Tony Denson on the back of the head, bounced back and hit the blackboard again, hit the pointer knocking it off the ledge which caused the erasers to fall off the ledge causing Mary Boyle to scream and the ball to finally roll down the first row, which woke up Sister Purifica. Sister Purifica, after my explanation, just looked over her light blue horned rimmed glasses at me, much in the same way Natasha was and said, "Oh Really!"

On cue, Natasha responds. "Oh Really!"

It sounds to me 'like who the "FUCK" are you?'

"Yeah really. Here's the game plan, with Gods'..." (Shit). "... I mean with our Regional Director's permission, I'm going to get one of our C/I's in here, get him consensualized, send him into the local PRD meeting to see what the hell is going on, and based on what is said inside the meeting we will go from there. What do you think John?'

"Sounds like a plan, I'll see you to the door Ms. Baylor; Sparky, you wait for me right here!"

As John walked Victoria to the door, I did the old make the telephone ring trick, and answer it just in time. John could hear me feigning talking to Tommy Litcello who needed me to come over his house as he just received some information he couldn't tell me over the phone.

"John, Don Cheech has something hot. I gotta run to his house and I'll be back as soon as I can and we'll get together to debrief." I yelled it as I ran out of the conference room knowing John was going to rip my head off.

If John really had laser beams coming out of his eyes, I was toast, however I escaped to live another day, as out of sight, out of mind, at least for now. We were still at DEFCON 3 and I was leaning toward 2.5; I wasn't going to turn my back on Natasha and where was Boris lurking? Where there was a Natasha, there was most certainly a Boris. When would he show his face? I would know soon enough.

***

Chapter 6

The Landing

"Up Periscope, Secure the Hatches, Dive, Dive, Dive"

Doc was unlocking the periscope on the Blackhawk's®
main surveillance tool, swinging his hat around, mimicking a
similar character, 'Von Stolberg' in the movie Enemy Below.

"Doc, everything OK big fella?"

I backed into the corner of the van, which wasn't saying
much; the entire compartment was five feet by five feet, if the two
Agents inside take turns breathing.

"Range 50 yards ...Ready Number one tube..."

I grab the mechanical arm supporting the digital camera
and swung it close so I could peer out the black onyx porthole
rhodium plated vent, which from the outside looked like an
ordinary chrome accent on a customized van. The panoramic view
gave me a glimpse into what set Herr Doktor off.

Daniel Croussano was standing outside PRD headquarters
greeting all the revolutionary party members as they pulled up to
attend the meeting.

Flash's red Cadillac went past my lens while he was
checking out the license plates of the attendees. I took the
opportunity to get relief.

"Doc, enough already...Flash, Oh Flash!!!" I yelled
through the radio. "This big mamaluke is goin' off again; we're
back in the war and he's sighting targets to hit with a torpedo."

"Am I in his sights?" Charlie shot back.

"I don't think so."

"You're on your own."

This is what happens when you are in cramped quarters for
hours at a time. We were recording the transmissions coming out
of the Philadelphia Chapter of the Revolutionary Dominican Party
meeting held inside 416 E. Allegheny Avenue in the *Badlands*.
Homey dropped us off within filming and receiving distance of the
meeting two hours earlier so we could get all the Party members

coming and going. G-Man would be sending the play-by-play electronically thanks to a special warrant. The speakers represent all walks of life. One minute a doctor is addressing the group, the next a street thug; like most meetings, the recorded conversations get heated at times. The voices are coming at us in a heavy Dominican dialect, so while I can pick out some quips here and there, I know I would need a full translation later. Just as well…can't get caught up in the conversation and lose track of the film and audio tape timing. The switch has to be perfect to preserve the continuity.

The time in between was a different story. You cannot leave or open a door. Although there was a separate generator to clean and cool the air; some bodily functions cannot be masked by any filter.

"We're under chemical attack," I screamed into the radio. "I'm melting, melting, melting…what a world, what a world…AHHH."

Doc grabbed the 150, "Sparky seems to have passed out, I don't know why. They say it's good for roses. Give us another hour until the meeting is breaking up. Send Homey over to drive us out. We'll all meet in the hole-in-the wall east of 95 at Allegheny to debrief G-Man and wrap up. By the way, anybody got smelling salts? I just kicked Sparky and he didn't move. I haven't lost my touch."

The hole-in-the-wall was the place we met to either pre-plan a joint start to hitting a place with a search warrant or to debrief after an operation with a C/I to take their wire off. The idea behind these holes is no one can enter the area without being seen so no one gets an extended view of our undercovers or our confidential informants. If we can get the manpower, a marked Police car blocks any access. It was normal practice to limit the amount of times a C/I goes to Police headquarters for their own self-preservation and anonymity.

G-Man pulled up in his wreck on wheels and climbed out in his signature all black jogging outfit. With a flash of his pearly whites against pitch dark skin, he grinned ear to ear. "I told you, I told you."

He excitedly started a string of phrases in Spanish, talking faster than I can catch. He's getting more frustrated every time I gave him the stop sign. I need Pineapple there to translate now; I can't afford to miss one detail fresh in his mind.

"Manny, where the hell are you?" I squeezed the radio transmitter.

"On the way to HDQTS."

I threw the radio back into the Blackhawk®, separating the battery away from the radio mainframe.

Flash picked up his 150 and proceeded to ball Pineapple out.

"Pineapple, I don't care if you have to cross over a barrier, run a light, or mow down few pedestrians. If you're not here in the next five minutes, you'll be back sealing up Section Eight housing before you chew the last bite of sandwich you're eating."

I could just see Pineapple's head bobbing from side-to-side, looking in his rear and side view mirrors. He'd later swear we have somebody following him; we don't. He was just such a creature of habit; everyone knew he took the first chance he could to fill his stomach.

"Listen to the a-hole screeching his tires." Dennis was squinting looking down the street. "If I was back in uniform, I would snatch the...hey, wait a minute, that car's coming right at us."

"It must be Pineapple; he has eight seconds left. I'd get on the curb if I were you." Eggs backed up as BNI's secret weapon came to a sliding stop.

"I don't want to hear any excuses, just tell me what G-Man is trying to get out, while we were waiting - you selfish sack of seething shit."

"Yo, Spark, why I gotta be ..."

The look I threw stopped him mid-sentence. Pineapple made a military about-face walked over to G-Man and started taking notes.

Near the end of the meeting, Daniel Croussano and some of the other speakers told the general membership to quash rumors of the PRD trafficking in narcotics as it can hurt Pena Gomez in the upcoming election. The members should not be concerned where the campaign money comes from and to mind their own business.

On February 15th, G-Man was again sent into the local PRD meeting. This time the speaker was from New York, a relative high-ranking figure named Rafael 'Fiquito' Vasquez.   In March, Fiquito said, Pena Gomez was coming to New York in the company of five to six bodyguards to collect $550,000.00 to take back with him to the Dominican Republic for his presidential campaign.

On March 25th, 1996, Flash, God, *Von Kook*, Wilson Primkin and I went to New York and met with DEA at 99 Tenth Avenue. Apparently, DEA group 2 in Philadelphia was told not to work with BNI- at the request of the U.S. Attorney's Eastern District office.   No reason given.   In New York we met with Supervisory Agent John Dowell and Supervisory Agent Joseph Sesami, group supervisor of Group D-534. Dowell stated William Dockler, the Associate Special Agent in Charge, was enthusiastic concerning the collaboration with BNI.   Guy Batrillo, Chief of Narcotics of the Southern District of New York accepted New York's related Dominican Revolutionary Party case (CK-96-01534) and assigned two assistant U.S. attorneys, Sharon Latvin and Robert Ferris.   New York DEA initiated their case using information from BNI's Investigation and made all references in their paperwork due to our initiative. S/A Dowell suggested BNI submit a DAG-71 (agency forfeiture sharing) form as soon as possible as there might be a large seizure of money soon.   S/A Dowell also agreed to promptly deputize any BNI Region 9 personnel or their designates.   This was a significant step to receiving OCDETF funding.

New York DEA S/A Don Denson gave me their investigative documents showing PENA-GOMEZ received at least $2,000,000.00 of drug money diverted into his campaign from a drug kingpin "PEDRO MARRERA" (CT-94-00412/MGC11) Naddis# 3314488. The other related New York DEA Files are CC-95-00114, GD-95-0105, CK-96-00153 and GFC1-96-40132.

In a memo to Robert A. Crymen, Special Agent in Charge, New York Field Division from Group T-135 dated February 9th, 1994 it stated in part:

"...Pedro Marrera is supplying the Jheri Curl Gang with at least 10 kilograms of cocaine on a weekly basis.   In addition, Marrera is the most vocal supporter and right hand man to Dr. Jose Francisco PENA-GOMEZ, who is running for President in the

Dominican Republic, under the Populist Party. By all accounts, PENA-GOMEZ will win the election slated for March, 1994. Marrera will become PENA-GOMEZ' Executive Assistant and entitlements to the political power of office. On January 21st & 23rd 1993, Marrera delivered one million dollars each time to an undercover detective in-group T-132 for deposit into an "Operation Pisces" account. The two million dollars is representative of the proceeds of 100 to112 kilograms of cocaine sold on a monthly basis. Group T-132 is investigating the drug profits going into the PENA-GOMEZ Campaign..."

The most significant document I received is a telecon from DEA Santo Domingo to N.Y. DEA listing all the members of the PRD in the New York Area. But it's the cover sheet that got my attention:

Manny,

Here are the requested documents per telecon. Please, Please keep me well informed on this one. Our Collective Asses are on the line.

Thanks in Advance.

Tim

This document was dated March 20th, 1996

BORIS Finally Surfaces

"Hey Sparky, it looks like Natasha's better half just signed in and John took him to the conference room." Marie, one of our secretaries, adopted our terminology in referring to CIA Agent Victoria Baylor.

I checked the sign-in log at the receptionist desk. Dave Torrence-U.S. Government was the only thing listed. I got out my trusty 007® Invisible Ink Spy Pen and wrote "aka BORIS" next to his name, believing the ink would disappear.

Cops are sarcastic sons of bitches and Narcs are no different. When we started working with the CIA all kinds of toy spy stuff started showing up on my desk. I started playing the role around headquarters goofing off with whatever gadget finding its way to my desk. I didn't bank on a fellow pranksters replacing the 'invisible' ink with indelible ink. I waited for my handwritten "BORIS" to disappear. It seemed like an eternity - no fading. Shit. Agent Torrence will have to sign out of the building. If the 'BORIS' signature doesn't disappear, I'd be leaving another lasting impression.

"Sparky and Charlie, come to the conference room."

Showtime.

"This is Dave Torrence with the Government. Sparky get me copies of the consensuals you made so far. We're going to share them with Dave who would also like to know the identification of your informant and what province he came from in the Dominican Republic."

"Government my ass; this guy's a CIA spook if ever I saw one, although he does look more like an accountant than a spy."

"No Fucking Way, I'm giving up my informant to anybody, let alone him. He just walked in. We don't know him." Flipping his left thumb in the direction of Torrence, "No offense." Flash pushes away from the conference table barely glancing first at Boris, and back at *God.*

"You got to be kidding me, what do you want to do, kill our informant? C'mon John you know we don't give up informants to anyone," adding my two cents.

"Agents, we just want to see if your informant has any ulterior motives for reporting what he says is going on concerning Pena Gomez and Narcotics trafficking. I mean come now; Pena has cult hero status and leads the most influential political party in the Dominican Republic." Boris seemed to be the political officer.

"And he's a Drug Trafficker" I added curtly.

"And he has zits." Flash is a smartass.

"We don't know for sure; this is just a lot of innuendo and supposition at this point Agent... can I call you Sparky?"

"You don't know he has zits?   Didn't you ever see his photo? I picked up where Flash left the line dangling.

"No!   You cannot call me Sparky.   That's reserved for those knowing me well enough to not ask stupid questions, like putting an informant out in the open and in harm's way."

My voice tends to rise when confronted with rhetoric over reason. I am at least two decibels above normal.

"Sparky enough; make copies of the consensuals and give them to Dave. As for the informant, I'll leave that up to you." John is bristling.

"He's Flash's informant so it's his decision. I know what and how I would tell you... go screw yourself."

"What Sparky says, in spades, and *you got something in your teeth*..."

Flash had Torrence unconsciously using his tongue to check his teeth, forcing him to keep his mouth closed.

Flash got up and walked out of the conference room. This wasn't the first time we had to tell some suit off for trying to muscle in a yes man to interfere in an investigation.

"John, can I see you outside for a minute?" Something was wrong and I wanted to know who put John over a barrel with this Spook.

"Not right now Sparky, go get those tapes copied and bring them to my office. We'll talk later."

As I walked out the door I overheard Boris heatedly complaining to John about not getting the cooperation he was promised, and asked for the nearest bathroom (I assume for a mirror for the non-existent need to check his teeth).

"Sparky, I got DEA on 1300; are you at your desk?" Marie came over the intercom.

"Agent, McLaughlin... Can I help you?"

"Sparky, Don Denson here, can you get up here with your Informant ASAP? Pena Gomez is due to arrive on the 4:50 p.m. flight from Miami to JFK. We have two undercovers we want your guy to introduce at the party. He just has to get them in the door. They'll do the rest. We can cover your hotel room but not a per diem. This is it, the Grand Reunion. It's time for a snatch and grab."

Boris was just ten feet away beating Flash's ear, still trying to get the bio on the G-Man.

"Flash," I can't resist, "start spreading the news ... we're leaving today...we're gonna beee a part of it...New York, New York. C'mon Flash sing along; screw the Spook. These vagabond shoes... are longing to pinch...right through the very heart of it ...Pena and the PRDDDD."

"Somebody get Sparky's Librium drip hooked up, he's over the rainbow again." Flash actually managed to crack a smile.

"Flash, Pena Gomez' plane is landing in six hours. It is DEA, New York. Road trip! They want to take him off and we're invited to the party. Bring your dancing shoes. I'll go see God and get the 'okie dokie'. Notify Pineapple to get G-Man warmed up in the bullpen. They're both coming. See Ya Boris...Ehh...Dave, we *gotta* beat feet." I *gotta* remember to watch my mouth.

"His plane's early. Come right to JFK. Each of you can double up with one of our guys when you get here. We have an unexpected problem; the Dignitary Protection Unit of the NYPD is assigned to escort Gomez around when he arrives because of some kind of death threat. One of the Uniforms told one of our guys the State Department is responsible for the escort request." Don Denson was genuinely surprised; I could sense it in his voice.

"BORIS"

Flash and I burst out with the exact same thought at the same time. An increase in force readiness is called for; the posturing required:

DEFCON 2

***

Chapter 7

"Say hello to mi pequeno amigo."

"Flash, we gotta give the G-Man another name to use up here. I don't want anybody knowing who he is; something's going south in Nueva York."

We were northbound just outside of New York in Flash's four-door candy apple red Cadillac Seville which he inherited from Tommy Litcello. The Seville was forfeited as an asset from one of our successful drug prosecutions and pressed back into service.

"Tony Montana." was the immediate response.

"OK I'll bite, How the hell did you come up with an alias so fast? He's not Cuban, even though he's dark skinned ...I don't get it."

"It's perfect, the black jogging suit, the gold hanging out from around his neck, his attitude; he can own this name. And with what he is going to do and the effect it will have in the long run, it's like having an M-16A1 and mowing down an established regime."

"Pineapple, you heard the man, tell G-Man he has just been re-born and baptized Tony Montana. Give me all his identification and check him thoroughly; I don't want one scrap of paper on him."

"Spark, I think he halfway understands, turn around and check this out."

G-Man aka Tony Montana had his hands posed; he was holding an imaginary old Thompson Sub-Machine gun and feigning shooting it, as Al Pacino did in Scarface.

We were on the upper level of the Verrazano-Narrows Bridge, as we made our way from Staten Island to Brooklyn, with an unobstructed view of the Statue of Liberty. I almost felt ashamed; the first image coming to mind was of an ink stamp of the Statue of Liberty on a glassine waxed paper heroin packet. Nothing was sacred in the marketing of heroin in the Dominican world of drug trafficking.

The words "Give me your tired, your poor... your huddled masses yearning to breathe free...the wretched refuse of your teeming shore; not give me your drug traffickers. I thought about what Emma Lazarus had in mind when she penned "The Colossus." Many have interpreted this next line as they see fit; I was no different.

"Keep, ancient lands, your storied pomp."

In my version it would be:

"Keep your bullshit in your country, we don't want it here."

We kept driving along the Shore Parkway and hung a right onto the Van Wick Expressway into JFK airport where along with the thousands of *not so huddled masses* was Don Denson and Rich Volholland of the DEA without any more information in relation to the unexpected news of Pena's NYPD escort.

We split up and jumped into their cars to see how close we could get to Pena and his entourage. A DEA Agent with a press pass tried to get closer to the cars lining up for Gomez, but was turned away. We do not want anyone to know our operation yet so the Special Agent stayed in character not using his Law Enforcement credentials to get through and reported his findings back to the group.

Our efforts were fruitless due to the NYPD escort, so DEA took us to the hotel to check in. At 8:50 p.m. we went back to DEA Headquarters at 99 10th Street and met with S/A's Rich Volholland, Don Denson, Supervisory Special Agent (SSA) Manny Brady, and Assistant Special Agent in Charge (ASAC) William Dockler and Assistant ASAC Anthony Senneca.

We reminded G-Man about his alter ego and he replied with his previous mock Thompson machine gun stance – winking as he mowed everybody down.

SSA Manny Brady asks if they could interview G-Man, and we agreed. We are thrown our first curve ball; we're not allowed to sit in on the interview. Manny says it was because the interview was also being attended by members of the DEA Sensitive Activities Committee.

Flash and I conferred. I had conditions to work in because of what I would play up as the informant's comfort zone issues. DEA could interview the informant without us present on two conditions. One was G-Man would not be asked any biographical information and the second condition was, all questioning will be done through Pineapple as the translator.

"We have Spanish speakers, and…" DEA SSA Manny Brady started into his spiel, but I stopped him abruptly.

"Let's go! Pack up, we are going home." On cue everyone stood up, even G-Man, and started grabbing their coats and headed toward the door (I planned to go just so far but not over the edge).

"Whoa, Whoa, wait a minute, we can do it your way, no problem." Brady recanted.

"Pineapple, can I see you and Tony one minute before you go inside?"

I wanted to give Manny and G-Man some final instructions. "Listen; tell G-Man everything I'm telling you in Spanish and tell him what I'm saying is to protect his identity from everyone else but us. It may seem crazy but trust me I know what I'm saying."

I wanted Pineapple's full attention.

"Spark, is there a problem?" Pineapple was catching on.

"Do you know what Sinn Féin means?"

"Irish Terrorists, wait a minute, I thought we are doing Dominican drug traffickers?" Pineapple's face was scrunched up in confusion.

"Ya goof ball, just making a connection. Sinn Féin means 'ourselves alone' and trust me, in the situation we are finding ourselves, the only people we know for sure we can trust, are the four…well…definitely the three of us."

I gave G-Man a wink in case he understood what I was saying.

"Pineapple, when you go inside, you open and close the doors, you pull out G-Man's seat, make sure he handles any glass, or plate with a napkin between his hand and the object."

"What am I, his maid now, besides his babysitter?"

"Pay attention, I do not want him handling anything anyone can take a finger print off and do not let him answer any question you feel, in any way shape or form, will give away even a hint of who he really is or where he comes from. If you do not like the question asked, you just say you are instructed not to let Tony answer anything you feel isn't appropriate for him to answer without the case Agents being in the room. If they give you a hard time you stand up, take G-Man, excuse yourself, and tell them you have to confer with the case Agents and Tony has to accompany you. Got it?"

"Absolutamente." G-Man jumped in.

I wheeled around. I was whispering or at least I thought so.

"So you Maricón, you speak English, and you now all of a sudden you have ears too, heh!"

"Sometimes-Poquito"

"Well, when you go in there," I pointed to the door behind the Authorized Personnel Only sign", you do not speak any English, comprende? Even if Pineapple doesn't say exactly what you have said, don't correct him. We have our reasons, and it's to protect you."

G-Man snapped to attention, he was in the military now, giving us a salute and started marching toward the entryway.

"¡Mira!" Pineapple called out to G-Man. G-Man did a military about-face.

"Where the hell do you think you're going?" Pineapple was putting his foot down.

"No comprende" G-Man was in full profile.

"I'll no compr…" I stopped Pineapple in mid-sentence by whispering in his ear.

"Acting?"

"¡Sígueme! G-Man fell in behind Pineapple dutifully as Pineapple told him to.

"Lead the way, Agent Brady, we're ready."

As Pineapple followed SSA Brady through the door into the interview area, G-Man apparently could not help himself. He turned around and gave us the OK sign with his right thumb and index finger and an exaggerated wink before he disappeared through the door.

"Oh shit, we might be in trouble; we just threw the sheep to the wolves."

Flash said what I was feeling, but we needed to wait and see. We did not really have a choice at this point if we wanted the investigation to proceed. We were in another Agency's backyard and it was their rules. They could always take the football and go home and we would not get invited to the Super Bowl.

"Flash, what time is it?"

"Spark, its fifteen minutes past the last time you asked me."

"Jesus, I've had enough. The next time they come out for a pee break we're leaving. DEA is breaking his balls all night, trying to poke holes in the information he provided. He's solid as a rock. If he's not out here in the next couple of minutes, I'm going in."

I intentionally started to raise my voice and move closer to the *Authorized Personnel Only* door. My not so subtle intention to be heard works. The door opens at 12:30 a.m. and G-Man, Pineapple and DEA SSA Manny Brady come out. I jumped on Manny Brady.

"We're leaving! Either you give us a ride back to the hotel or we will walk. Either way, we're done here. You are not keeping our C/I in there all night and turning an interview into an interrogation. You apparently forgot he is on our side and is working for us, not the bad guys. I'm not letting you or anyone else treat him like he's done something wrong here, because the opposite is true and you know it, or your *collective asses wouldn't be on the line.*"

I threw the quote from Tim on the Telex back in his face. I was pissed off and I wanted him to know it. He got the full picture immediately and tries to wash his hands and play the good guy. Everyone knew if we were right, U.S. Policy in the Americas screwed up once again, and it would embarrass the Clinton administration.

"Sparky, I agree with you 100 percent. I told them they were keeping you guys too long but I'm a peon like you. I was overruled; I'm on your side. I want these bastards as much as you guys. You gotta know though, what we're planning to do is not only going to affect a whole country, but the whole Caribbean region."

"Yeah, so?" Flash, Pineapple and I sarcastically blurted out the same thing within a millisecond of each other.

"Are you driving us back to the hotel or what?" I'm tired of this shit.

"Yeah, you're from Philly." Even Manny Brady laughed at our matter of fact attitude.

We have a reputation for not caring who someone knew or what politics were involved. If you are trafficking drugs in our domain, and we got the goods on you, you were history.

At 11:00 a.m. Thursday the sun was shining bright or at least it appeared to be. The view from my window was brick and mortar shadowed by the Empire State Building. I was straining against the hotel window trying to see the peak, when a knock came at the door. I backed up suddenly and fell over the edge of the bed. It was the smallest hotel room with the largest price per night I ever stayed in. I made my way to the door where I was greeted by the Chief of the Southern District of New York, Assistant United States Attorney Guy Betrillo and another AUSA Robert Ferris.

"I'm Chief Betrillo AUSA. This is Bob Ferris who handles the prosecution should we be able to prove any viable case here. I'm a little confused. I went to the front desk to find out where Police Officer Hernandez was staying with the C/I and the clerk told me he wasn't registered here." He was rocking back and forth with an attitude believing we will succumb to his mere presence.

"Correct." I'm going to make them work for it.

"Well, where are they?" he was stuttering in anger.

"Close by…I relocated them."

"Excuse me?" The tone was indignant.

"Acoustics are a problem in here...I said I relocated them. We have concerns after the questioning of the C/I and subjects I explicitly told Supervisory Special Agent Manny Brady, were out of bounds. My partner and I decided no one was going to have access to our informant again without us present without clear guidelines established."

"Agents, I assure you…"

"Tut, tut, tut, I don't want to hear it. Now if you want to question the informant, my partner Charlie and I are present and our translator Manny Rodriguez is the translator used and there will not be any questions posed as to the identity of the informant or where and when he is born. If you're agreeable and my partner, who is the C /I's handler, feels comfortable, we will contact the C/I and have him brought to us here while you wait in our room."

"I guess we don't have a choice." Betrillo smirked. "But why the fuss? He's just a common street thug trying to shave off some time, isn't he?"

"Yeah you have a choice, there's the door." Flash was always impatient with suits.

"We would appreciate it if you called the C/I over here Agents," AUSA Ferris jumped in to break the tension.

Instead of getting on the cell phone or the landline, I opened the door and gave a loud whistle down the hallway.

"You prick!" The head suit jumped up from the sofa stepping out of character.

"Now, now Counselor, your crudeness is showing."

Pineapple and G-Man walked in the room, ten seconds later.

"OK, OK, you made your point. But I did bring good news." Guy Betrillo handed me a memorandum.

"Proceed with your questions, counselors."

I let the questioning go on for an hour before breaking in and telling the AUSA's we needed to sync up with the DEA agents to go over the plan for tonight's main event.

*****

Chapter 8

Manhattan War Dance

At 8:30 p.m., the PENA-GOMEZ entourage arrived at 76 Wadsworth Street in Manhattan at PRD Headquarters and Flash sent G-Man in to pave the way for the New York DEA undercover Agents. The DEA undercover agents, Carlos and Marisa (who were consensualized) were supposed to be traffickers out of Florida with connections to Colombia and Cuba. They looked the part, at least the way Latin American traffickers are portrayed in mass media. They were *dressed to the nines* all decked out in black, both with sleek physiques, looking like they were going to a Hollywood premiere instead of a DEA Special OP. We're getting the play-by-play via the DEA's car-to-car radios by Special Agent Don Denson.

"OK, Carlos and Marisa are at the door and Tony just gave Carlos a bear hug like he hasn't seen him for years and he...Whoa!!...Wh...Where'd you get this guy, he just planted a wet one on Marisa, Tony should get a *Tony* for this performance."

Flash quipped "Are they in?" sarcastically.

Don came back "Oh yeah, no problem, Tony's acting like he owns the place. He just introduced them to Pedro MARRERA."

We just recently learned of Pedro Marrera, he was in DEA's Narcotics and Dangerous Drug Indexing System Number with a NADDIS # of 3314488.

Pineapple gave us the lowdown on our own 150 radios; he was listening in on Carlos' wire. Carlos told Pedro they represented people wanting to make a contribution of $250,000.00 a month to the campaign of PENA-GOMEZ in exchange for letting them land five airplanes a month in the Dominican Republic, no questions asked, should he be elected President. Pedro was overheard inviting them to stay through the meeting and attend the Grand Reunion at the Waldorf-Astoria in Midtown Manhattan. The two DEA Agents exited a short time later followed by Tony and are picked up separately.

"Aha, I tol' you, I tol' you, but you no believe me." Tony was visibly excited; sweat was rolling down his cheeks.

"Relax, you're not done yet, we want you to go party a little bit." Flash was helping him into the back of a black window tinted sedan.

"Qué chevere!"

"Oh great, huh, we bring you up to New York and all you say is Great! You get to go to a big party, maybe eat some *chicharron de puerco*, do some merengue, and get paid for it. I was breaking his stones; couldn't let him off easy.

"No chicharron de puerco, 'pork fritters' gives me the winds, but I can Merengue!" I swear this guy didn't speak English only when it was convenient. Tony aka the G-Man was dancing from the waist up with an air chica instead of an air guitar. He was even faking some dips. Too much commotion for a guy we normally couldn't get out of bed on time. The New York lights seemed to agree with him.

We drove to the next staging area within walking distance of the Waldorf Astoria. I rattled off some last minute instructions through Pineapple to Tony but his mind seemed elsewhere. He got out of the car and started doing the Merengue on the sidewalk, again with an air chica.

"Flash, do something with him, he's back in the DR."

"I'll handle it, Spark."

Flash got out of the car, but instead of bawling out Tony, Flash grabbed his outstretched hand and started dancing with him.

"You son of a ... oh well, what's the use."

This was a scene to behold. A Dominican Dark as the Ace of Spades and a White Ethnic Russian Boy from Philly dancing the Merengue in Midtown Manhattan to an unseen band in the town that never sleeps, in the middle of an International narcotics investigation.

DEA pulled around the corner and came to an exaggerated stop at the floorshow before them. Rich Volholland, usually reserved, was first to get a one-liner in. "I'll give them a seven but I need to know which one's the woman."

"What woman? This is a manly thing only men can do with other men. Don't you guys get recess up here?" I wasn't giving them an inch.

"Last call gentleman, you don't have to go home but...you can't stay *queer*."

"So do you guys have to go through a yearly psyche eval or is it bi-annual?" Manny Brady walked up, shaking his head.

In tandem, and on cue, Flash and Pineapple pointed at me and said, "He's got Papers!!!"

I took the customary bow.

"My other nickname was Psycho, a long story, however the papers they were referring to stated I was perfectly sane, just persistent and unwavering. "Shall we get to the mission at hand? We can't stand around dancing all day; you guys at DEA will just have to get your dance lessons somewhere else."

I think we stopped the DEA in their tracks. No one spoke for what seems like minutes but in reality was only seconds. They stood frozen with puzzled looks on their faces.

"Yo, guys, snap out of it. I got dinner on the stove and it's getting cold. Are we gonna do this or what? Where's *Darren and Samantha?*"

"You mean Carlos and Marisa?" Don Denson just wasn't in the spirit.

"Darren and Samantha, Carlos and Marisa, whoever, let's go work some magic and take off this glorified Narco-Trafficker." Boy, these guys didn't have any fun in their job...

"Pineapple, tell Tony to jump in with the Feds; you go with him. Let's get this show on the road; whose got the eyeball?"

***

Chapter 9

Double Cross and the Potomac Two-Step

We were moving now and Tony was dropped within sight of the Waldorf Astoria with the DEA Agents walking from the other direction. They met at the entrance and Tony gave Carlos the bear hug; Marisa was prepared and extended her hand. Or so she thought; wrong move.

Tony was *'on'*. He grabbed her hand and twirled her toward him in a dance move, but gallantly he swirled her into the arms of Carlos. I hoped these two agents were at least friendly or was it going to be a long night.

Once inside Tony again found his way to Pedro and like a good little host, according to plan, he mingled and made separate observations.

Marrera introduced Carlos and Marisa to Rafael 'Fiquito' Vasquez, who was the National Coordinator of the PRD in the United States. Pedro was overheard on tape telling Fiquito about the offer the DEA Agents have made. Fiquito walked up to the dais and whispered in the ear of Dr. Rafael Tantigua who Vasquez said was the PRD's Executive Commission President in the United States. Tantigua, a seemingly scholarly man, spoke softly and agreed to discuss the proposition at a later date; numbers were exchanged with Carlos and Marisa. Tantigua was extremely cordial and told the undercovers, he would reach out within two days.

Carlos turned to leave with Marisa in tow and they both started to scan the large room for Tony. They found him cornering another Dominican male; the task of rounding him up unfortunately fell to Marisa.

"Venga, por favor."

Tony gave his compadre a big smile, which was returned immediately, and was led away by an impatient Marisa.

However, instead of heading toward the dance floor which was Tony's plan, Marisa's grip forced a "Guay mi Mai" out of Tony.

Tony's expression brought a smirk to Marisa's face; they met up with Carlos and walk back to the staging areas in two different locations in case of counter surveillance.

When G-Man (Tony) returned, he said the guy he was talking to was Vinicio Sanchez, back out on the street after beating a murder rap in Philly. He told him that the Philadelphia Chapter brought $10,000.00 and Nelson Cuello was bringing the grey duffle bag of cash to the Grand Reunion. There were 50 people standing in line at a side room guarded by an extremely large dark Dominican male; everyone was carrying a bag of money. The fund raiser was expected to net $500,000.00.

G-Man recognized Bernardo Diaz seated at the dais and was introduced as the Secretary of Finance for the PRD.

"Flash you got Stan Breward's number on you?"

"Yeah, why?"

"I'm pretty sure, but I just want to confirm. Brewmiester told me Bernardo Diaz was on lifetime parole for trafficking and he had an outstanding warrant for deportation."

"OK, I'll hit him up."

"Brewster, it's Flash, you awake?"

"No, at the sound of the beep, leave a message for Stan Brewarrd, BEEEPP!"

"Are you drunk?"

"Not yet, but I am very tired, only one beer…just got in after 16 hours straight. If you need me, just pick me up. I ain't driving."

"No, no. Just a quick question. Do you remember if you have a warrant to deport Bernardo Diaz?"

"Yes."

"Yes to which?" Flash was getting reeled in.

"Who?" Stan had him.

"Who? I just told you who, Bernardo Diaz."

"What?"

"I don't know…what the hell are you saying?"

"I don't know, he's on third."

It took Flash a few seconds before realizing he was Costello to Stan's' Abbott.

"Hold on a minute, Stan; Spark wants to talk to you." Flash reached across the car held the phone to the squelch on the radio, cranked the volume, and hit it quickly with a loud blast.

"YES...yes, I got a warrant. I answered you the first time." Stan recovered enough to answer quickly and without the radio show.

"Spark, Stan's got a warrant."

"Tell him I said thanks, and to go back to bed."

Everything was going as planned. The money was there; at least $500,000.00, if not more, collected in paper bags. The head of the PRD, who was approached with a proposition to land five planes a month in exchange for $250,000.00, did not have the DEA undercover agents thrown out of the party; did not alert the authorities or tell the DEA Agents to go to hell. He did, however, exchange pager numbers and agree to meet later to discuss the arrangements after this event, making it clear he was speaking for Pena Gomez.

We waited patiently watching for the entourage to leave for the airport. We already checked on the return flight and the same crew that flew in would be on the redeye tonight. Doubtful they'll be declaring the cash money going out of the country; we'd be ready to pounce as they were loading it onto the plane. We would seize all their funds and once a forfeiture hearing was held our Agency would get its fair share. Feeling good!

"Sparky, we're going to regroup at DEA headquarters." It was SSA Brady coming over DEA's car-to-car radio.

"I'm sorry, my radio must be breaking up; it sounded like you said we were getting off of these guys. I'm sure I have bad reception."

"No you heard right; don't kill the messenger."

"Somebody's gettin killed if you're telling us we just wasted our time the past couple of days."

"See you inside." Manny Brady's weary voice trailed off.

Someone from Washington stepped in and crushed our attempt to seize over $550,000.00 in proceeds from narcotics sales laundered as fundraising for a third-world political campaign. Further, several dozen law enforcement officers stood by on orders from the DEA Sensitive Activities Committee or some other nameless DC entity as these funds illegally left our country. No one was touching Pena Gomez or his entourage. With no jurisdiction, we were powerless.

In Summation (Wilson would be proud of me) as Pena Gomez, et al, were not associated with any diplomatic immunity; according to the U.S. Customs website:

"You may bring into or take out of the country, including by mail, as much money as you wish. However, if it is more than $10,000, you will need to report it to CBP. Ask the CBP officer for the Currency Reporting Form (Fin Cen 105). The penalties for non-compliance can be severe.

"Money" means monetary instruments and includes U.S. or foreign coins currently in circulation, currency, and travelers' checks in any form, money orders, and negotiable instruments or investment securities in bearer form."

None of those conditions were met. In fact a good portion of the money was from the illegal proceeds of narcotics sales. We had first-hand electronic evidence corroborating this fact. The Good News AUSA Barillo handed me earlier at the hotel was a memorandum from AUSA Samantha Jo Black addressed to Carlos XXXX stating her office was going to secure interviewing certain material witnesses and she would support significant prosecutable federal cases derived from the investigation.

What the hell is going on?

***

Chapter 10

Triple Cross – 'Why can't we all just get along?'

I learned many years later through dogged determination we would have embarrassed the current administration, so the DEA Sensitive Activities Committee -- in conjunction with the other three-letter agencies -- put off Operation Crown Jewel http://www.justice.gov/usao/nys/pressreleases/December03/crownj ewelindictment.pdf until 2003.

My bonifides say one of the fugitives missing was Carlos Alberto Villavizar Guzmán who was listed on our hand written notes by Wilson Primkin on March 25, 1996, a sample of which is provided below.

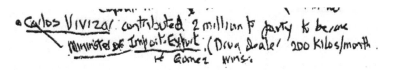

Carlos wasn't arrested until 2005; he was connected to the PRD in multiple other documents, which I will not reveal at this time. http://www.justice.gov/usao/nys/pressreleases/June05/reyes-mendozaextra.pdf

I am, however, getting ahead of myself.

We drove back to Philadelphia in silence. Flash drove, Pineapple and G-Man slept and snored what sounded like "you got screwed," over and over all the way home. My usual migraine - *nicknamed 'Mikey'* - proliferated to such an extent, I renamed it Michaeleen.

We had a couple of days off and got right back in the game.

April 3rd, 1996

I got a call from Sixes as to the address 60850 Pacmetto Street. He gave us information on the same organization at 13245 E. Luzerne Street on 03-04-96 leading to the arrest of five individuals and the seizure of $129,590.00 of heroin.

I sat on Pacmetto Street for days. Neighbors actually called the Police on me twice, saying I was acting suspiciously.

Early one afternoon just as I was about to move to another location to check out an anonymous tip. I watched a Maroon Chrysler come up the street, noticing an expired inspection sticker; and as the vehicle turned in front of me, I noticed a Pennsylvania license plate also expired and it was the wrong plate for the issued year.

"H-46. Hey Joe, do me a favor; run this tag and see what comes up. It's hanging on a Chrysler."

"Spark, Radio says it's registered to an Acura. If it's a Chrysler, it's a *pause for cause*."

I could almost see Joe Dank grinning.

I moved, getting a better vantage point so I could see the doors of the apartment complex better. The Hispanic male who drove the Chrysler in, was leaving carrying a large trash bag. I told Joe to stop him away from the area and when he does, Joe gets on the air.

"Spark, he's acting real nervous. He doesn't have a license or any paperwork for the car and guess what? The VIN (vehicle identification number) is missing from the doors and the dashboard."

"Well, I don't have to tell you what to do. You know our motto:

"Cuff 'em and Stuff 'em."

"Done and done."

I watched as Joe put the Hispanic male in the back of his patrol car. There is only one other place the VIN is readily accessible, the trunk. Since we didn't know who owned the car and would take it into custody, we'd be inspecting the trunk anyway.

I'm back a bit, but within range to back Joe up if he needed it. I saw him open the trunk and he started jumping up waving wildly to me. I held my '150' out the window by its antenna, my usual signal to get on the Radio.

"We hit the Motherload! It's a trash bag full to the top with bundles of crack cocaine. Unbelievable."

"Alright, I'm coming up the street. We need to get the car off the street and out of sight in case anyone is looking for this guy to make a delivery. Call for a wagon; we'll take him in and see if he'll flip."

I got on the air quickly. "Flash, you out here, you got your ears on?"

"Go ahead Spark, I got you."

"I got one en route. We just cornered the crack market. Meet me in headquarters and bring your pajamas, it's going to be a long night."

"901 to 926."

"Jesus, he comes out of the woodwork; do you know if Von Kook is in headquarters or on the street?"

John D'Amato heard me talking to Flash over the air.

"You're on your own, Spark, go to channel one and face the music."

"Yeah, you're right; I'll switch back to two after I let him know what we're doing." I reluctantly reached out.

"926 to 901, John we have a good hit and I think it may lead elsewhere."

"I'll meet you inside."

While en route to HDQTS, Jose Rato said he wanted to cooperate. I had prior knowledge there was an ADA Weinstein in the Philadelphia District Attorney's Office, Dangerous Drug Offender Unit who was working a prosecution concerning the same narcotic trafficking group. It was *'Dogface'* whose countenance resembled a bulldog, thus the moniker. I asked the permission of Deputy Attorney General Neverlong to contact Philadelphia ADA Weinstein to come down to BNI for the rest of the investigation. The resulting seizure was $397,320.00 of heroin, $55,600.00 of cocaine and $30,000.00 of crack cocaine. ADA Weinstein worked with our Agency 'til at least 2:30 a.m. in the morning, approving all of my warrants. He even went out on the street with us to see the job to its conclusion.

I argued with Jay over having the cooperating defendant sign a consent to search for properties he controlled. I wanted search warrants; Jay said it wasn't necessary. I reminded him how the Philadelphia District Attorney's Office and our Office, at above-our-pay-grade levels, are like oil and vinegar; they just didn't mix.

Jay said for this investigation, he represented the District Attorney's Office and he guaranteed what he said goes. He would co-sign the consent to search. Case# 9012134-96 was in the bag.

There was a Philadelphia Assistant District Attorney with us throughout the entire case except for the original stop. He consensualized the defendant who wanted to cooperate. He witnessed the defendant's phone call to the eventual co-defendant and finally after being on scene at the execution of the warrants, ADA Weinstein approved all of the charges against both defendants.

We had tapes and cooperating witnesses. Slam, bam, thank you Ma'am.

***

Chapter 11

DEFCON 1 – 'Ourselves Alone'

April 23rd, 1996

Walt Bunter, a local Television News Reporter from BRM in Philadelphia, was in our headquarters parking lot by the sign identifying the Pennsylvania Attorney General. It was right before the 12 p.m. news and he was setting up for a noon shoot and I just happen to be driving through the parking lot and notice the commotion.

"Do we have a press conference today? Walt Bunters' outside and he's getting ready to go live." I was asking a general question to Flash, Dennis, and Eggs, who were sitting at their desks kibitzing.

"No, the General's not here, there's nothing new going on that I know of." Eggs was interested. "Von Kook has a television, call him on the loudspeaker, and tell him *God* wants to see him. When he runs upstairs, we'll go in his office and turn the deadbolt and lock him out. Sanderson just went out to get a sandwich; Von Kook will never know what hit him."

It worked like a charm. Von Kook was muttering out loud relevant to God calling him on the loudspeaker, instead of the phone, and he had enough of his mightier than thou shit.

We piled into Kook's office and tuned in his television just in time to hear. "This is Walt Bunter standing outside the Bureau of Narcotics Investigation of the Pennsylvania Office of Attorney General where I have learned a group of Narcotic Agents are now under Federal Investigation and the United States Attorney's Office and The Philadelphia District Attorney's Office is now refusing to take their testimony on any cases brought for prosecution in through either of those prosecuting authorities."

We looked at each other in disbelief. No one spoke. I thought for a second, and went over to the Kook's calendar.

It was exactly 15 days from the day we refused to give the CIA our informants' biographical information. They retaliated. I am certain of it.

I knew to start circling the wagons, there was a war starting.

It was inevitable. I realized it now. We were at...

DEFCON 1

My initial reaction was to start photocopying everything I had. The news reporter didn't say why exactly, and who the Narcotics Agents were, but you can bet being so close to what just went down in New York; we were on the chopping block.

There was an ongoing probe in the Philadelphia Police Department that started in the 39th Police District and somehow moved into the ranks of the Philadelphia Highway Patrol. The news naturally extended the connection to our office. Well this time they weren't wrong, in fact they may have even helped the CIA and the current administration in DC by spreading rumor and innuendo without the facts to support it.

However what wasn't being reported and hasn't been reported to this day in any newspaper or any other media was before becoming employed as a Narcotics Agent for the Attorney General's Office, in the course of doing the background investigations of any potential employee; one of the most basic requirements was the taking of an invasive Lie Detector Test.

Since I wasn't hired with BNI until February of 1995 and my background would have been done around August to November of 1994, with the lie detector being administered on November 10, 1996, means my tenure as a Philadelphia Policeman from the years 1977 through 1994, approximately 17 years, were all under review and scrutiny of the Lie Detector Technician.

Not only did I pass, but I did so with a comment from the technician--he never met anyone who answered as truthfully as I did. I revealed some personal things when asked, and answered every question with the highest form of integrity.

Again as Veteran Police Officers we find some of the questions a little odd and responded sarcastically.

"Did I ever have sex with an animal? Well, depending on your definition of an animal. Some women call us pigs and at *last call* at the FOP, we have called some women the same thing when they turn the ugly lights on, you know, last man standing and all."

"Officer McLaughlin, the question requires a yes or no answer."

The tech said this several times trying to maintain his composure; he was used to the sarcasm; but I don't think the background teams were ever used to all of us.

I remember the MMPI psych test they gave to all of us together in one conference room in Harrisburg being semi-monitored. There were a bunch of us from Philly getting hired and we weren't worried about these kinds of things as we went through it before.

However, there are those, like a guy I'll call "D-Man."

We were running through the test like we loved everybody, are social, didn't want to be forest rangers, wanted to be teachers, yadda, yadda,…and when the monitor would leave, there would be guys yelling out the answers across the room or laughing at the questions.

"D-Man" was having a heart attack. He was the kind of guy whose Mom still laid out his clothes every day. When we got to the academy later we actually *dimed him out* to one of the instructors. He was setting up ammunition in his room. We were getting worried. We were undergoing firearms training; we were not issued weapons yet, nor ammunition, but this guy was lining up bullets along his desk.

Yes, he did graduate, but didn't last long with BNI; those types usually don't; he's a good guy, he moved on to another three letter agency. Frankly, 'Bravo Investigator', was all I had to say.

Getting back on track. I awoke the next morning to a call from Flash.

"Yo, Did you see the Sentinel?"

"No, Why?"

"This guy Mazollo was writing front page shit concerning BNI?"

"Screw him, not to worry, circulation must be down; see you inside after Court. I have the 'Dogface' job with ADA Weinstein."

When I got to court I saw Jay and I also saw 'Dogface' in the gallery talking to a guy with a spiral tablet, indicative of a reporter in those days.

I approached Jay and he told me to follow him outside.

"Sparky, the case is getting continued; 'Dogface's' attorney Sly Gialla requested a long date because of another commitment. My guess was he didn't get paid yet. Which reminds me, something's fishy; our Nebula hearing got tanked. Somehow the papers weren't served in time on his cash bail."

The guy who was talking to 'Dogface' interrupted our conversation and introduces himself.

"I'm Largo Mazollo from the Sentinel. I was wondering Agent McLaughlin, if you would like to comment regarding BNI being investigated."

"First, as far as I know we're not being investigated. Second, I'm not permitted to speak to the media; you are referred to Harrisburg. I assume you were already aware of the policy."

"And you ADA Weinstein, are you going to prosecute the case Agent McLaughlin is here for today?"

"We are definitely going forward on this case."

"Can I quote you?"

"Yes."

In retrospect the "Yes", and Jay being there, when we needed him, seeing first hand everything we did was on the level, probably cost him his career, as later he too, suffered the fate of the *alphabet soup* disease. He drank from the poison well of the Red Team and bled red too.

Later at night when I returned home angry and upset relevant to this *rag writer* confrontation, I was greeted by a message on my home answering machine from the same *poison pen scripter* I left earlier in the day.

Now I was really pissed as I paid extra, like most in law enforcement, to have my phone number unlisted and I purposely did not give it out to any credit company, etc. I gave out my cell phone, instead.

I called Regional Director John Sanderson and made a complaint through him to internal affairs. Someone gave out my home phone number to the press. I called the Philadelphia Police Dept. and make a formal Complaint on District Control # 96-12-23879, which Sgt. Nick Sanini took, who I happened to know from when we both received 'Hero' commendations for a fire rescue. We chuckled for old times' sake.

The next morning the Headlines in the Sentinel read:

Drug Cases in Doubt, State Task Force Work Questioned

These headlines became a daily way of life for us; both in the Sentinel and its sister paper the Noon News. It was a constant display of negative press and all the time tried to link us to the corruption probe of the Philadelphia Police department.

On April 29th, Lou Camiel, and Jim Maggiano came to the Office at BNI and told all the Agents, we will only be doing i nvestigations, able to be brought before the Statewide Grand-Jury. Those are prosecuted by our own Deputy Attorney Generals.

Well this at least looks like a positive step for us, Screw them all. We will do our own jobs from beginning to end.

'Ourselves Alone.'

***

Chapter 12

The Bastard Squad

May 9th, 1996

The Blackhawk[e] was taken out to the corners in the Badlands to film Narcotics transactions. A couple of corners were especially highlighted showing sales of heroin stamped "Super Buick." This brand was causing overdose deaths. It was being cut with scopolamine.
http://www.cdc.gov/mmwr/PDF/wk/mm4522.pdf

We told the BNI administration as far back as 1991 heroin was being cut with Rat Poison from the Dominican Republic. This Rat Poison was basically undetectable unless you specifically looked for it; its name is 'Tres Pasitos.' Tres Pasitos contains Aldicarb. Aldicarb is a carbamate insecticide, which is the active substance in the pesticide Temik. "Tres Pasitos," a mouse, rat, and roach killer containing high concentrations of aldicarb, is illegally imported into the United States from Mexico and other Latin American countries. The product is highly toxic to animals and people, and according to the EPA "should never be used in the home." http://en.wikipedia.org/wiki/Aldicarb. The name literally means *three steps* for the reasoning; the rodent should only be able to take three steps before it dies.

We had an informant telling us as early as 1991 Dominican traffickers, when opening up a new corner for heroin sales, will first cut the heroin with "Tres Pasistos," give out a few testers of this combination to local junkies, and if they died, it would appear they overdosed because of the purity of the heroin. Well established junkies built up a tolerance to the amount of heroin needed to put them in their special place.

The other denizens of this netherworld, after saying things like:

"Man "D'you hear, Slim kicked?"
"Yeah, man, he is alright...it must be some good SHIT!"

"You right, we need to take it easy, "
would line up around the corner before the heroin ran out.

Marketing 101 by Dominican traffickers. They take *taste testing* to the extreme, and once they established a *following* to the corner, they would put out the regular Heroin, cut with other additives, less deadly.

No one would listen to us, it wasn't until recently I sought out Dr. Kyle Oysterman after finding an article he co-authored concerning aldicarb related poisonings where he stated there are adult Dominican suicide attempts using 'Tres Pasitos.'

However looking at the suicide rate of both Dominican Males and Females by the World Health organization in 1994 shows zero percent suicides for both genders.

My opinion was the rodenticide, which is readily absorbed through the skin, was being ground and mixed in with the heroin, before packaging. The adult Dominican males showing up at emergency wards certainly are not going to say they are bagging heroin. The next best thing when readily supplied, and confirmed by directed chemical testing is, "Tres Pasitos" poisoning, will only get the Police involved if it is not listed as an accidental poisoning or if necessary, they would succumb to the idea in the U.S. to a suicide attempt, which would get them social services and some free health care.

Either way they won't get a home visit by the local Police, which they were trying to avoid at all, cost.

These are not suicides; they are inhaling their own product. Now our agency was filming the corners of the same traffickers with another deadly 'cut', not as it should be, to be used as evidence against these deadly dealers. They are killing people. Junkies are people too, no matter what your belief, because addiction is a sickness.

At least I know it will come out as a counter offensive against the press and those other agencies who are talking smack about us, and they will want the tapes as evidence. Everyone would see what we say in our reports and affidavits for search and seizure warrants. It will be out in the open, on the television. OK, way to go Home Team!!!

The next day word comes down from Lou Camiel who was the Deputy Chief of Investigations, not to use the videos made the day before, of all the drug transactions of various dealers shelling out the deadly heroin.

It's incredulous. I had a warrant typed up and ready to go based on an informant who told us there was a kilo of this tainted heroin coming to 19000 Kale St. in Northeast Philadelphia where Flash and I videotaped the occupants of the house several days earlier.

In fact, Flash, the *bold brazen article,* as Sister Purifica would call him, was almost caught by counter surveillance, as he needed to get the tag of the vehicle backed into a driveway.

"Flash, where the hell are you? The guy's standing on his porch steps."

"Spark, radio silence from now on, I'm under the car in the driveway. Give me one squelch on the radio if he goes inside, two if it's safe to come out from underneath."

"OK, if you hear me playing *Wipeout*^{e} on the squelch, you're screwed."

Well we had enough for the search and seizure warrant. I finally got DAG Dick Mattingly to answer his page to approve the warrant. *God* was pissed at his failure to respond, and even more pissed, he, meaning Mattingly, was giving me a hard time concerning the approval. *God* pulled the phone halfway out of my ear and started listening to our conversation. When he realizes it had nothing to do with the probable cause aspect of the warrant, and the politics of playing nice-nice to the DA's Office came up; *God* ripped the phone out of my hand taking the earing right out of my ear. Regional Director Sanderson was giving Mattingly a tongue lashing usually reserved for one of us in the cheap seats.

This was a rare occasion, being a spectator, instead of feeling like a spec of sand on life's biggest beach, but I couldn't revel in it. The lid was slowly closing on the coffin of our careers.

May 15th, 1996

Attorney General Bobbit stated to the Press he had pulled five or six agents off the street, replaced the Regional Director, and sent in two prosecutors to review cases. Bobbit referred to many ex-city Police that were hired with their "BAD HABITS." Bobbit verbally bashed his own Agents.

Flash, Dennis, Eggs and I got a letter from Personnel stating Harrisburg was going to turn over Personnel folders to the Public Defender and if we wanted to fight it we were to get our own lawyer. Bobbit said in a press conference that the Agents in question would never get their regular jobs back.

On June 5th, 1996 Deputy Chief Lou Camiel held a meeting in Philadelphia with Flash, Dennis, Eggs and myself and said we could only investigate cases by ourselves and not have any interaction with any other Narcotic Agents in any Investigation.

"In effect, you guys are the Bastard Squad," Lou said without a smile.

Dennis was first, cocking his head back, "What did you just call us?"

"Whoa now, wait a minute Dennis, I meant to say…"

"Wait, shit, we all heard you loud and clear, you called us Bastards." We all got up in unison and started walking toward the door.

"Now come back here!" Lou was calm but trying to be authoritative.

No one turned around, but I quipped in a similar calm authoritative voice.

"Not a good idea."

We walked downstairs feeling for the first time in our professional careers like lepers. We were branded. Not only did we have to circle the wagons, we needed to build a fort, a moat, start a treasury, and what I would find out later, pat down everyone, at least mentally, we came into contact, telephonically, electronically or in person.

***

Chapter 13

"Occupation Requested"

Unbeknownst to management I learned my lesson while still a Philadelphia Policeman and I kept a digital diary of everything that had happened, since we recovered the PRD documents. I was now taking notes on all my movements and anything I felt germane to the events as they unfolded.

On May 21st, 1996 I interviewed C/I 9021378-96 and he/she revealed Jose Francisco PENA-GOMEZ only won the election in the Dominican Republic by twenty percent and there would be a run off on July 1st, 1996. There were 24 deaths in the Dominican Republic in reference to the election.

PENA-GOMEZ told party members they would have to buy votes and to raise a lot of money. Philadelphia Chapter member Vinicio Sanchez (Photo#74208893) told members they would have to sell a lot of cocaine and heroin in order to get the required funds to buy votes in the Dominican Republic.

The C/I further stated 354 kilos of cocaine were found in the Dominican Republic and this seizure was tied to the Revolutionary Dominican Party (PRD). A later check with DEA New York confirmed the seizure and they also stated "Fiquito Vasquez" went to where the defendants were being held and tried to post bail. One of the Dominican Nationals arrested, admitted to the Dominican Drug Control Directorate (DNCD) he took a large cache of cocaine to land, donated to the Dominican Revolutionary Party. The Dominican Revolutionary Party and its candidate Pena Gomez were supported by the United States for the Presidency of the D.R. until the Red Team, now labeled with the pejorative term, the Bastard Squad, told the CIA of the connection between drug traffickers and the PRD.

May 28th, 1996

CIA Agent Torrence contacted Wilson Primkin and stated due to the decision of the Undersecretary of State, Tim Birth, the

CIA was out of the "loop." He just happened to be the national Co-Chair of the Clinton-Gore campaign. He led U.S. foreign policy in the area of Narcotics along with other functions (http://en.wikipedia.org/wiki/Tim_Wirth).

DEA was now in charge and the CIA refused to give BNI their translations of the consenuals made inside PRD headquarters in Philadelphia. BNI does not have the time or expertise to translate the consenuals. The State Dept. was actively supporting Pena-GOMEZ for president of the Dominican Republic.

June 12th, 1996

I made a request through the Intelligence Unit to request Interpol confirm the large seizure of cocaine on PRD land. This request was to reinforce the information supplied by the C/I because N.Y. DEA was ordered not to give BNI any documentation.

The rest of the summer it was more of the same, bad headlines, extreme stress and a great deal of the unknown.

September 19th, 1996

However in New York it was a late summer night in Manhattan, and there was a fundraiser at Coogan's Irish Bar in Washington Heights. The Blue Book of New York's Democratic machine was there, including the Vice President. The DNC is hoping to attract contributors of all ethnicities with deep pockets. In this year's campaign, the Democrats are determined to stage a comeback, and they needed money. The network of Dominican drug dealers in Northeastern cities have plenty of cash, and they owed this administration. The CIA and DOS have been looking the other way while these drug dealers produced funds for their own political machine back home. Now it was time for them to fork over funds here in the host country. It's you-scratch-my-back-I-scratch-yours.

Conspicuously still listed as of this date under the FEC column for *Occupation* for most of the ethnic Hispanic surnames on the New York State Democratic Return is one word, *Requested*, handwritten. Each one of these *contributors* listed as donating a minimum of $1000.00 to the VP's Election Campaign through the DNC. A couple of exceptions list Associated Supermarkets and Los Primos Meat Market and again the same thing on **October 21, 1996.**

October 15, 1996

Federal Election Commission
Office of Public Records
999 E. Street, N.W.
Washington, DC 20463

Re: October 15, 1996 Quarterly Report
ID No.: C00143230

Dear Madam or Sir:

Enclosed please find the October 15, 1996 Quarterly Report of the New York State Democratic Committee. This report reflects activity covered during the period July 1, 1996 through September 30, 1996.

If you have any questions with regard to this report, please do not hesitate to call David L. Cohen, Director of Operations, at (212) 253-9696, ext. 248, or me at my office (212) 972-4000, ext. 295.

Sincerely,

Marcia Allina
Treasurer

cc: Judith Hope, State Chair
Gerard Harper, Esq., Counsel
Marc Sloane, CPA

10 East 20th Street, New York, NY 10016 • Telephone 212/929-4823 • Fax 212/721-0867
34 East Bridge Street, Oswego, NY 13126 • Telephone 315/342-4831 • Fax 315/343-1897

In the later investigations, it seemed everyone just happened to miss these glaring *occupation requested* donations permeating this report and several others. Everybody who audited the donations seemingly forgot, drug traffickers with dubious identities and no occupations, should raise a Red Flag.

The later investigations referenced here http://www.washingtonpost.com/wp-srv/politics/special/campfin/background.htm are headline news. While the Dominican traffickers and the link to Narcotic Trafficking fall to the wayside. Even though the November Group had some major problems, which can be found here as well. (http://www.inthesetimes.com/article/4602/what_went_wrong/)

There was still no hard look at this report, and the report covers October of 1996. One has to pause after seeing the extent to which the Investigation was allegedly thoroughly investigated and at least ask; Why?

During this time the Dominican Traffickers and legitimate businessmen were part of The Federation of Dominican Businessmen and Industrialists who eventually merged or became known as the National Supermarket Association who were also known as "The Corporation", who are also known as the Bodega Management Corporation. They were first incorporated in New York but the informant said they found people could find the names of the officers on the corporation paperwork and trace their financial movements, so they up and dissolved this corporation and incorporated in Nevada where no one can look into the corporation paperwork without filing a lawsuit, which usually failed.

I had the paper trail. My wife says I fart in triplicate. Lucky for me I have a fresh supply of briefs, because the shit was going to get much worse. I didn't know at the time but I would also require a bevy of the legal type as well.

Chapter 14

"Do You See The Light?"

OK, enough already!! We were not getting any answers and we were under a gag order by our own agency. The subpoena finally came down for our personnel files from the public Defender's office and our office was not going to fight it. Our personal information regarding our families was in those files. None of us have any disciplinary actions, so this information isn't germane. We were being treated like bastards.

I went home later and set up a war room eventually taking over control of my entire three-story row house.

It was my daughter's nursery room. I remember my Mom and Dad, the wallpaper team of *Heckle* and *Jeckle*, who came to all their children's houses. Mom pasted and Dad plastered and papered the walls, all the time kibitzing back and forth, with Mom backseat driving.

I sat down at my makeshift desk and computer. The letters were rubbed off the keyboard from the Demon Princess dancing *ever so gently* across the keyboard at 120 words per minute.

I was motoring; hell, my index finger on my right hand to this day is shorter, than my left, from all the legal research and data mining I had done over the years. I would only stop for the occasional "Jo, I can't find the "R" key", or some similar exclamation.

However, at various times I would hit on something strengthening my resolve, and telling me we were on to something much bigger and it involved cover-ups on a national level.

***

"Will the Bastards come to the small conference room please?"

Moments later, Eggs, Dennis and the Flash came into the room.

"Close the door and lock it. Look at this shit I found, and look at the date and remember the day the story broke and what is suspiciously missing from the report."
http://www.fas.org/irp/gao/nsi96119.htm

Report to the Chairman, Subcommittee on National Security, International Affairs, and Criminal Justice, Committee on Government Reform and Oversight, House of Representatives
April 1996
DRUG CONTROL - U.S.INTERDICTION
EFFORTS IN THE CARIBBEAN DECLINE
GAO/NSIAD-96-119
Drug Control
(711161)
DEA - Drug Enforcement Agency
DOD - Department of Defense
JIATF - Joint Interagency Task Force
ONDCP - Office of National Drug Control Policy
USIC - U.S.Interdiction Coordinator
Letter
B-271376
April 17, 1996
The Honorable William H. Zeliff, Jr.
Chairman, Subcommittee on National Security,
International Affairs, and Criminal Justice
Committee on Government Reform and Oversight
House of Representatives
...*The executive branch has not developed a plan to implement the cocaine strategy in the transit zone, fully staffed interagency organizations with key roles in the interdiction program, or fully resolved issues on intelligence sharing. U.S. officials noted that neither the Director of the Office of National Drug Control Policy (ONDCP) nor the U.S. Interdiction Coordinator (USIC) had the authority to command the use of any agency's operational assets. ...*"
...*"Various U.S. officials told us that, despite changes in governments, corruption is still widespread throughout the Caribbean. Drug traffickers' influence in the region is evident.*

Payoffs are a common form of corruption, particularly in countries with poorly paid public servants. <u>Law enforcement and State Department reports support these statements.</u>

<u>**A February 1996 law enforcement agency report on one island Indicated that corruption may be occurring at high levels of the government.</u>

<u>This report stated that there are indications that the leader of a political party is linked to the illegal drug trade. Furthermore, the report also stated that there are numerous allegations regarding corruption in the country's customs operation at the airport. ..."</u>

..."On one island, there are continuing rumors and allegations regarding the corruption of high-ranking government officials (including officials in the Police department). **Also, the current administration and opposition party are both perceived to be involved in illegal activities. ..."**

..."Various agencies stressed those decisions to reduce the funding devoted to drug interdiction are often beyond their control. For example, **<u>DOD noted that a resource shift from the transit zone to source countries did not occur because its overall drug budget is reduced in fiscal year 1994 by $300 million, $200 million of which is taken from transit zone operations....</u>"**

..." *****The executive branch has not developed a plan to implement the U.S. antidrug strategy in the Caribbean. DOD, the Department of State, and law enforcement agencies have various agreements to implement the national drug strategy in the Caribbean region. <u>However, counternarcotics officials expressed concern over the lack of overall responsibility for implementing the current cocaine strategy in The Caribbean...."</u>**

"OK, you *Bastardos*, ain't this some shit? These sons of bitches knew all this shit was going on. They backed this guy Pena Gomez anyway and they withheld it from Congress when they knew we already had a guy on the inside. The FBI turned down the investigation with ties to the whole East coast, international shipping and the weapons trafficking in the cars shipped back to the DR in engine blocks. Customs, who was working with us, stopped the collaboration. DEA was crying that this shit was not right, yet you could see who had the ball in their court. We had all the evidence and were able to tie in the entire Eastern Seaboard and bring National attention to a failed Drug Policy from a simple car-stop in North Philly.

***

"Boys", Dennis was shaking his head, "what has this psycho bastard got us into; I think even I need a beer; let's stop out tonight to the FOP, we need to strategize."

"Sounds like a plan." I agreed.

Eggs just nodded in agreement giving his usual shitty grin.

"Spark, what kind of wine do you drink? I think I'm gonna need to switch up a little."

I opened the conference door and there was Homey and the Doctor, caught listening at the door.

"All we heard was, road trip to the FOP... we're in."

The Doctor replied "UN-GAhhh."

***

Chapter 15

"Do You Know the Way To San Jose?

"Homey, what the hell are you singing now? It's not the Temptations…Dionne Warwick, isn't it?"

We were at the FOP and Skippy the DJ was taking a personal and left a tape on and Homey was singing "Do you know the way to San Jose?" by Dionne Warwick. For a Ninja Turtle he has a pretty good range of vocal tones.

"Yeah, I didn't know you were a switch hitter" Dennis jumped in.

"Who said he was *switchin?*" Doc grunted.

"Holy shit, an idea just popped into my head; Think San Jose." My mind clicked to an article I read back in August.

"Popped? I'm going on the other side of the dance floor; I think you guys switched sides." Flashed looked back as he feigned walking away.

"No you ass. Back in August, Gary Webb from the San Jose Mercury News ran a story about the CIA/Crack connection in Los Angeles. He might have some insight to share or some resources we can use, to see what the hell is going on."

Everybody now started walking away slowly.

"Sure, Spark, sure…is he armed?" Eggs quipped.

"Yeah, and I got two legs too; and I'm going to the back bar, and call him right now, smart ass."

"Oh wait, he's on your speed dial, right? What's his number, 1-800-spook busters?"

"Yeah, I bet he's in a Webb of problems right now and he's gonna stop, just to talk to you." Doc joined the critics.

Doc and I worked the Door at the FOP, so we had privileges other employees of the FOP had as well.

"Operator, can you connect me to the San Jose Mercury News in California?"

"What city, Please?"

"What city? You really didn't just ask me what city the San Jose Mercury News is in did you…I didn't think so."

After convincing the City Desk editor I actually was a Narcotics Agent calling from Philly inside the FOP, and not the usual lunatic, I was connected to Gary Webb author of the Dark Alliance Series.

http://www.narconews.com/darkalliance/drugs/start.htm

"This is Gary Webb."

"Gary, I'm Sparky McLaughlin and I'm standing here in an FOP in Philly with three other Narcs. We are having one heck of a time with Dominican Drug Traffickers and the same people you were investigating back in August."

"You mean the CIA," Gary was direct.

"Well the way we see it, yes. Without getting into the particulars of our investigation, can you tell me if while writing your article on the CIA and the CRACK connection you found the CIA tried to destroy the Agents and Officers reputation and credibility who uncovered the connection?"

Gary Webb stated "Most Certainly."

"Shit."

"You know, that about sums it up, you're in for a long road full of shit; I'm already up to my neck in it, but I'll give you one word of advice. Document your every move, and document it over again and send your information to several attorneys who have no connection to each other." Gary wasn't kidding.

He went on, "Listen, I assume you have e-mail, send me your address and I will send you some references and contacts; one you should get ahold of right away is Orazio Cosentino of the Law Enforcement Defense Foundation of America. It sounds like you and he have a lot in common, maybe even too much, he's retired-INS."

I got off the phone after exchanging e-mail addresses and inquiring faces wanted to know what was up.

"Well the guy is pretty down to earth and straightforward and said yes, we are getting screwed, but we ain't seen nothing yet, pardon my English."

"I'm buying."

The next day I drove to our Allentown Office to attend a meeting and while at the meeting I received information from

Interpol describing an organization of Dominican Drug traffickers with ties to the Cali cartel in Colombia dating back to at least 1991, and it also documented hundreds of kilos of cocaine seized as well as approximately one hundred people either arrested or had outstanding arrest warrants. This organization had ties to the Dominican Revolutionary Party headed by Jose Francisco PENA-GOMEZ who was being backed by the U.S. Department of State in the last election.

One piece of vital information fell into my lap from an earlier request. Here it was in black and white, the PRD is connected to the biggest trafficker in the Dominican Republic, Rolando Florian Feliz.

October 15th, 1996

I took a bold step and called Senator Arlen Rectors office in an effort to get more information as to why the United States is backing the PRD for the presidency of the Dominican Republic when the State Department should have known of their (PRD) connection with Narcotics Trafficking. We gave the CIA absolute proof of the connection in an undeniable format. A woman named Joyce stated she would contact the Intelligence Committee and have them get back to me.

October 21st, 1996

At Senate Rector's direction I contacted Leslie Earhard of the Senate Intelligence Committee at xxx-xxx-xxxx who in turn gave me the phone number xxx-xxx-xxxx and told me to call the Senate Intelligence Committee.

October 22nd, 1996

Leslie Earhard from the "Committee" called me and stated she was drafting a memo to the chief council of the Intelligence Committee. OK, I was getting somewhere now, at least it looked that way.

October 24th, 1996

John Heller, Chief Council to the Senate Intelligence Committee called me at 4:45 p.m. and spoke until at least 5:15 p.m. and he kept trying to get the CIA off the hook, making odd unrelated excuses I kept shooting down, with factual information, telling him I had the documents to back it up.

October 28th, 1996

I got a return call from John Heller, Chief Council to the Senate Intelligence Committee who wanted me to come to Washington, DC and to fax documents to him, which I needed to decline. As far as I knew, they were not law enforcement and I did not have a subpoena.

October 29th, 1996

The partisan politics came into play as Colleen Bander from the Republican National Committee called me and tried to talk about the Revolutionary Dominican Party. I declined again as I knew she was not law enforcement and she lacked authority.

I received permission to speak to Senator Rector from a sympathetic supervisor who will remain anonymous.

The day before Halloween was eventful, beside Dennis coming to work in costume, a leprechaun as always, on October 30, 1996, we first heard another often used word by a supervisor in the Attorney General's Office when referring to or speaking about us.

Supervisory Agt. Lyman told Doc Siednich he refused to send Agt. Manders to Philadelphia because she might get "tainted" just being in Philadelphia, even though she requested a transfer to Philadelphia.

In the afternoon at around 3:05 p.m., Ed Mummer called me and stated he was more directly responsible to the Senate Intelligence Committee and he wanted me to come to Washington, D.C.

I told him the same thing I was telling everyone else. I was glad to come; however, the office more than likely would not let me, without a subpoena.

At 5:05 p.m. I again talked to Andy Sharemann who told me he was on the staff of the National Security Advisor and stated he was very interested in the situation and Ed Mummer was a Democrat so he might be giving Agt. McLaughlin a little bit of a runaround, but Shareman states he would make sure the proper inquiries were made. Sharemann gave me all his contact numbers to reach him, xxx-xxx-xxxxxxx-xxx-xxxx

Pager 1-800-xxx-xxxx PIN# xxxxxx

November 1st, 1996

I knew to play it safe and document everything, so I turned in a memo through the chain of command and asked permission to appear before the Senate Intelligence Committee. I requested the memo be faxed to Harrisburg.

I waited until 4:00 p.m. and finally Lou Camiel called with an attitude asking, "Who gave you permission to turn over the PRD tapes to the CIA?"

"John Sanderson, the Regional Director of Philadelphia ordered me to turn the tapes over and further, a property receipt was signed by CIA Agent Dave Torrence on March 27, 1996 as per orders."

"Fax it to me." Lou was not happy; he thought he had me. Thank you, Gary Webb.

Fifteen minutes later at 4:15 p.m., Bill Banton called me and stated, (concerning the request to appear before the Senate Intelligence Committee), "one hell of a memo" and further stated "Don't get this the wrong way, but we might want to send an attorney with you to make sure you don't disseminate third party information. This came from the Attorney General but as a matter of protocol a letter should be sent to the Attorney General from the Intelligence Committee."

I offered the telephone number to the Committee but Banton declined. I called Ed Mummer from the Committee and asked him to fax a request to the Attorney General, for me to appear.

On another front, First Deputy District Attorney, Daniel Horshack, testified before Judge Fields, the reason he Nolle Prosed 53 of my cases was because of the Rivera case. The Rivera case was where I made a grammatical error in an affidavit for a search warrant, which I explained to ADA Wenstein. He did not have a problem with my explanation, further stating it would just have to be explained at a suppression hearing, which probably would not happen as the defendant normally proffers witnessed by his attorney and ADA Weinstein. Rivera wanted to plead guilty and cooperate with BNI Agents.

November 4th, 1996

The Intelligence Committee faxed a subpoena to the Attorney General and a copy to me requesting permission to come before the Senate Intelligence Committee.

November 5th, 1996

I found out why a precedent was set in the Philadelphia District Attorney's Office.

Deputy Attorney General Larry Chesky gave me a copy of the transcripts from a trial, from when First Deputy District Attorney Daniel Horshack testified and he stated all of my "cases were Nolle Prosed because of the Rivera case in an "abundance of caution." So in essence, the Philadelphia District Attorney's Office wanted people to believe they released all of these felony drug traffickers because I made a typo in a search warrant.

They knew who the informants were on the search warrant, because each of the informants gave information on their main supplier and each of the informants proffered with their attorney present, and in fact there was a third informant involved, but I only listed two, and two was more than enough.

Based on my conversation with Bill Banton, I called Ed Mummer and set up an appointment for November 8th, 1996 to go to Washington D.C.

November 6th, 1996

Deputy Attorney General John Barnett came to BNI Headquarters and reviewed all of my investigative documents as to the Revolutionary Dominican Party and he was surprised I was giving all the documents voluntarily. I told him Chief Banton told me to do so. He left but called back a couple of hours later and asked who gave me permission to go before the *Committee.*

This is getting old, but I told him again, Chief Donnolly OK'd going before the *Committee* and he said my documents needed reviewing and Barnett just finished the review.

Right on cue, I got a phone call from Ed Mummer who was calling from the *SSCI* and asked if I am still coming to Washington. I replied,

"Yes, but they're starting to tap dance."

The following day, November 7th, 1996 I am given a memo, which ordered me not to go to Washington; I was pissed.

"Sean, you can't do this, enough of this shit; here."

"What's this?"

The new Regional Director was Sean Boyle. He could have been brought over under different circumstances and he wouldn't have been treated so badly to begin with; but the Attorney General at the time was only concerned with his press and not his employees. He came over from the FBI task force. His background was from Internal Affairs in the Philadelphia Police Department. This automatically put a stigma on us; and it showed in the press. Again, we felt like, and are being treated, like dirt.

"Sean, this is a copy of the Whistleblower's Law and I'm just going to take off and go on my own time."

"I'm ordering you not to go" Sean insisted.

"You better read the law Sean, you're violating my Civil Rights, and I'm taking off, I'm not a sick abuser, and I have plenty of 'time', you have no possible reason to deny me the day off. You have us sitting around the office doing nothing but taking trash out and mopping floors; I'm not a prisoner, no matter how much you try to make us quit, I'm not quitting either."

I took an annual leave day the next morning and did it by the numbers, calling in at the correct time. Regional Director Boyle started paging me, and he left two messages on my home answering machine. It appeared the 'Crystal Palace' was upset and thought I went to Washington D.C.

The Attorney General faxed a letter to Senator Rector stating if Agt. McLaughlin went to the meeting he would be in violation of Pennsylvania law.

The next day I was given a copy of the faxed letter.

Regional Director Boyle told Supervisory Agt. Dever that if I went to Washington on my day off, the Attorney General was going to fire me.

"Sparky, come to my office," it was unusual for John Dever to use the intercom.

"Yeah, John, What's up?"

"Now, don't shoot the messenger, and I mean it literally...are you carrying?" John started laughing.

"Always." I smiled.

"This is coming from the 16th floor and I have to ask; did you go to Washington yesterday?"

"Where?"

"D.C."

"Virtually, physically, or telephonically?"

"Spark...C'mon man, quit break 'in my balls, you know what I mean."

"I was ordered not to, and...you know...I... Never...Ever...Disobey an Order. If you want to verify my whereabouts, you can check the Philadelphia Public Library, I signed in there. You can check the Federal Building, I signed in there as well...I was taking pictures of the opposition. I also went to the FOP and signed in there also. It pretty much went like this the whole day."

"You are a Mother Fu.."

"Now, Now, you know the policy on swearing," we both start laughing aloud.

I got what I needed. The Attorney General himself was so embarrassed he sent a fax with his name on it to the Senate Select Committee on Intelligence. I got the attention I wanted; now I knew somebody would make sure I got down there; the hand played. I won a minor victory. We would not be ignored.

***

Chapter 16

Collateral Damage

John Dever is part Cherokee Indian and I'm not sure what difference it really makes except when Homey found out he started wearing tee shirts with American Indian motifs on them.

John has one patch of genetically altered white hair on the back of his head, or scalp (pun intended) and one on his beard, when he is sporting it.

Homey is African American and when the mood hits him, fills in as the unit preacher, whether we want him to or not. I'm not sure what particular persuasion he is but he definitely should be filling the pews in the Baptists Churches.

John allowed Dennis during 'Special Investigations' to go out and hit the supermarket and cook food for the entire office. Homey said a blessing and the smell of gravy permeated the building once you open the back door with a takedown or two.

This is a family within a family and it is slowly disintegrating as all this trumped up bullshit continues to play out over the days, continuing into the many months.

God was the first to go back in May. He was given the choice of *retire now*, or be removed without cause. Pennsylvania is an "at will" state, meaning anyone in our management team can be fired without cause, just as a reduction in force, or a reorganization.

God was a good guy, had a good reputation and a great many years under his belt.

When I first got hired, I made the mistake of asking a question while at the new Agents Academy out in St. Josephs during self defense class. I already, like most in my class, transitioned from the Philadelphia PD wherein if officers struck a person with a baton anywhere other than a clavicle, another designated pressure point or clearly designated area being clearly defined, they better get themselves their own attorney, if sued, for any misplacement of a strike, in a self-defense move. It does not matter if the suspect is moving or fighting with you or if he turns into the baton, you are on your own.

The question I asked was during a gun grab maneuver. Now the trainers were teaching us if we had a weapon pointed at us, in close range, we were to use this certain move to attempt to take the weapon off the suspect. OK, sure. I was back over the rainbow, or at least in a Chuck Norris movie. Therefore, I think I was correct in asking:

"If I think my life might be in danger, and instead of doing your move, I step to the side and shoot Zippy, will the AG back me, or am I on my own."

Ed Yale seemed frustrated when several of the guys from Philly jump in.

"Yeah, what's your answer?"

"Yeah, man what do you think we are Kung Foo dudes?"

Ed Yale just walked away.

I turned around to the guys and asked:

"Now you all know I am trained in martial arts, but even I'm not crazy, if I can disable the guy going to shoot me first, before he shoots, isn't it the right thing to do?"

Lou Camiel, who was the Assistant Deputy Chief of the West, came storming in.

"I understand we have a problem."

We all looked around.

I stepped up.

"Boss, there's no problem. If you're referring to a question I asked; it was only a question concerning support of the agency if we think we are going to be killed or injured severely and we use extreme force to disable the attacker, and everything being equal, it is a *just shooting*; would the agency back us?"

Lou said "Sure."

I said "Thanks, I think it was an easy answer as well. I don't know why Ed left."

Someone whispered which was overheard.

"He's a rat."

At lunchtime, Agent Mark Shockley got a call from God on the classroom phone and God was cursing him out a blue streak. All I heard was on one end with Mark saying,

"John it wasn't me, it was Sparky."

"Mark, give me the phone" I reached over for the receiver.

"John what's up?"

"Sparky, you mother fucker, you guys didn't graduate yet, I'll see you don't, you son of a bitch; what the fuck are you fucking doing out there?"

I was holding the phone a foot from my ear and I went back in for a shot at getting a word in edgewise.

"John, all I did was ask a question."

"You did what?"

"John, I asked a simple question of this guy who was teaching the class regarding support. If I found it necessary to shoot somebody instead of doing the move he was teaching; the other guys agreed with me and he up's and walked away without saying a word."

"Are you shitting me?"

"No."

"Go back to lunch."

The next thing I knew the instructor came in and tells me I was to report to Lou Camel's Office.

The guys started breaking my balls.

I walked into Lou's office and he had a great big smile on his face and he called me by my nickname.

"Sparky, c'mon in, sit down; there seems to be a big misunderstanding. In no way was I disciplining you. I meant nothing derogatory or in any way was I trying to demean you in front of your peers."

"Huh?"

"Earlier today in the gym."

"What are you saying?" I didn't say shit to anyone, but apparently either he or his trainer called the Crystal Palace in Harrisburg to complain.

"Well Sparky, I just want to make sure you know we don't have anything against you guys from Philly."

"Sure; are we through?"

"Yes, and I'll be over to explain to everybody it is just a misunderstanding."

"Not necessary; as far as we are concerned, nothing happened."

John Sanderson has 'weight.' *God* has pull with the 16th floor somehow. His influence must have been the hundreds of thousands of dollars in assets and drugs seized we were bringing in; more than the rest of the state combined as part of the Philly team, even before we became Agents.

Now we lost *God*, and the writing was on the wall. The family was breaking up. The Pennsylvania State Police pulled out of the Task Force and left the building. The Immigration and Naturalization Service Agents were pulled back. The Housing Police Task Force left us and pulled Pineapple, and now we knew our greatest ally, Daniel Letzman's days were numbered. He was the Assistant Regional Director and the Community Liaison.

The anti-drug community was outraged over our removal and Daniel took no small part to see they are fed information and kept them informed as to what was happening to us. Daniel was also well entrenched in the local FOP and one of the original Granny Squad Stakeout members. His reputation was beyond compare both inside and outside the Police Department in the City of Philadelphia. He was loved by everybody and he was the drug traffickers' nemesis.

He came out with us one time on a round up and we were running up the street grabbing guys and he grabbed a guy putting him up on top of a hood of a car, *ever so gently*, and said:

"Don't move! You scum sucking druggie."

"OOhh, Dannn." Flash walked up and whispered in his ear; "wrong guy."

"Right guy!" Dan pulled out a gun from the guy's waistband.

"Damn, he still had the eye."

"What... *He's got my money* not good enough; you got a new slogan?"

The money reference was the takedown signal when Dan dressed up as a Granny Decoy. When he got robbed, it was his signal for the other Stakeout Cops to come on the run, one of which was always walking Monty the Giant Schnauzer, who was handled by a cross designated K9/Stakeout Policeman for the robbers doing the *Stop n Snatch* and wanting to make a run for it.

So here we were. Besides our law enforcement family suffering through our degradation consistently played out in the press; our internal families inside the thin blue line, having been developed for over 20 to 25 years in some cases, were pulled apart, by an unseen force. There was no tangible rhyme or reason other than to cover-up political foils at the highest levels.

Until you go through doors, repeatedly, facing the unknown and bleed true blue inside; seeing the blood flow red outside, seems insignificant. It's the *blue blood* flowing, seen through the soul of the cop next to you, when he dies in your arms, and through the eyes of his wife and dependent children; gives one, an unobstructed view. You've never witnessed a truly bloody crime scene as when you stand, much like they did in 4000 B.C., according to the Chaldean scriptures, and listen to the bagpipes playing Amazing Grace,[e] just as they must have played some unknown tune for the Egyptians and the Persians.

http://gaitasturiana.files.wordpress.com/2011/06/1911-the-story-of-the-bagpipe-william-h-grattan.pdf

***

Chapter 17

Jack Blum, ESQ and SSCI

November 19th, 1996

Today started out like any other morning lately. I woke up, walked outside with Blitz, crossed the street to the park, and waved off all the little rat-tails whose owners would rather let them be hors d'oeuvres running by, instead of securing them on a leash. I was frustrated today about one guy who kept letting his dog loose running around the park. Today would be different.

The dog came charging at me and Blitz once again and the owner again ignored my "Hey buddy, call your dog, please." Blitz, who was used to me strangling him up in the air and swinging a stick or whatever was close, to fend off the attacker, now found himself on a loose lead and was able to stand his ground.

He stood like a rock, he did not bark; but his ears were fully forward on alert and he was not straining on the lead. The other dog kept coming and as he got close, he started putting on the brakes but slid right into Blitz who hit him once on the neck, shook him, barely moving, except to throw him to the ground. The dog quickly got up yipping as he scampered away, with his owner chasing after him. I did not praise or correct Blitz. He did his job; I would not stop him anymore from defending us, and again, I marveled at the mechanics and the instincts of the trained German Shepherd Dog.

***

I was reading my notes over when I was contacted by Special Agent Don Denson of the New York field division of DEA who stated in the early morning hours, that date, Fiquito Vasquez came in to DEA Headquarters and identified himself as the leader of the PRD (Revolutionary Dominican Party) in the United States. Agent Denson seemed to think Vasquez was on a fishing expedition. Vasquez listed several people whom are contributors to the campaign of Jose Francisco PENA-GOMEZ whom DEA knew are connected to drug trafficking. When questioned in reference to Pedro Marrera, Vasquez stated Marrera was in charge of publicity for Gomez' campaign and he is president of one of the chapters.

"So Don, I really have to tell you, I am surprised to hear from you."

"Well, Sparky, we were surprised as well. Fiquito whose real name was Rafael Vasquez walked into our Headquarters and asked to speak to one of our agents in reference to the Revolutionary Dominican Party and allegations of drug trafficking."

"Are you shitting me? So what happened?"

"Hey, we took advantage of the opportunity and showed him the leaders of the Party in a photo spread including Pablo Espinal, and Simon Diaz. He started shaking. He told us he knew they were into drugs and whenever the Party needed money, they would go to them and they would come back with buckets full."

DEA Special Agent Denson stated, in a recorded conversation between undercover agent and Dr. Tantigua, a high ranking member of the Revolutionary Dominican party, the undercover said his contact was willing to pay 250,000.00 a month in order to land five planes a month, in the Dominican Republic without any interference from the Police or Military. He confirmed Dr. Tantigua was amenable to the conversation and stated they set up an appointment to meet the undercovers at a hotel and discuss the proposal. At the last minute it seemed like they got tipped off and canceled; they never reported the attempted bribe to the authorities.

I hung up the phone and told Flash to meet me in the parking lot.

I walked around the corner of the office after asking the cleaner if it was safe to pass, (as it was the only way to get to my vehicle from my desk), found myself flying up in the air and flat on my back.

Sean Boyle, our new Regional Director who was a clean freak, had the cleaning person wax the entire office floors, during day working hours.

"Boyle you freaking Asshole", I was on my back screaming in pain. I hit my back and head, hard. Everyone came running, and I rolled over and got up and put my fist threw a wall.

Granted the walls were only plaster; but the tension was building. Boyle took all of our chairs and piled them at the top of the aisles so the front of the office was in a traffic jam and all of the back aisles were being waxed.

Boyle heard me from upstairs and came down.

"Sean, I almost broke my back; don't you have any sense? I'm serious, all due respect."

"What do you mean; don't you like a clean area?"

"Why don't I call the Fire Marshall and see what he says."

"Go ahead."

I picked up the phone as Sean stormed away.

"Can you give me the number to Jack Blum in Washington, DC; he's a private attorney."

Flash stepped back. "You're suing him already?"

"No, this is the guy doing those Iran-Contra hearings. I want to call him but I didn't want Sean checking up on me. I figured me yelling at him regarding the Fire Marshall would keep him in his office and out of our hair. I did hurt my neck though. "While I'm trying to get this guy on the phone, can you get me the injury report paperwork?" This should piss him off even more. I'm not going IOD; I just want to get it on the record in case I'm worse tomorrow.

"No problem."

I talked to DC lawyer Jack Blum and asked if he ever heard of the State Department and the CIA trying to block investigations. Jack Blum was the special Council to the Senate Foreign Relations Committee on the Iran-Contra hearings. Blum stated "Yes" and he would talk to sources inside the State Department.

November 26th, 1996

I talked to Bruce Badinov, our Human Resources Director. I wanted to see my polygraph examination as although it may not be allowed to be used in court proceedings, it would be a good defense mechanism against the constant barrage of bad press and the attempts to link us to the Philadelphia Police Highway Patrol Officers, going on trial shortly, for alleged corruption. Badinov stated it was against policy to show me the results.

Jack Blum from Washington, D.C. called on December 18.

"Sparky, Washington on line 2" comes over the intercom. Marie was instigating.

"Tell the President, I'm busy" I thought she was messing with me.

"Where you at, 1384?"

"Shit, who is it?"

"Jack Blum, I don't know, it sounds like Blum."

I picked up the receiver.

"Agent McLaughlin?"

"This is Agent McLaughlin, eh Sparky fits better, How are you sir? I'm surprised to hear from you."

"Why? I told you I would check into it and I would get back to you. Well you were right. The State Department is backing Gomez for President of the Dominican Republic and at the same time DEA was targeting Gomez for Narcotics Trafficking. How the hell did you start stepping on these toes from Pennsylvania?"

"Would you believe from a car-stop in North Philly tying into an East Coast door to door drug delivery service and they all tied into this Revolutionary Dominican Party. The Dominican Party was shipping guns and money back home to buy votes and our Government appeared not to be doing anything about it, in fact, the suits have jumped to the other side. We are supporting this candidate and by "we" I meant the current administration. Now didn't he just have the same problem with Columbia?"

"He sure did. Now don't despair, you're doing the right thing. I'll go to the press my damn self if the Senate Intelligence committee won't do anything."

January 29th, 1997

I woke up; got out my black three-piece suit. I always wore three-piece suits; one because I hate suit coats and once you walk into a place you can usually take the coat off and still look presentable in a vest and a tie. The second reason was because as you get older and your waistline expands it doesn't seem to be a change in your fashion regimen when you are seen wearing a three piece; as your shoes disappear.

I went in to headquarters first and found someone ripped open my sealed box of documents I taped, to take with me. I made a complaint with the Regional Director, not that it will do me any good. He was probably under orders to go through my stuff. They are definitely afraid of what I am going to say.

I called Jack Blum on my way down, on the train and he said he would represent me, free of charge.

"Listen, they will shit if I walk in there with you."

"I really appreciate it, but I haven't done anything wrong, I'm doing the right thing, I'm telling the truth."

"Listen Sparky, there's truth, and there's the truth they want to hear."

"I'm sure they will want to hear this."

"Suit yourself."

I wouldn't forget Jack Blum's prepared statement and especially this one line:

"...If you ask whether the United States government ignored the drug problem and subverted law enforcement to prevent embarrassment and to reward our allies in the Contra war, the answer is yes..."

http://ciadrugs.homestead.com/files/blumprep.html

I arrived at Union Station for what must have been the second time in my life. I was walking around Washington D.C. and unlike the last time, I was on my own and feeling that way as well. I walked across the street and as luck would have it, I came upon the Senate Hart Building.

The first thing I noticed when I was finally announced was I felt I was entering a hull or a gangway of a submarine. The door was thick and when it opened, a whooshing sound was heard, only louder, like opening a vacuum-sealed can or jar. This knocked me into, and right back out, of a thousand memories of old movies.

"Shit, shit, what have I got myself into?" I remember thinking.

I settled down across from a raised podium and three people identified themselves to me, one being from both sides of the senate, and the third allegedly a neutral. Just the way they introduced themselves and made sure I knew their political party affiliations, told me that we were right from the beginning. This audience was not referencing our investigation. We were right on track. This concerned the political ramifications of what we knew and what effect it will have on the political system, both in country and out.

I looked to my right as a court stenographer was whipping out what appeared to me to be an old oxygen mask from a fighter plane, and he was pulling it up into place around his mouth. Think Darth Vader in a suit and tie, typing and breathing heavy and trust me, you can hear the heavy breathing. I found out later this was a secure form, and a backup for stenography, called a *stenomask*. In this situation and how uncomfortable I felt, inside this submarine for a room, I thought I was being measured for a nuclear suit.

I went through my spiel and the panel who seemed dead faced asked if I wanted to say anything further. I said politely:

"Why yes I do, we're the good guys, we're supposed to be on the same team. Why are you fucking with us?"

This got a reaction from the lone female on the panel; her left eyebrow went up higher than the right eyebrow.

She must have gone to the Natasha School of Intelligence.

"We'll get back to you should we need any more information. Thank you for coming Agent McLaughlin."

I gathered up my documents and charts, walked out, grabbed an earlier train, and headed home wondering what I stirred up and what it meant personally for me as well as for the Bastard Squad.

***

Chapter 18

Firebomb

In early February Philadelphia First Deputy District Attorney, Horshack, admits on the record in front of a Common Pleas Judge, he may be unfairly stigmatizing the Bastard Squad by taking the actions he has taken. At the same time, Tommy Litcello and I met with David Marash of Nightline who takes an interest in our situation. Tommy talks for me and I listen as Dave says he wants to see the 'smoking gun' in all of this before going forward. I'm still employed and cannot give up anything more than is already in the public venue.

In like a lion out like a lamb didn't hold true in our case. The end of the March brought a new revelation by Assistant Deputy Chief Tony Maggiano.

"Spark, do you know what this maricon just told me."

I heard parts of Flash's heated exchange with the Assistant Chief and only heard the occasional profanity.

"Well, I heard you getting pissed off, but not much else."

"This dickhead said our office made a deal with the DA's office. The four of us will never work the street again."

"Did you get it in writing?"

"No, he'll deny it later, you know it."

"Looks like it's time for one of my memorialization of a conversation memos. You have to document this shit right up to the General himself."

"Spark, you write; I'll tell you what he said."

I not only started a diary and insisted all my partners keep notes as well but I also documented everything said and not put to paper by management.

Mid-March things take a turn for the worse. I was inside the FOP lounge talking to U.S. Customs Agent Tom Bambros who stops me to say he was ordered to close the investigation into the Revolutionary Dominican Party.

I received an emergency page from Pineapple.

"Yo, why aren't you out with some Senorita?"

"Spark, G-Man's car got firebombed and they tried to get his house too."

"Shit, I'll be right up there, is he hurt?"

"No, but he's freaking out. He says someone gave him up; he's on the run."

"Get ahold of him again. We will get him a hotel until we sort this out and put your ear to the ground. I'll send you Highway for a backup."

Meanwhile we must fight their continuing attempts to discredit us in the media, and within the law enforcement community. These incidents are punctuated by conflicting orders, and setups aimed at creating situations where the Attorney General will get the justification to fire us.

It was time to start looking for legal representation. We needed a good offense for a prevent defense. I start pounding the pavements with my memos and facts in hand including 'hearing' testimony and civil suit defense testimony wherein we won every case and many based on the complainants credibility. The complainants are jumping on the hysteria the media created, trying to ride the money train.

Well I reached my point of "No Return." It suddenly hit me after every high priced attorney in Philadelphia listens to our plight. They are utterly fascinated and always impart the proverbial 'but' to end their spiel.

This last 'but' was well intended; it might as well have been a kick in the 'butt' and the 'don't call us, unless you come up with a $25,000.00 retainer and of course there's the court costs.

Well I got up off the floor mentally, after falling in a heap onto a chair in frustration. I just couldn't think anymore. I need another lead. I call in to Dennis, who said:

"Hey you mamaluke; these pieces of shit are violating our civil rights, right?"

Wearier of the history lesson; now the exasperation was permeating from my voice.

"Tell me something I don't know."

"We're fine upstanding citizens, are we not lad?" His fake brogue was kicking in.

"DENNIS, Get to the point."

"Call the Civil Liberties Union, you Psycho Bastard! They gotta protect us citizens of the Commonwealth."

Damn, what a Great Idea.

"Dennis, you're a genius; give me their number."

"Hey Jerky, do I look like Joe Yellow Pages? I think not."

Finally getting the number and 'dropping my dime,' I proceeded to explain my tale of woe to this new attorney.

"Come on over, was his response."

He went through all the paperwork I had, lifted his head, started to walk away and said:

"Sorry, I can't help you; we sue Cops."

***

Chapter 19

Chickenman

Again crushed, I plowed on, and oddly enough Orazio Cosentino from the National Police Defense Foundation called me and told me somebody want to take our case, and he made us an appointment for the upcoming Friday at Sam Strettons office. Sam needed everybody to be there.

We piled in to Eddie's classic Caddy and take the ride to West Chester, Pa. and I am prompting the guys to be cool. We don't want to scare this guy off right away.

Upon arrival, an unassuming heavyset male is in the lobby of the three-story row house and is quietly reading.

We all got up simultaneously as soon as a secretary said Sam Stretton would see us. To my surprise, so did this very large man, and he walked to the extreme rear of us, and we kept cracking jokes half under breath, saying we going to the last roundup, and we were going to get whacked.

The interview went rather quick once Don Bailey, a heavy-set man, identified himself as a partner of Stretton:

"I was reviewing your case downstairs and listening to you guys I believe in you and even if Sam doesn't take you on, I'll take you on. You are getting screwed. We need to hit them hard and as soon as possible."

Relieved, I mentally unstrapped the Body-Armor. However this is going to turn out, We are not going down without a fight.

Again, we find ourselves the next day with a serious case of the "blue flu" and finally arrive at former Congressman Don Bailey's house.

Don brings us back with an odd conversation starter.

"Did anybody bring something to sweep the room?"

Eddie gives me the look of death, while Dennis, ever so subtly says:

"Sparkster, what have you gotten us into??"

Don quipped, "Seriously fellows, you've entered the dark world now."

"Adrienne, keep those five chickens on a warm oven for now, I gotta take the boys upstairs to the soundproof room, so we can name names."

I got tripped all the way up the steps by each guy, mouthing the words "Let's run before we get whacked." We got to the top stairs of the tiny attic, now a converted office, and froze as Don worked his way around the front of his desk to his chair.

Our eyes are all fixed on the hand grenade sitting on the corner of the desk, and an automatic weapon leaning against the wall behind the desk.

We were pushing each other around to try to get out of being closest to the hand grenade. Of course we didn't know whether it was live or not, but weren't going to ask the big fella and risk getting him stirred up. Apparently he had a bit of an appetite and hadn't eaten.

"ADRIENNE! Now where the hell did I put my pen?" Immediately my three partners reached into their pockets and are holding pens in the air. They are on the quick draw. We broke for a light snack down in Don's kitchen.

When he saw five chickens and four of us he told Adrienne to throw another one in the oven.

Now these weren't squabs, game hens, or small foul of any other variety, these are chickens you could get at your local super market on the rotisserie.

Well as I walked around past the back door, I saw the chicken inventory running around with Adrienne doing a scene from Rocky II.

Time to go.

"Don, we really got to get back, it's a long ride. The guys looked at me; saw the *face* and got up from their seats.

"OK boys, get me the information I asked for and send it to me. We're going to strike and strike hard. Too bad you'll miss this chicken, it's fresh."

We got out the door and started our trek for Philly; Jody foster didn't have anything on our nightmares that night. This was how Don Bailey, one of the highest decorated soldiers in Vietnam got his moniker, the "Chicken Man." Not for his spine which is indomitable but for his voracious appetite both in and out of the courtroom.

Congressman Don Bailey served in the 82nd and 101st Airborne Divisions in Vietnam. He was awarded the Silver Star, three Bronze Stars, two with the Valor device, one for meritorious achievement, Army Commendation Medal, with "V" for Valor, Air Medal, and a second Army Commendation Medal for meritorious service. He became our primary attorney and battlefield commander.

We were at war.

***

Chapter 20

Whoops

October 8th, 1997

Chicken Man called late in the night, which wasn't unusual; but what he immediately said as he spoke made me sit back in my chair and ponder what we were really ready to do.

"John, (Don rarely called me by my nickname when he was being serious) I want your permission to attach your journal to the lawsuit."

"My what?"

"Your description of the daily events for the last couple of years; it is damaging to the defendants and no one can tell it like you from your own words. You see if I make it an attachment, the Jury has to be able to view it during deliberations."

"Oh, shit, shit...Don, I name *names* in there. I have some Sensitive information in there and some even above the Sensitive Level. I could possibly get somebody hurt if that saw the light of day in its entirety. It was never meant for public view."

"I know, I need you to come up to my office tomorrow and redact it. Blacken anything you don't think should be seen by any civilians because of Law Enforcement Sensitivity."

"OK, you're the attorney, I trust you."

"John, we have to do it; it is damaging. There is raw emotion on each and every page and it is the God's honest truth and it is seen as such."

On my two-hour trip to Harrisburg and the several rest stops to relax my neck, diagnosed with a herniated disc at C5-6, I started to acquire some of the Chicken Man's perceived paranoia. He became a good friend, besides an attorney, and as any good friend,some of his idiosyncrasies, got on my nerves from time to time.

I sent him documents and I had to send them repeatedly. He would either lose them, shred them for fear of them falling into the wrong hands, or say he never received them after I faxed them.

I arrived and spent a good hour with a black magic marker redacting my diary, copying it and redacting it once more for good measure. I should have done this for a living; this document bled black ink. I went home and did not tell the Demon Princess what I did; it would have just made her worry.

The phone rang sending Blitz into an alert mode.

"John, It's Don Bailey... we strike tomorrow."

"OK, I'll tell the guys."

The next day October 14th, 1997, I got a call from Don and in a low guttural tone, he said: "Now John, I'm going to tell you something and you are going to get upset but it's my fault and I'll take all the weight on this."

"What happened?" I was finding myself lowering to the stair-step beside the phone.

"Well, we both know you came up here to my office and redacted your diary and all those documents...and the reason I'm saying this is because if those son of a bitches are listening, they can go..."

"Don, stop with the bullshit, what happened?"

"I turned in the wrong copy of your diary as an attachment to the lawsuit."

"What do you mean the wrong copy; turned it in to who?"

"The court clerk"

"Where?"

"The Middle District"

"Get it the fuck back."

"Now, you know I can't. I don't know how it happened. My office is a mess. You know how it looks; I really have to get around to..."

"DON!"

"Yes, John"

"Jesus, Don, I'm going to get fired"

"No, it's my fault, you did your job; I goofed up"

"Do you really think the Crystal Palace cares?"

"Don't worry, it's all true, so I'm the only one that screwed up"

"Don, I gotta go, I gotta call the guys and prepare them for the royal screwing coming our way."

"OK but don't worry, I'll call Sam"

"Yeah, while you're at it, tell Sam Stretton to keep his Crimes Code up to date as well as the civil procedure. We are really screwed."

***

Chapter 21

Blitzed

On November 7th, my wife and I took a trip and I had to kennel my new puppy; however I made the conscious decision to leave my trained K9 *Blitz* at home asking my Dad to come and feed him and give him water. Usually I would ask my brother who lived a short distance away, but the last time he entered my house after I was injured as a Highway Patrolman, left him a little leery, and Dad wanted a shot at it anyway.

My brother was one of the oldest new recruits at the Philadelphia Fire Academy and one of the top in his class. I remember him telling me from my hospital bed after one of my 'on duty' incidents.

"Yo, Johnny (Note, only my brother and sister have ever called me Johnny and got away with it) the fire Lieutenant came into the classroom and was looking down at a paper and said: "One of you guys have a Highway Cop as a broth..."

"Before he got the words out I was up out of my seat saying; what hospital is he in and is he alive?"

The Lieutenant said: "Methodist in South Philadelphia and yes; as I brushed past him."

"I know Frank, and I appreciate it but you know I can't let Mom and Dad see it on the news before you tell them"

"Yeah, after I called the hospital, I stopped to let Blitz out and he almost took my hand off; he bit the side of the door, until he recognized my voice, I guess. He scared the bejesus out of me."

"Sorry" was my response, but Blitz, when I am home is the most lovable canine you could ever meet.

There was some odd stuff going on at work since we filed the suit, with files missing, etc...so I wanted everyone to know I was going away and I made no mistake of telling everyone I was kenneling my dogs.

We arrived home and when I put my key in the door, I called out to Blitz and his bark was higher pitched than usual. I opened the door and he jumped up but ran toward the kitchen, and I noticed an odor usually associated with crime scenes.

I backed Joanne out from behind me saying I thought Blitz made a mess and I knew a shitty mess would stop Jo cold, as she has a weak stomach.

I went through my small living room to my dining room where I could see my mail with what looked like blood splatters dropped around it and on the Formica.

As I turned into the kitchen, in front of me was a pool of what seemed to be coagulated blood and led down the cellar steps. Blitz ran down the cellar and I was in hot pursuit. My files were down there in metal cabinets, the drawers were a little open, but Blitz and the drip trail went to the doggy door.

I found a bit of cloth in the door, and what I believed to be blood, going through the door. Blitz was salivating and in my face, as I was looking through the door. He started barking at me, seemingly trying to say; "I got the son of a bitch."

I knew to clean up quick before Jo came back in, but I needed to call my Dad to see if he has any inkling as to what went on.

"Hellooo"

"Dad"

"Yesss"

"Are you alright?"

"No I'm half left, Get it. You fall for it every time."

"Enough with the corn; any problems with Blitz?"

"No why? Did he complain? Gotcha again."

"Dad, Dad, listen, please, did you cut your hand or anything on his teeth, or on the door bringing the mail in?"

"No, Why?"

"Nothing, I just wanted to make sure he wasn't too rough with you."

"Ruff, I get it; you can't get me, I'm 2 and 0"

"Thanks Dad, goodbye"

"Ruff, Ruff"

My German Shepherd Blitz had done his job, and repelled the invader, but the physical evidence did not lead me to the perpetrator, or whoever hired him. There was a lot of blood on the kitchen floor and counter, but the injured black-bagger got away without any sign of forced entry. At seven hundred fifty pounds of pressure per square inch I could only assume the intruder still has nightmares of the land-shark not letting go. I needed to go shopping for another finless wonder, this time a solid black Czech GSD to protect my wife, call name, Faolan.

The stakes rose with this trauma. My wife spent her thirty-fifth birthday curled up in a ball, sobbing uncontrollably. I vowed to find justice for all of us.

My source at the Department of Defense found out many years later the name of the Black Ops guy was a "Matt Gunner." He was from Los Angeles and he was brought in to Philly to do a job. The cover story was, he fell down a flight of concrete steps and screwed up his face, his arm and hand. His face was so bad he needed plastic surgery and he still walked with a limp. He allegedly has carpal tunnel syndrome. An Indian or Pakistan Doctor, who was later deported because of tax problems, allegedly treated him at Einstein Hospital in the Northwest part of Philadelphia on Broad Street. However the story goes the DOD paid him three to four times the value of his house to help him with his tax problems through the Department of Defense Logistics. They got him a job at an Embassy overseas. "Matt Gunner" was allegedly still with the Agency and living in the Los Angeles Area.

***

Chapter 22

Siberia aka "Operational Requirements"

On November 11th, 1997

I was hand delivered a memo from our new Regional Director Ed Larner recently, of the *Beacon Hill Larners,* of Boston. He came over from the Secret Service and to say he knew nothing of being a gritty street cop, was putting it mildly. He apparently had a good reputation in the *Service* as he so often referred to the Secret Service. However; not being one to be shy, I constantly reminded him that he is not in the *Service.* He was in BNI, where to get your street *creds,* you might have to stand knee high in rat shit in an abandoned house for hours, while listening to Dennis croon '50s melodies on the 150 radios, which would drive a sane man to drink, let alone a *Bostonian.*

The memo from Chief of Investigations, John J. Qatar, stated because of Operational Requirements effective November 17th, 1997 Agent McLaughlin was assigned to Greensburg and another memo said Agent Micewski was assigned to Wilkes-Barre.

"Operational requirements? What operational requirements are there, making me drive 306 miles every Monday out to almost Ohio, and back to Philadelphia every Friday? Now could you explain this thinking to me."

"You have any questions; ask your chain of command."

"All due respect sir, you are my chain of command."

"Not anymore; as the memo states, you have been temporarily detailed to Regulatory Compliance and Intelligence."

"I'm already this Region's Intelligence Agent; why am I being moved?"

"Dennis is staying here; you've been detailed out."

"You mean because Dennis doesn't send any memos, or has written any diaries, he gets to stay home, while Charlie and I are sent 450 miles apart and away from our families."

"Listen, Spaarky, When I was in the Service, I was in the middle of my daughter's coming out party arrangements and I…"

"Sir, again not to cut you off, but this isn't the *service*, and I didn't do anything wrong to be treated like a memory; to be exiled to the other side of the mountains, and I'm not going to take this from you or anybody else in the Crystal Palace."

"Watch yourself Sparky."

"Respectfully, I call you Sir, and or Regional Director. I am formally requesting you address me as either Agent or Agent McLaughlin. Sparky is reserved for people I know are not out to screw me and that have my back both physically and mentally. You do not fit the criteria. Am I excused?"

"Don't leave the building unless I know."

"What? Now I'm a prisoner?"

"You have your orders, dismissed."

I was seeing a Chiropractor around the corner from headquarters for quite a while since my fall a year before, for neck and back injuries. I know the injury was related to the fall, but going up against the State, in a State Workmen's Comp hearing, proved a task too much. The State inadvertently sent me one of their internal memos from their attorney to the coordinator stating they would get a "favorable report" from this *independent* doctor, the State bought and paid for.

I never wanted a disability; I just wanted treatment so I did it on my own, including epidural steroid injections, into my cervical spine.

Well now I was not allowed out of the building, and I was expelled to *Siberia*, or Pennsylvania's version of it. I was going to take long term sick to attend to my injuries as I accumulated enough sick time. I called the Attorney General's Personnel department and asked for the procedures for "long term sick" and turned in a memo on November 17th, 1997 through the Chain of Command requesting long term sick leave, because of disturbing news over the weekend compounding my resolve to stay in the area to see my own doctors.

November 16th, 1997

My mother called and said my Father's was rushed to the hospital because of a heart attack.

Anyway, I had a subpoena to meet with Chief Deputy John Smallburger to go over some trial testimony. While in with the Chief Deputy, he received a call, left the room, came back agitated, and asked if I was ordered to be in Greensburg today. I told him no, as number one, I took off long term sick, and number two, he sent me a subpoena to meet with him, and number three, my Father suffered a heart attack and was in the hospital and may have to have an operation.

"Leave here and report to your Regional Director in Philadelphia."

I walked in to headquarters, went up to the second floor, and stood outside the Regional Director's door. I could overhear someone on an intercom talking (whom I later identified as First Deputy Mike Mappert).

"Is he dangerous?"

"No, he's just upset about the whole situation, and now this memo, and his Father's heart attack."

"Alleged heart attack."

"Mike, even he can't fake a heart attack, let's be real."

"I want the son of a bitch in Greensburg, tomorrow, do you hear me?"

"Yes, Sir."

The Regional Director opened the door and it was clear, I caught him with his hand in the *cookie jar*. No one knew I was outside listening, they did not know how much I overheard, and I was not going to let them know either.

Larner recovered his composure,

"What are you doing standing there?"

"I was ordered to report to you by CDAG Smallburger."

"How long have you been standing there?"

"Long enough."

"Come into my office and sit down."

Larner walked out and came back shortly with another memo and handed it to me. Again, it is from Chief John J. Qatar and it stated that I have violated a direct order by not reporting to Greensburg by 3:00 p.m. If I did not report to Greensburg by 3:00 p.m. on November 18th, 1997 I would be terminated from employment for insubordination.

Now being the Vice President of the Union and the head of the contract committee I knew every BNI directive and policy there was. I did not violate any of them, and I proceeded to quote everything the OAG violated, and threw in some federal employee laws, just for good measure.

Larner's answer was as much as sticking his thumb and fingers to his nose and waving them at me. It did not matter what he said, he was telling me to 'fuck off.' It was his football and if I did not want to play by their rules, I was off the team, one way, or another.

I had two dependents and a wife to help support. I was never fired from any job I ever held. I received excellent job performance evaluations my whole career. I earned everything I accomplished. No one ever gave me anything and I never asked.

My Father was going to have to undergo heart surgery and I was being forced under duress to travel over 300 miles away. If something went wrong and my Dad became critical or even died, I wouldn't be there, because of the State Attorney General of Pennsylvania.

To say I was angry was to say Vietnam was a "Conflict."

***

Chapter 23

"So a Narc walks into a Shrink's office…"

It was time to vent to an uninvolved third person. I called Don Bailey and Sam Stretton, and my Union Reps, and they all were saying they are filing TRO's on my behalf.

"What the hell was a TRO?" I found myself on the web because I didn't want to seem like I wasn't in sync with the program.

"Temporary Restraining Order? Temporary?!!"

I was in the realm of having chest pain, which I know was nothing more than stress and anxiety. The word temporary never even entered my mind. I thought I'd rely on A.F.S.C.M.E and my attorneys and they would nip this in the bud. The word temporary kept hitting me in the head like the migraines I used to get earlier in life. The throbbing was blinding. I needed to talk this through; I wanted to talk to a third person so I knew I was not crazy.

So I found a Psychologist who took pity on me and agreed to see me forthwith and I ran down to Center City Philadelphia into one of those endless high-rises. This one was on Chestnut Street. My insurance covered the visit and I found myself in a small elevator rising to the 13th floor, my lucky number.

As I got off the elevator, I found the hallway a bit dingy but navigable and easily found Dr. Jamey R. Zindel. I opened the door to a small waiting room and no receptionist. A note on the door said:

"Five minutes before your appointment, knock on the door lightly three times."

Oh shit, where have I gone? I'm back in OZ.

"No one gets in to see the Wizard, Not no way, Not no how."

I looked at my watch as the second hand hit 2:55 p.m. and knocked on the Door.

Knock…Knock…Knoc…

Suddenly the door flew open, scaring the piss out of me and there stood before me, sans shoes, was Dr. Zindel.

"You must be John, come on in, sit over here by the desk. Let's get some preliminaries out of the way and we can see what we can do for you."

OK, a little different, but OK.

"Alright, now the admin is out of the way; what brings you here today,from the beginning."

"Well Doctor, I'm a Narc, the longer version is a Narcotics Agent. Myself and three other Narcs, later called The Bastard Squad, got involved in an investigation in the Badlands of North Philadelphia, ultimately taking us to a tiny island in the Caribbean, and the backing of a Presidential candidate for this tiny island by the United States Department of State, the CIA and DEA Sensitive Activities Committee. We also tracked this candidate's dirty campaign money and this Dominican Trafficking Organization into New York where they were giving heavily to a Presidential campaign here in The United States."

Now Doctor Zindel, who was four feet from me, managed to double the distance, in the time I finished my first paragraph.

"John, let me interrupt you for one second. Now I do not want you to get offended and this is purely a diagnostic housekeeping thing I have to ask you."

"Sure, Doc, What's up?"

"Do you have any law enforcement identification?"

I dropped my head and started to chuckle.

"Yeah, Doc, here."

"And could I see the badge as well?"

"Sure."

"You understand it isn't every day someone comes in and tells me a story like this and…"

"It's not a story. I am reciting the facts of what brought me here and why I am under so much stress, and I not finished."

"There's more?!!"

"Much more."

I finished reciting basically a dissertation, as I knew everything by memory, including dates and times and when I was done Doctor Zindel, aside from being totally aghast, started writing on a pad and spoke:

"I want you to take these Xanax as needed and we will follow up next week…"

"Doc, I appreciate it, I really do, but you don't get it. If I'm not in Sib…I mean Greensburg by 3:00 p.m. I'm toast."

"They can't; I'm totally disabling you. You can't work under these conditions."

"Again I appreciate what you say, but they don't care what a Doctor says."

"I'm the adjunct Professor in the Department of Psychology at Jefferson Hospital University. You send them…What is their fax number? I am faxing them my note right now and you take the original. You can't travel, the meds I put you on and the pain from the dislocation in your neck could cause you to get killed or seriously injured."

"Now, I think you understand what I'm dealing with; I'll call you from one of the rest stops on my way to the nether regions tomorrow."

"How do you like to be addressed John?"

"Doc, you can call me Sparky,"

"Well Sparky, I'd be surprised if you found yourself anywhere but home tomorrow."

***

Chapter 24

"Follow the Yellow Lined Road…"

"Surprise, Surprise, Surprise." I was daydreaming in pain as I drove across Interstate 76 writhing in pain from my neck and my back as I spent the arduous journey into what an Eastern Agent would term as Siberia. Using the Marine's voice on the old Mayberry show would be a great voicemail to leave for Dr. Zindel.

The yellow painted lines on the blacktop seem to blend into one long hypnotizing mass of puke yellow and all I could do is try to make sure I stay between them and not fall asleep from the narcotic I am on for the pain, as prescribed by my Neurologist.

I finally arrived at Region 5 at St. Joseph's Seminary and after identifying myself to the secretary, Helen, she buzzed me in.

I asked for the Regional Director's office and knocked on the door of Regional Director, Tom Mavis.

"Sir, Agent McLaughlin reporting as ordered, can we agree it is 2:55 p.m.?"

"What? Who are you, and what's that about the time?"

"Agent McLaughlin, and I am requesting you check your watch to agree on the time of day I have reported to you."

"Yeah, Yeah, it's 2:55 p.m. Now what the fuck are you talking about?"

"I was told to report to you by 3:00 p.m. or I am terminated from employment with the Office of Attorney General. Sir, can you have someone direct me to my desk and can you tell me what my important assignment is? I am allegedly needed here so urgently, I was not allowed to be by my Father's side while he undergoes a lifesaving operation."

"Marie!!! Get Harrisburg on the phone. You… what did you say your name is?"

"Agent McLaughlin Narcotic Agent II from Region II Philadelphia, Sir."

"Well listen Agent, I don't know what the hell is going on, but I didn't request you, and I don't even have a desk for you and furthermore I have no idea what you're doing here. Just go outside in the 'bay' and find a place to sit until I sort this out."

"Sir, so you understand, I'm not being smart with you. What I told you is all what was told to me, not once but twice, so I can only assume there is an urgent need for a Dominican Drug Trafficking expert out here for some important mission.

"Dominicans? What Dominicans? What the hell is going on? Helen did you get somebody yet?"

So here I am, in Siberia, literally, there is ice and snow all over the ground. The images are ghostly. The office was empty. There are no Agents in the bay and none are expected. In this area of the State the Agents go out to local task forces and run the task force for the State so the Task Force can get State funds and the State Attorney General gets credit for the seizures.

RD Mavis came out after a half hour on the phone and said:

"Listen, from what I now understand, you're here all week and you travel on Friday, right?

"Yes, Sir."

"Did you check into a hotel yet?"

"No, I came straight here, I was afraid of being late."

"Go check in, get yourself situated and come back tomorrow. Hopefully I'll have some answers."

"Sir, isn't Agent McInenney still your Intel Agent for the Region?"

"I haven't received anything telling me any different, and you can quote me."

"Thanks for being straight with me."

"Hey, I'm not the enemy; I'm just following orders like you."

"Boss, I know your following orders, however so am I. We both understand. I was told there was an "Operational Need."

"The typical organization consists of the integration of many different functions," wrote Howard J. Weiss and Mark E. Gershon in Production and Operations Management.

"The two most obvious functions are to provide the product or service and to sell the product or service. Operations management focuses on the function of providing the product or service. It is concerned with the planning and controlling of all activities necessary for the provision of the firm's product or service. Aspects of operations management, then, include products or services to emphasize; facility size and location with respect to customers and suppliers; marketing strategies to attract clients/customers; techniques and equipment to use to make the goods or to provide the services; work force management and training; and measurements of quality assurance. Operations managers apply ideas and technologies to increase productivity and reduce costs, improve flexibility to meet rapidly changing customer needs, enhance product quality, and improve customer service."

None of these principals were applied in the deployment and detailing of the "Bastard Squad" to faraway places, to do nothing, while travelling two days, of a five day work week. The expense for vehicle maintenance and lodging for two agents including the impending legal actions made no fiscal sense.

No, these actions taken by the Pennsylvania Attorney General were nothing more than vindictive nasty retaliations for daring to file a 1st amendment civil rights action against the Pennsylvania Attorney General and daring to expose the connections leading directly from the sandy beaches of the Caribbean to a back room in Coogan's Restaurant in Washington Height's in New York. The Vice President was photographed and the campaign workers at his benefit, collected numerous donations from Dominican Narcotic Traffickers. Their occupations are all listed as "Requested Never Received." Several of those in attendance also carried NADDIS (Narcotics and Dangerous Drugs Information System) numbers next to their monikers. This should not have been lost on any advance team scanning the invitee list pre-event. Facts are the facts, and they are open-sourced.

***

Chapter 25

"We have Ways of Making You Talk…"

So I spent my first three days in Siberia sitting at someone else's' desk doing absolutely nothing for eight hours a day with two fifteen minute breaks and a half hour for lunch in which there was nowhere to go, so my lunch was out of a vending machine. I was told by Assistant Chief Maggiano I was not allowed to use the state vehicle for personal use. At 5:00 p.m. I would stick my head in to the Regional Directors Office and make sure he knew I was still there, which meant he was still there until 5 as well. I am sure he was appreciative of my keeping him according to the rigid time clock. Hey, two can play the game and I was not going to be broken.

Friday, after a fully satisfying week at work, (insert sarcasm here), I traveled home relieved to see my front door. Yet when I opened my door I was greeted by an all too familiar flashing light on my answering machine which told me only one thing; it was some suit from the crystal palace, not satisfied with ruining my week, they were out to ruin my weekend as well.

It was another Assistant Deputy Chief, Jim Muckert, revoking my pre-approved personal leave days I requested for the following week and ordering me to report to Internal Affairs in the Norristown Office. It was termed the ERO, (Eastern Regional Office). I will be met by Von Richtofer, actually his name is SSSA Richtofer (Senior Supervisory Special Agent) but with the ethnic name and his chosen unit, and hey, cops are corrosive sons of bitches, and if you are on the 'dark' side lovingly known as Internal Affairs, you are getting a monocle. Whoops, I mean a moniker hung on you as well.

I hit up Flash and Dennis and they were summoned for interrogation as well. OK, well I knew this concerned the lawsuit, their questioning seemed illegal, so I called the *Chickenman*.

"Don; Charlie, Dennis and I are being called on the carpet at IA, for what yet, I don't know, but I'm sure it has something to do with the lawsuit."

"John, don't worry. This just shows how scared they are. I'll make myself available. If they ask you anything regarding the lawsuit, you tell them this exactly. You tell them you fully want to cooperate with any Internal Affairs Investigation as a condition of employment; however you are doing so under duress, and you are also aware it is illegal for them to ask you anything in relation to your lawsuit without your attorney present. You tell them you want to speak to your attorney and get me on the phone in front of them."

"OK, I'm counting on you Don."

"We got them on the run; they're really worried to do this."

I was first to go under the lights and cameras, and I mean literally. I visited, by request, Internal Affairs in my career as a policeman for shootings I was involved in and also as a union rep for other Agents, but never was I involved where the interrogation was 'under the lights and on film.'

"Sparky, come on in; can I call you Sparky?"

"No."

"OK, well Agent Mclaughlin let me tell you why we are here. You filed a civil law suit, right?"

"My attorney has advised me I am to cooperate with you under the expressed fear of termination and under extreme duress and once you mentioned the lawsuit I am to ask for my attorney which under Civil Federal Code I am allowed to do."

"Stop filming. OK now John all you need is union representation and ..."

"I want to speak to my attorney. Are you denying this right while I am in custody?"

"Custody, what the hell are you saying? We're just interviewing you."

"We both know this isn't just an interview, your acting like Nazis and we are being treated like prisoners, denied council."

"Call your attorney; if you want, I'll speak to him."

"Fine."

"Don, Von Richtofer wants to talk to you; they are interrogating me about the lawsuit under lights and on camera."

"Mr. Bailey, it's not sinister. There was an attachment to the lawsuit. We in the Attorney General's Office consider it *privileged*. It is an Attorney's work product."

"I understand your position Mr. Bailey but all we are concerned with, is how it got attached and if your clients have any knowledge."

"Here Agent, Mr. Bailey wants to talk to you."

"John, we both know you, Charlie and Eddie did not know where I got the report, and furthermore I told you, it is none of your god damn business where I got it."

"I remember Don."

"I'm ready for your sweating, Agent Richtofer."

"I really wish you wouldn't refer to my questioning as such."

"I really wish you would stop violating my civil rights, but we both can't have what we want, can we sir?"

"Let's move on."

"Do you know how the report, we will term the Eric Noonan report, attached to your Lawsuit, came to be attached?"

"No."

"Would you agree the report is favorable to you and the other Agents in question?"

"Not only is it favorable, it clears us and any other Agent at BNI of any wrong doing whatsoever for the years 1991 until present day."

"Do you have any knowledge of anyone who may have given the report to your attorney?"

"No."

"Have you ever had this report, prior to it being filed, in your possession?"

"I'm not sure."

"What do you mean?"

"This is my diary (pointing to the document on the table) attached to the lawsuit" As I reached for the packet lying on the table, Von Richtofer pulled it away.

"I am just trying to find the exact date."

"What date?"

"It is back in the summer of, I believe July 1996, I think around the 16th when Regional Director Sean Boyle called me from his home and told me to ask *Mikey Cars* to go get the envelope off of his desk and for me to bring it to his house in Delaware County.

When I got to the RD's house, I met him at his back door. He asked me in, and I declined. I gave him the envelope and he said it was important. It was Eric Noonan's report. Why I said I am not sure, was because I did not see it, but if what Boyle said was true than I did have it in my hands. Now if you let me see my diary, I can give you the exact date."

"Not necessary; who is Mikey cars?"

"Oh sorry, Agent Mike Carvello is our Motor Maintenance Agent, so we call him Mikey Cars."

"Did he look inside the envelope?"

"Not that I know of. It was sealed when I got it; in fact I wrote the directions to the Regional Director's House all over the envelope, because I didn't know where I was going."

"Why do you think he asked you to bring it, and not Agt. Carvello?"

"Not my department; however everyone knows my parents live in Wallingford which is just past Granite run, so I assume he knew. They are often ill and I have to rush out to them."

"Do you have anything else to add?"

"Yeah, I need an operation and you are violating my civil rights by threatening to fire me if I take off sick to attend to my medical needs."

"Cut the camera."

"Hey, you asked."

Now I knew what got their shorts all bunched up. The Eric Noonan report cleared us of all wrong doing and the fact Eric who was well respected even in the US Attorney's Office was beyond reproach. If Eric said we were clean, and it was publicized, the Attorney General would not only look bad, but also the conspiracy we uncovered held some weight in the public eye. They also did not realize their own argument was invalid. They said only the Attorney General and Eric Noonan saw the report and they are claiming *privilege*. However, even an investigator like me can read cc's and footnotes. In fact the person who typed the report was not Eric Noonan. It was clearly listed on the report. It was typed by his secretary and read by three top executives in the Attorney General's office. So every time they stated in court, as officers of the court, only the Attorney General and Eric Noonan saw the report, they in fact, were not telling the whole truth.

But I'm the one turning on the spit.

***

Chapter 26

"The Hypocritical Oath or Who's on First..."

I prefaced this Chapter by drawing attention to the original Hippocratic Oath attributed by most to the Pythagoreans of the late Fifth Century B.C. It was translated below from the original Greek:

"I swear by Apollo, the healer, Asclepius, Hygieia, and Panacea, and I take to witness all the gods, all the goddesses, to keep according to my ability and my judgment, the following Oath and agreement:

To consider dear to me, as my parents, him who taught me this art; to live in common with him and, if necessary, to share my goods with him; To look upon his children as my own brothers, to teach them this art; and that by my teaching, I will impart a knowledge of this art to my own sons, and to my teacher's sons, and to disciples bound by an indenture and oath according to the medical laws, and no others.

I will prescribe regimens for the good of my patients according to my ability and my judgment and never do harm to anyone.

I will not give a lethal drug to anyone if I am asked, nor will I advise such a plan; and similarly I will not give a woman a pessary to cause an abortion.

But I will preserve the purity of my life and my arts.

I will not cut for stone, even for patients in whom the disease is manifest; I will leave this operation to be performed by practitioners, specialists in this art.

In every house where I come I will enter only for the good of my patients, keeping myself far from all intentional ill-doing and all seduction and especially from the pleasures of love with women or with men, be they free or slaves.

All that may come to my knowledge in the exercise of my profession or in daily commerce with men, which ought not to be spread abroad, I will keep secret and will never reveal.

If I keep this oath faithfully, may I enjoy my life and practice my art, respected by all humanity and in all times; but if I

swerve from it or violate it, may the reverse be my life."
http://en.wikipedia.org/wiki/Hippocratic_Oath

Now the reasoning behind my prefacing this chapter in this way should become quite apparent as I tell the tale, that would have Abbott & Costello thinking, copyright infringement, if they were alive, based on their famous routine.

On November 26th, 1997 Chief Qatar was outside a courtroom with me and says he was sorry to hear about my Father's heart attack and he did not know. I replied I found it hard to believe as my memo concerning my Father was required to be seen by him, since it was addressed to him.

On December 1st, I received a phone call from the head of my section of A.F.S.C.M.E. who stated they talked to the Chief of Personnel and he said I misconstrued something as I was certainly allowed to take sick time.

On December 2nd, I notified Harrisburg again I was taking long term sick and upon arrival home I was met with a letter on my FAX machine. It was from the Assistant Deputy Chief of the Western District stating if I was not in Greensburg by 3:00 p.m. on December 3rd, 1997, I was terminated from employment. Wait it gets better.

I arrived in Greensburg on the 3rd and I was given another written order faxed by Assistant Deputy Chief of the Eastern District, Maggiano, stating I was to report to a Dr. Samuel Kline in West Chester on the 11th of December. In the meantime, on December 9th, my attorney, Don Bailey, got a phone call from the Attorney Generals Senior Deputy Attorney General, defending our civil suit, who said if I dropped the lawsuit, I would suddenly find myself back detailed within 1 hour of Philadelphia, which would mean the Norristown office.

Hmmm, if you are still following along, you are thinking what happened to the "Operational Need" in Greensburg?

Grinding on.

On December 9th, I forcibly drive 6 hours to Greensburg, for 2 hours of sitting in a desk doing nothing. On December 10th, I'm ordered to drive back to Philadelphia so I will be on time for my appointment in West Chester, Pennsylvania on the 11th. Again another 6 hour drive and no work completed.

On December 11th, I met Dr. Samuel Kline and I am forced to take an intelligence test, an MMPI personality test, and also *draw the male and female body.*

Thank God, for my art by mail class, when I was a kid.

After preliminarily reading my results, the conversation went a little like this:

"So Agent McLaughlin, what's going on?"

"I thought you, were supposed to tell, me."

"No, I was just told to evaluate you."

"Well?"

"Well, I see you are intelligent and have an incredible memory. Your ability to recall the string of numbers backward is a little out of the ordinary."

"So Doc, does my eidetic memory make me nuts?

"Hell no; Why?"

I proceeded to tell the Doctor everything from the beginning to the present time including my recent travel back and forth to get to his appointment.

The Doctor's next words are, and again I am quoting:

"Man, the Attorney General is out to fuck you; whose toes did you step on?"

"Doc, I am just doing the job I was paid to do. Can I leave?"

"Sure, are you on anything for stress?"

"Yes, my Doctor totally disabled me, because of what is happening."

"No doubt; so why are you working?'

"Because if I take off sick I'm terminated from employment."

"Huh?"

"Yeah, that's what I keep saying."

On December 22nd after travelling back and forth to Greensburg during the Holiday season away from my daughter who was 6 years old and my wife who was having a difficult time handling my K9's and the household by herself, I got another order. Amidst the facts we uncovered, we found out once again there was an arrangement made between the Philadelphia DA's Office and The Attorney General's Office to keep us off the street permanently. It should be noted again at that time, the DA's office was Democratic as was the White House and our office was Republican.

This time I was ordered to travel in one of the worst ice and snow storms to Pittsburgh to see the Attorney General's Neurosurgeon to evaluate my C5-6 Spinal Injury. My shift was forcibly changed to 11 a.m. to 7 p.m. to accommodate the appointment set up for me with their Doctor. I barely arrived on time and that visit went like this:

"I'm Dr. Drinkwater; do you have reports for me to review?"

"No Sir, this is an Attorney General's evaluation. I was just supposed to report to you."

"How am I supposed to evaluate you without an MRI or at least a MRI report?"

"You would think the Attorney General would have thought of that, wouldn't you. Listen Doc, I am not trying to bust 'em for you. I just happen to have my actual MRI films with me, because I knew they would pull a stunt like this. They are in the car. I'll be right back."

After viewing the films Dr. Drinkwater said the following:

"Well it's simple; this shows you have a severe herniated disc at C5-6. I don't understand, what else I am supposed to be looking at. Are you having this treated?"

"I was, until I wasn't allowed to take off to get treated."

"What? You're not treating for this condition? Are you at least getting epidural steroid injections?"

"They won't let me see my Doctor."

"Huh?"

Next in the batting cage was Dr. Gary Bass in, you guessed right, the Eastern part of the State, in Wayne, Pennsylvania. The Attorney General apparently didn't like the answer they got from the Psychologist so they are sending me to their designated hitter, a Psychiatrist.

"Dr. Bass I'm Agent McLaughlin, reporting as ordered."

"So tell me what brings you here."

"The Attorney General ordered me to come."

"Why?"

"Don't you know?"

"I'm asking you?"

"I don't know, I'm just following orders."

"Listen, we won't get anywhere if we keep going like this."

"You're not my Doctor, I have one."

"Well, can I talk to your Doctor?"

"Sure, but not concerning me."

"I assumed you understood, I meant in regards to you."

"You didn't say that, now, did you? Remember I do this for a living as well. You can ask me a direct question and I will give you a direct answer if I know it, and if it has to do with my employment."

"Well maybe there are issues outside your employment which are affecting your job."

"No, I need an operation and I am in great pain and the Attorney General said if I took off sick to attend to my illness, I was terminated from employment. Pretty much sums it up."

"Oh."

So this was how it went from November 18, 1997 till April 9th, 1998 when I was travelling home from Siberia. I got paged four times and when I got to my front door I finally returned the page and it was Assistant Deputy Chief Maggiano who said as of April 13th, 1997 I could now use my sick leave.

There are many incidents during this time in Siberia but the one most noteworthy was a call from Dr. Zindel on St. Patrick's Day March 17th when he stated:

"I think your friends were here last week"

"My friends? What friends?"

"You know the ones vilified in movies as lurking in the darkness."

"Doc, give it up; what's going on?"

"My building was burglarized last week on the 10th, and everybody got hit; but all that happened to me was...my files were gone through. I mean I have all those medicine samples lying around and not one was taken. It just doesn't make sense. I think the people after you, just visited me looking for information on you."

"Screw them. I'm sick of this shit, I'm gonna start fighting back." Burglary reported to Philadelphia. Police on DC# 98-6-4817369.

***

Chapter 27

"Pineapple Gets Peeled..."

January 21st, 1998

I got a call from Dennis saying "Did you hear what happened to Manny?"

"What? Pineapple? What's wrong?"

"He got pinched by the Feds."

"What?"

"Yeah, after the Housing Police left us, he apparently kept working the street with Housing and it was related to something regarding a search, without a warrant, on a car."

"On a car? What, after they hit a Section 8?"

"I don't know, it's all real quiet."

"Jesus, that's really bad news; they'll also try to connect this shit to us, you know."

"How can they? We've been off the street for almost two years now."

"You just mark my words."

January 30th, 1998

I just entered my house from my return trip from *Siberia* and I was walking my K9 Blitz when my cellphone rang.

"Yo Spark, it's Manny."

Oh shit, I don't know what to do? Did the Feds try to get him wired? Whether he did anything or not, is he trying to hurt us to help him? Wait a minute, we have not done anything so screw it; just be careful.

"Yo Manny. Man what the hell have you gotten yourself into?"

"It's fucked up, real fucked up. Can I talk to you?"

Oh shit, here we go

"Yeah sure go ahead."

"Not on the phone, in person."

"OK, where?"

"I don't want to go by headquarters; you know the Double D?"

"Dunkin Donuts? On Lindberg and Island? OK, When?"

"Well I'm close by; whenever you can get there, you just live around the corner right?"

"Yeah, I'll be right around, give me a few minutes."

Shit, I guess he knew I wouldn't refuse him.

I purposely drove around the extended parking lot of the Double D looking for Surveillance Platforms like the one we have in the Blackhawk© . I was reasonably sure there wasn't anything within range, again if Manny was wired, I'm sure it would be cutting edge. The Feds know I might suspect and take him somewhere or have a RF (Radio Frequency) detector on my person.

I saw Manny and I approached his vehicle and made sure he understood, I was not getting in.

We gave the customary handshake wherein you shake with the right hand and give a quick hug with the left. I purposely didn't do anything extra to make him feel awkward as he obviously did, by his first comments.

"I swear to my mother I'm not wired."

"I didn't ask."

"Man, I am in deep shit."

"What happened?"

"This Dominican called me and said there was major shit coming in on the Peter Pan at the terminal."

"Yeah, but there's no Housing there Manny. Why didn't you call the PD?"

"This was only the second time this guy called me and it was supposed to be going to a Housing property."

"OK, go on."

"I watched a guy pick the mule up from the tag I was given and I followed him with some Housing guys and I pulled alongside and as I was coming up I saw the passenger pulling out *fingers* from a yellow bag and show the driver. The passenger then gave it to the driver and he reached under the driver's side and it disappeared."

"You saw everything?"

"You know how it is; I'm darker than they are and in North Philly they don't care because I'm Spanish."

"So, OK then what?"

"I call the uniforms, we stop them and I went to where I saw them put the *shit* and take it from a hidden compartment and we lock them up."

"OK so what's the problem?"

"I said it was in plain view."

"What the hell! You said you saw them put it there; you said it was what you knew to be *fingers of heroin*, why the bullshit?"

"Because the guys I was with said I should have gotten a warrant and they weren't going to say they were there, unless I put it down like I did."

"Well you are screwed. Why didn't you call somebody? We could have helped you type a warrant? No matter if you saw the guy even on video; this is Philadelphia. You have to know by now there is the law and there is the Philadelphia District Attorney's Law; two distinctly different entities."

"What should I do?"

"There's nothing you can do but tell the truth. Get a good attorney and tell the truth. Just so you know; the Feds will try to come after us through you and so just tell them the truth. We never did anything wrong, and neither did you."

"OK Spark, can I call and talk to you?"

"Sure, anytime!"

April 30th, 1998

Manny went on trial in Federal Court at 6th and Arch and *The Bastard Squad* were all there in his defense as character witnesses.

Before the trial began, I had asked his attorney about Manny's notes of interrogation from when the *Feebs* interviewed him. Manny took verbatim notes during his interviews with the FBI and the difference between the official FBI-*Sixes* as their investigative reports are called, and what Manny wrote are astounding. The unofficial handwritten reports of Mannys' mostly concerned *the Bastard Squad* and how we were "on the boat waving to Manny on the dock as the Boat is pulling out' and how Manny was being left behind if he doesn't say the Bastard Squad did something wrong.

The Feds, it seemed, were barely interested in Manny's indiscretion. It was only a stepping-stone in their unyielding attempts to try to pin anything on the BNI Agents. Manny even mentioned our meeting in the Double D in both the official and unofficial record, and to be fair, the Feds actually reported I told him to tell the truth.

Manny was found not guilty on three counts. He was found guilty on one count, of falsifying an official document. Defense Attorney Melbert will appeal this, however, as Manny's' memo (to which the count referred) was never actually entered into evidence as a document. He should never have been convicted.

However later, as sentencing usually is unequal against Police Officers more than anyone else; Manny got hit hard with 36 months incarceration. He does 30 months in a hell-hole in Texas. I wrote him often and sent him funds and the newspaper; but I couldn't help but think the only reason he got slammed so hard was because he wouldn't lie and say we did something wrong; in fact he wrote in his notes to the FBI interrogators:

"Listen if you're saying it will help me if I say the BNI guys did something wrong; tell me what to write and I'll sign it. If you're asking me if they did something wrong, no they didn't."

AUSA Mary Bobber states she would have given Manny immunity if, in exchange, he would have testified BNI agents did something wrong.

"Whatever happened to Truth, Justice and the American way?"

***

Chapter 28

"N.Y. Times Breaking News – Death by Editorial..."

'Neither Confirmed nor Denied'

A year earlier in late April of 1997 The New American printed an article written by William Norman Grigg entitled *Smuggler's Dues* and went into the connection between the Dominican traffickers of New York's Supervisory Special Agent Orazio Cosentino of INS and BNI's traffickers and the connection to the Presidential elections in both the Dominican Republic and the United States. It was an explosive article given the revelation of our country's backing of Samper of Colombia and its favored Nation status.

I am *shaking the tree* by writing FOIA's (Freedom of Information Act) requests to every federal agency we dealt with, in all of our names, after getting permission to do so.

Chickenman also had his investigator, who he only refers to as *Big Tony* checking his DC connections and trying to find who exactly has it in for us, and why. He also is fielding calls from various news outlets. May 10th, 1998, our little daytime drama, exploded on the national stage with a center page mention of our investigation. In the middle of a series on the Dominican Drug Trafficking problem, by Larry Rother and Clifford Krauss of the New York Times was an article entitled "Dominicans Allow Drugs Easy Sailing."

http://www.nytimes.com/1998/05/10/world/dominicans-allow-drugs-easy-sailing.html?pagewanted=all&src=p.m.

Mr. Vincho Castillo, the Dominican Republic Anti-Drug Czar said:

"This is the greatest problem we face in these elections. Not only that, narcotics traffickers from New York are putting their own people, by which I mean their brothers and cousins, into the campaigns, and some of the candidates know that."

The article referenced our investigation, "American officials have long harbored similar suspicions of the Dominican political process. During the 1996 presidential campaign here, in fact, the Drug Enforcement Administration, responding to a Central Intelligence Agency inquiry, took the highly unusual step of organizing a sting operation in the United States against Mr. Fernandez's chief opponent, Jose Francisco Pena Gomez, in an effort to determine whether he and his party are involved in drug trafficking.

Mr. Pena Gomez was running well ahead of Mr. Fernandez in election polls when he took his campaign to New York City's large Dominican immigrant community early that year. At a rally at the Washington Heights headquarters of the Dominican Revolutionary Party, or PRD, members of his staff are approached by a couple who said they are representatives of a Colombian cocaine cartel, but in reality, are Drug Enforcement Administration agents working undercover.

The pair offered the Pena Gomez campaign an immediate $50,000 and said $250,000 more would be forthcoming each month if Mr. Pena Gomez, once elected, would agree to let five planeloads of drugs land unobstructed. Such an agreement is already in place with Dominican military and Police authorities, they said, urging Mr. Pena Gomez and his aides to check the authenticity of their claim with the officials involved.

One of his New York representatives later met the drug agents at an office at Columbia-Presbyterian Medical Center, but Mr. Pena Gomez eventually rejected the overture, and shortly afterward he sent a letter of protest to President Clinton. American suspicions are again aroused, however, when, just days after Mr. Pena Gomez won the first round of the election and declared himself "virtually president," several of his party members are detained and a shipment of 778 pounds of cocaine seized, according to Dominican officials."

Almost at the same time I pulled over on South Broad Street in Philadelphia, reading the Sunday Times, I got a call from Flash.

"G Man called."

"Yeah? Long time, since we heard from him."

" He said they killed Pena Gomez and he hung up."

"What?"

"I checked on the internet, Pena Gomez died that day from an alleged pulmonary embolism."

"Are you shitting me?"

"No, Spark, they *did him*, man. You know he was going to say something."

"Shit, one hell of a coincidence."

"You know the *little general* is reading a book on assassinations in headquarters."

"You mean our National Guard personnel?"

"Let me hit him up, stay on the three-way."

"Yo, General. Did you ever hear of anybody from that three letter agency whacking anybody by giving them an embolism?"

"Hell, yeah, there's a book by Richard Camellion, called *Assassination: Theory and Practice* (Paladin Press, 1977) describing a form of *refined cyanide* that *can* cause or appear to cause embolism."

"Why, are you guys getting whacked?" chuckling.

"No, but our PRD investigation may have just been closed *with extreme prejudice.*"

***

Chapter 29

"ET TU (fill in name here)..."

Between May of 1998 and when I finally have the surgery at my C5-6 disc, I was the subject of at least two attempts of subversion or persons approaching me wearing a wire to try to make me say something damaging; quite possibly three, but two for sure.

The first one involved a stone cold heroin addict who was an informant we will call "Albert." Albert always called me from the same phone number without fail, no matter what, for any reason and would always put in the number '3' after the return phone number, to let me know it was him, which really didn't matter, because he was the only one who ever called me from that number.

Two things the Feds didn't know before forcing Albert to wear a wire against me. The first was in the Spring of 1997 while off the street, I often visited my parents when I could, due to their illnesses and their proximity to the Granite Run Mall in Media, Delaware County, Pennsylvania. This practice gave me the chance meeting, to come upon Albert, walking around the Mall with his, I assume, either US Marshall or FBI Agent handler on the second level near the Men's fashions. I assumed they were trying to get him dressed up for Grand Jury testimony as apparently he was *dried out* as he had put weight on, was clean and must of weighed at least 175lbs.

So when his eyes met mine he put his head down in shame but did not speak. I got the message loud and clear. He was *humbugged* by somebody and I needed to find out by whom.

I wasn't worried and as I went past him in the mall he looked back and I gave him the 'OK' sign, and he turned his eyes up to heaven in despair.

I checked my informant's record the next day, which I was actually required to do and saw quite an unusual arrest on his jacket.

Aggravated Assault on Police, impossible! Got to be a mistake. Albert couldn't assault a Police officer if he tried. Half the time he is *on*, meaning high on heroin. I pulled the initial investigation report. I see who arrested him and I knew it was a humbug. A humbug is a bullshit arrest. No Police Officer likes to believe they exist; however sometimes it was a fact of life. I never personally saw one; however the team who arrested Albert had a reputation for putting their grandmother on the books, if it would make them look good on paper. I found out many years later that one of the members of this team killed himself.

So mid-May I got a page with the coded threes, after the return phone number; however it was not from our usual phone, which was located in the 1100 block of Lehigh Ave on the South side of the street. Tip-off number 1.

"Yo Sarge, what's up?"

"I don't know, Albert, you tell me."

"Oh nothing. Can we do something?"

"Like what? I haven't heard from you in ages and I'm sure you heard I haven't been on the street, and from what I hear, neither have you."

Dead air.

"Well yeah, I got caught up in one of them Bench Warrants."

"Well you remember, when I ran you, we could only run NCIC because the Police Dept. Bench Warrants didn't show up in NCIC (National Crime Information Center) only PCIC (Philadelphia Crime Information Center)."

"Yeah I know, but can we talk?"

"Sure but where are you; I know you're not up the *WAY*."

"Yeah I just got out, but I'll meet you at the same spot."

"OK, a half hour."

Now I knew he was not getting, from either 8th & Race, or State Road prison to 12th and Lehigh on foot in 30 minutes if he was walking, so he must have a ride, most likely with a Fed.

I told Charlie to gear up and follow me. I wanted somebody to watch my back as I knew I was being watched and taped.

I arrived, and in a few minutes, Albert showed up and got in my Pathfinder, a state unmarked Police vehicle.

"Albert, I'm off the street so I can only take your information and pass it on and if somebody hits on something, you have to come in and get re-signed with that Agent, but everything has to be straight–up, just like always."

"Oh yeah, you were always straight-up, no playing around with you Sarge, by the numbers."

"OK, he's going overboard. He's telling me he's wired and if he opens his eyes any wider I'm going to think I was back in an old Abbot and Costello movie.

"OK, all I have is $20 bucks; I'm not making any overtime, here."

"Thanks, OK I'll see you, and if I have anything, I'll call you."

"OK, Albert, thanks for everything."

The second time wasn't as pleasant.

It was odd. I started seeing my old partner who was now a Sergeant in North Philadelphia showing up wherever I went to have a meal, before I stopped down the Fireman's club to get away from everybody. Now it seemed whenever I showed up in Northern Liberties at this small bar/restaurant where I ate steak au poivre, there he was. He would have some people from his squad there but basically he was always hanging out with this african american female Officer.

This is odd to me as Joe didn't go out, in fact since he got married he never showed up at the usual cop spots. He was a Northeast Philly guy and only rarely, did he go out with the guys.

One night after I left for the Firemen's I was surprised to see Joe and a table full of his squad at the front of the Fireman's club. I went my way and stayed with my guys and didn't pay him much mind until he called me over and committed the mortal sin. Any veteran Police Officer will tell you what he next said as the first sign of a rat in your midst.

I was in the firefighter's club awhile and what I do when I went out on a Friday night was; I go to the restaurant in Northern Liberties and drink wine with dinner, approximately two glasses. I then went to the firefighter's club and drank diet coke the rest of the night. No one knows whether or not there was a mixer in it and I never got drunk anyway, but just because I stayed out; there may have been those, federally speaking, who thought I was inebriated after a certain period.

Well I wasn't, but apparently Joe or his handler must have hoped I was off my guard, because when Joe called me over to his table, he said:

"Spark, do you remember when…?"

Any cop worth his salt knows when you are under an FBI investigation, for any alleged infraction of the law. You have been vilified in the press for over two years, and the former unit you and the person you are speaking to, just got slammed with several persons indicted, by a Federal Grand Jury, the one thing you never say,when out *drinking* is, "Do you remember when?"

It didn't matter what followed those four little words. I knew he was wired or one of those Police Officers around him were. Most likely the african american female who was sitting so cozy next to him, almost in his lap.

My response not only was the truth, but probably upset Joe more as he most likely didn't tell his handlers, he had these little habits.

"No, Joe you must have me confused. Maybe you are talking about after I left and you hid your one man vehicle and work three man cars with so and so."

He almost choked.

His head went down and he started stuttering and said "Oh, Oh I guess I was wrong."

"Yeah, Joe, I guess so" as I put my face directly in his face, he couldn't look me in the eye.

On Wednesday, I found out anonymously what tour of duty he was working in North Philly and showed up unannounced as he was dismissing his men.

"Joe, I need to see you alone outside, right now."

He was ashen.

We stepped outside and I controlled myself, actually much more than I ever thought I would.

"Joe, I'm really sorry for you if you're in any kind of trouble; but if you try to hurt me to try to help yourself; this would be the most cowardly thing you could ever do, and you know me, and you know how I would react."

He couldn't look me in the eye. His head was down and he was gulping.

"Sorry Spark, I swear, I wasn…"

"Stop, don't lie anymore to me; in fact, don't ever talk to me again for any reason whatsoever."

I never looked back.

***

Chapter 30

"Damnatio Memoriae"

In the fall of 1998, I had major surgery to repair damage to my back and neck. My recovery was long and painful, stretching into the spring of 1999. This came after a long deterioration, many visits to doctors and hospitals, and constant on-the job harassment concerning these health issues. The AG's harassment was just one part of the overall effort to stop my partners and I.

The same month I had the surgery our attorneys file our retaliation lawsuit, and started taking depositions for eventual use in court. They got the venue changed from Pennsylvania's Eastern District court in Philadelphia, to the Middle District court in Wilkes-Barre, but this suit was destined to drag on for years. I fielded calls from David Marash from Nightline, Will Grigg from the New American and several other major media outlets, however if I talk, I knew I would be fired.

I was ready to go back to active duty and I was told I was going to be shipped again back to Greensburg, some 300 miles away, even though we were cleared by the US Attorney. I was sent back to Siberia for another month. Still no work. Don Bailey filed a Temporary Restraining Order to bring the OAG to heel. I'm temporarily sent to a desk job in Norristown, Pa, twenty miles from the streets of North Philly. Flash was also in Norristown but had responsibilities still in Wilkes-Barre. The following September the Third Circuit Court of Appeals reinstated our second lawsuit (the one filed in '98), and this one was assigned to Pennsylvania's Middle District. The state's attempts to get this one dismissed fail.

We went through the next four years fielding insults and the daily internal grinding grief of not being allowed to do our jobs. We were denied promotions; we were denied the status and prestige of meeting with outside agencies as representatives of our Agency. We were told internally not to associate with any new Agents officially, at least on paper, but the regional people would appreciate our expertise if we could help find hidden compartments or sit in on an interrogation.

We finally got back to Philadelphia after Dennis forged our signatures on a document stating we would never fight getting our regular jobs back. Dennis knew it would never stand scrutiny, but he wanted us back in Philly so we were all together physically at least.

We are hidden away in a back room and leashed to a computer and became the Intelligence Unit. Although the idea was to *disappear us* like the Russians used to do; we won't be ignored. Other Agencies find if they need some information they call the guys from Philly, as we could find, identify, and target anybody based on a thread of information.

"The *damnatio memoriae* method of disappearance is practiced in the Soviet Union. When an important political figure is convicted, for instance during the Great Purge, artists would retouch them out of photographs; books, records and histories would be recalled, rewritten or re-enacted; pictures, busts and statues would be taken down; people would be discouraged from talking about them, and the government would never mention them again. They are made to have never existed - unpersoned - in the same way as is used by the Ministry of Truth in George Orwell's novel Nineteen Eighty-Four. Notable examples range from prominent Russian revolutionaries who took part in the Russian Revolution but disagreed with Bolsheviks, to some of the most devoted Stalinists (for instance Nikolai Yezhov) who fell into disfavor.

Since 2001, as part of its War on Terror, the United States' Central Intelligence Agency has operated a network of off-shore detention facilities, commonly known as black sites, which are used as part of the system of extraordinary rendition used to hold and interrogate "high-value" foreign combatants captured during the US's wars in Iraq and Afghanistan. The ACLU has stated they consider extraordinary rendition to be an illegal form of forced disappearance and called for the detainees to receive trials and the camps to be closed; the US government argues   since the combatants are captured while participating in active military conflict against the United States and officially designated as "Illegal Combatants" under the Geneva Convention, the detentions are legal under international law.

The International Convention for the Protection of All Persons from Enforced Disappearance, adopted by the UN General Assembly on 20 December 2006, also states that the widespread or systematic practice of enforced disappearances constitutes a crime against humanity. Crucially, it gives victims' families the right to seek reparations, and to demand the truth about the disappearance of their loved ones. The Convention provides for the right not to be subjected to enforced disappearance, as well as the right for the relatives of the disappeared person to know the truth. The Convention contains several provisions concerning prevention, investigation and sanctioning of this crime, as well as the rights of victims and their relatives, and the wrongful removal of children born during their captivity. The Convention further sets forth the obligation of international co-operation, both in the suppression of the practice, and in dealing with humanitarian aspects related to the crime. The Convention establishes a Committee on Enforced Disappearances, which will be charged with important and innovative functions of monitoring and protection at international level. Currently, an international campaign of the International Coalition against Enforced Disappearances is working toward universal ratification of the Convention.

Disappearances work on two levels: not only do they silence opponents and critics who have disappeared, but they also create uncertainty and fear in the wider community, silencing others who would oppose and criticize. Disappearances entail the violation of many fundamental human rights. For the disappeared person, these include the right to liberty, the right to personal security and humane treatment (including freedom from torture), the right to a fair trial, to legal counsel and to equal protection under the law, and the right of presumption of innocence among others. Their families, who often spend the rest of their lives searching for information on the disappeared, are also victims. http://en.wikipedia.org/wiki/Forced_disappearance "

Screw Them.

We will not go away and we will not be ignored.

***

Chapter 31

"Justice"

"It is a Cold Day in Hell…"

Well it certainly at least looked like a frozen and abandoned hellish tundra as we arrived in the town of Wilkes-Barre on February 2nd, 2003 the night before our jury trial was set to commence.We went through the center of town; Flash was driving my SUV as I still had a problem driving distances.

The town not only had seen better days but the section from the hotel to the courthouse looked like it was abandoned and frozen over, for years. We arrived on the cusp of a snow and ice storm with blizzard like conditions lurking around the corner that would arrive mid-week.

The saying when it rains it pours took on new meaning for us.

It was now five years of constant harassment by the Attorney General's Office and we were crucified in the press with only *under the radar* media outlets taking up our plight to the extent of articles that made us out to be conspiracy theorists.

What the rest of the world didn't know was for everything my attorney said either to a reporter or in a pleading; I had the facts to back it up. The factual information I was referring to was not from my own internal reports. It was from DEA, Customs, CIA reports and Dominican Drug Control Directorate reports.

Unbeknownst to my chain of command and even my attorneys, I established an international informant of my own who had direct ties to the Presidential Palace in the Dominican Republic. Whatever I needed or wanted for my case, having to do with the Dominican Republic, found its way to me.

I was able to prove without a doubt, the defense attorney Sly Gialla turned in a fake birth certificate for a Dominican National and falsely testified before a Common pleas Judge and he was one of the main catalysts fueling the media circus against us. If this concerned credibility the Attorney General should have welcomed the information and backed his men. This never happened which fueled even further the following summation opening at the trial on day one by our attorney Sam Stretton.

Now I strategically sat at the end of our table closest to the Jury because I wanted to employ a strategy as well.

Sam's opening was sometimes wordy but masterful:

IN THE UNITED STATES DISTRICT COURT

FOR THE MIDDLE DISTRICT OF PENNSYLVANIA

JOHN MCLAUGHLIN and

CHARLES A. MICEWSKI   )

    Plaintiffs

      v.

MICHAEL FISHER, ET AL,

    Defendants.   3:00-CV-521

BEFORE: HONORABLE A. RICHARD CAPUTO

    United States District Judge

    For the Middle District of Pennsylvania

    at Wilkes-Barre, Pennsylvania,

    Jury Trial, Volume I,

    on Monday, February 3, 2003.

A P P E A R A N C E S:

For the Plaintiffs: SAMUEL C. STRETTON, ESQ.

    301 South High Street

    P.O. Box 3231

    West Chester, Pennsylvania 19381

DON BAILEY, ESQ.

4311 North 6th Street

Harrisburg, Pennsylvania 17110

For the Defendants: REED, SMITH, LLP

BY: ROBERT DORFMAN, ESQ.

KARL FRITTON, ESQ.

P.O. Box 11844

213 Market Street, Ninth Floor

Harrisburg, Pennsylvania 17108

"Well, first you get to know my clients. Charlie Micewski is a Philadelphia officer since 1974, worked for the Philadelphia Police Department, retired in 1995 and then became hired by the Attorney General's Office, very decorated Philadelphia Police Officer.

John McLaughlin, Philadelphia Police Officer starting in 1977, worked there until 1995, I guess that's what, 17, 17 and-a-half years, had a job opportunity to work as an agent in the Attorney General's Office. Also a very decorated Philadelphia Police Officer. And both of them are working in the Philadelphia Police -- I mean, in the Attorney General's Office as agents in the Bureau of Narcotics Investigation, investigating narcotics activity, primarily in Philadelphia and surrounding areas.

As part of their investigation they discovered something involving the Dominican Republic a presidential candidate, bringing in heroin and drugs by individuals who are coming in under diplomatic immunity.

Now, as a result of their discovering something, a complaint is filed because they are mistreated, allegedly. I'm going to read to you the complaint, portions of it, because this is not the lawsuit you're deciding. This is not the lawsuit you're deciding. "The Plaintiffs," and that's Mr. McLaughlin and Mr. Micewski, extremely dedicated and successful narcotics agents to the Philadelphia Attorney General's Office began gathering evidence on the PRD, a Dominican political party supported by the United States.

A Dominican party supported by the United States, which indicated that illegal drugs are being prolifically sold at will in the United States to our Black and Hispanic populations. This money is even being put into American elections. But when the Plaintiffs went to the Federal authorities with certain sources in the PRD, they are suddenly ostracized, my clients, and became the target of vicious unfounded attacks on their credibility and careers by the Federal Government. From on or about 1991 through 1994, the Plaintiffs, those are my two clients, are diligently working at the investigation and prosecution of criminals involved in the sale and distribution of narcotics in Philadelphia. "On or about October 20th, 1995," John McLaughlin, that is, my client there, opened an investigation into the Revolutionary Dominican Party, PRD, and its leaders. The PRD is supposedly based in the Dominican Republic.

The Plaintiffs learned that the PRD had an extensive network for the sale and distribution of drugs into the entire Eastern seaboard of the United States and they operate with impunity in Philadelphia. On October 20, 1995, the same date Mr. McLaughlin, my client, opened the PRD investigation, he and Mr. Micewski my other client. This is Mr. McLaughlin, this is Mr. Micewski. received PRD, that's the political party, documents during an arrest that demonstrated direct involvement in widespread unlawful drug activities.

The FBI is contacted in November of 1995 and they did not wish to become involved, citing lack of jurisdiction. On January 20th -- on January 30th, 1996, the CIA, Central Bureau of Investigation -- CIA, Central Intelligence Agency.

On January 30th, 1996, the CIA indicated that any arrest of Pena should be cleared with the State Department. He is a presidential candidate.

On March 25th, 1996, McLaughlin and Micewski are informed that the Philadelphia Drug Enforcement Administration people are told not to work with the BNI, Bureau of Narcotics Investigation, by the U.S. Attorney's Office, that's Mike Stile's office who is the U.S. Attorney then in Philadelphia, in the Eastern District of Pennsylvania. However, New York DEA is excited about working with the Plaintiffs. They had two Assistant United States Attorneys assigned to the project.

The Plaintiffs discovered a plan to make a large seizure -- the Plaintiffs discussed plans, discussed plans, to make a large seizure of drug money from Pena, that's the presidential candidate of the Dominican Republic, who had organized a fund raising trip to the United States to collect drug money in New York, some of which came from Philadelphia. Also on March 25th, 1996, McLaughlin is given a memo listing PRD members, as political party members, in New York by the Santo Domingo DEA office with a cover sheet that reads as follows: *Larry, here are the requested documents per telecon. Please, please, keep me well informed on this one. Our collective* -- and then there's a word for the buttocks, *are on the line. Thanks in advance, Jim.*

When Plaintiffs, that's my clients, met with the Defendant Lawrence he is intensely interested to know who is the confidential informant and what province he came from in the Dominican Republic. In other words, my clients are working with a confidential informant, obviously. Plaintiffs had grave fears for the CIA's role in the entire matter because they seemed to center more on gathering information rather than on sharing it to further a common goal.

McLaughlin received an urgent call to bring the confidential informant to New York because Pena, the president candidate, is to arrive soon. However, upon arriving in New York, BNI, that's Bureau of Narcotics Investigation; personnel are informed that Pena is under protection of the New York Police Department at the State Department of the United States' request because of alleged death threats.

But on the same day New York DEA agents debriefed the confidential informant and later collected information on PENA's fund-raising where drug proceeds are turned over to Pena.

On April 16th, Arnold Gordon, First Assistant in Philadelphia, District Attorney in Philadelphia, met with the AG's office and explained there is 'an ethics problem' with the Bureau of Narcotics Investigators in Philadelphia.

On April 23rd, 1996, Channel 13 News in Philadelphia did a lead story comparing the Plaintiffs to a situation where a group of Philadelphia officers created false crimes and caused terrible injuries. The Plaintiffs are ordered by the Defendant in this case, not our case, Gentile not to respond to the inaccurate press reports.

The Defendant, Tom Corbett, who is then Attorney General of Pennsylvania before Mr. Fisher, publicly announced on May 15th, 1996 that the agents involved, my two clients, would be reassigned and never get their regular jobs back.

On or about June 3rd, 1996, the Plaintiffs, my clients, are told that the DEA in New York could no longer work with the Philadelphia Bureau of Investigation.

On July 16th, 1996, Chief Deputy Eric Noonan, after investigation, including interviews with the Plaintiffs' confidential informants, reported to the Defendants, that is, Defendants in this case, there is no evidence of any corruption regarding my clients."

So that was basically Sam's opening statement with all the wordiness taken out. While Sam was speaking, it was our job, Charlie and I, to take a good assessment of the jurors. The only juror bothering me was the older white woman closest to me, who would squint down her glasses in our direction, from time to time, and her cheeks would cave in like she just sucked on a lemon.

It was time for me to take the stand on direct examination.

A few of my major moments come when first I am asked by my own attorney:

Q. At some point are you taken and prevented from continuing to work on the street?

A. That's correct.

Q. And when is that, sir?

A. It is approximately 11 days after we refused to give the CIA the names of our...

MR. DORFMAN: Objection, Your Honor."

I made my point and followed the first rule of testifying; I was looking the Jury straight in their eyes when I framed my answer in such a way the correlation was made and the time frame was established. The CIA didn't get what they wanted, so we got yanked off the street. Mr. Dorfman only put fuel on the fire jumping to his feet as I slid the three little letters into my testimony I knew would stick in the Jurors mind, *CIA*.

In his cross-examination, Mr. Dorfman kept trying to drive the point home I could not testify and I could not make prosecutable arrests, neither of which was true.

Since there was no evidence we did anything wrong and the Eric Noonan report made it very clear along with the US Attorney closing its investigation into BNI without any charges being levied, we should be back in action. Additionally, the Philadelphia District Attorney stated on the record, "He may have made a mistake, it is a gut feeling." In any courtroom no evidence amounts to *ZILCH* or better yet *Bullshit;* I had every right to answer Mr. Dorfman consistently with "I can testify" and "my cases can and should be prosecuted by the Pennsylvania Attorney General under the Commonwealth Attorneys Act. It stated The Attorney General may petition the court having jurisdiction over any criminal proceeding to permit the Attorney General to supersede the district attorney in order to prosecute a criminal action or to institute criminal proceedings. Supersession shall be ordered if the Attorney General establishes by a preponderance of the evidence that the district attorney has failed or refused to prosecute and such failure or refusal constitutes abuse of discretion."

In any court in the land I have more than enough physical evidence to prove my case. We finish day one of testimony with Bob Dorfman looking a little foolish in his vague attempts at trying to discredit me.

***

Chapter 32

"Justice Day 2"

"Psy Ops and Mappert's Swiss Cheese Defense..."

We walked the three blocks from the hotel to the courthouse in the falling snow, across the ice laden sidewalks. They weren't shoveled, I assume because of the abandoned stores, we were passing as we trekked along. We felt we were going through the under bowels of the great winter of despair.

We approached the courthouse. I saw Don Bailey get out of a dark black ford sedan with spotlights on the outside, and I recognized the driver from one prior meeting.

As I got closer, I could see a DOD sticker in the windshield and on the bumper.

"Who the hell is this guy?"

I remember Don's first statement when he saw us.

"Well fellas, let's go slay the beast."

We walked ahead with Tony, an ominous figure bringing up the rear until we approached any door and Tony scurried past us not saying a word and grabbed the door until we all passed through.

We took our seats, Sam was already at our table, and again I made sure I was on the outside with Flash to my right and he opted to sit back a bit. Big Tony set up residency directly behind me and had his own psy op plan afoot.

The judge came out and did some preliminary housecleaning, as it is termed, which was brought to the courts attention by the defense attorney.

"Your Honor, we think it is unfairly prejudicing the jury to have Mrs. Bailey crying every time Agt. McLaughlin is testifying."

"Mr. Stretton, your response?"

"Well your honor, as you can see for yourself on the defense side of the room beside the defendants there are at least fifteen people in the gallery that have snickered and made little comments that I have heard but haven't said a word about, and on my side of the room I have Mrs. Bailey and a Federal Investigator."

"A Federal Investigator?"

"Excuse me your honor" Don rose to his feet. "May I present Anthony Marceca who is a Federal Investigator who does work for me from time to time and is the investigator on this case."

Sam continued, "So your honor if Mrs. Bailey has an honest emotion that comes out during live testimony it is not prejudicial; what is prejudicial is the amount of people on that side of the room (pointing behind the defense table) here to try to damage my clients further."

"I object."

"Over-ruled, you opened the door Mr. Dorfman. I will allow Mrs. Bailey to remain in the courtroom and just ask her to try to control her emotions and will take judicial notice of any excessive human emotion, Mr. Dorfman."

Hmm, The Judge just zinged the defense attorney, not a bad way to start, I thought to myself.

Before the Jury came out, I got up to run to the Men's room and Big Tony got up with me and was following me out the door.

"I gotta hit the head, damn BP medicine, I know I'll be peeing all day."

"Yeah, I could stretch my legs as well," Tony related.

"Uh oh, what the hell was going on?"

Tony stayed outside the Men's room though, and I noticed no one else entered. He was an imposing figure, 6'3" 300lbs, Italian in a black suit.

I came back in the courtroom and got my briefcase ready as the jury took their seats. I purposely had photographs enlarged of many of the great seizures of drugs and cash we made and hoped we could use them in some way to show what kind of investigators we were and what we confiscated off of the streets in our short tenure. I told Sam Stretton he kept cutting me off on Monday and he needed to stop doing that, as just as he had a rhythm, so did I. I needed to get my story across in my own way as I was also an expert around juries. I could joust with the best of defense attorneys and have proved it time and again.

Apparently this isn't true of First Deputy Mappert. What Sam Stretton did to the First Deputy on the stand was nothing short of a surgical cutting of his entire prepared script. Mappert started out calmly, speaking in a monotone and in a professional manner, but by the end of the day Sam had him stuttering, reaching for water, looking up and to the left, a thorough indication of lying, and just generally contradicting himself. He made Peter's betrayal of Christ in the garden, look insignificant, compared to the blaming he was doing in the morning session until I guess he got his marching orders in the afternoon session.

In between various slices by Sam's tongue, I got up to run to the *john* followed by my shadow, Big Tony, who I guessed sensed my uneasiness and stopped me outside the courtroom.

"Sparky, listen, me following just you, when you get up to leave every single time, sends a psychological message to the jury that you are in danger. That I am here protecting you. It gives them this picture in their head whether they want to see it or not. Check their faces when we walk back in, it's undeniable."

"Well, you do have a point." Even Charlie made it perfectly clear on direct examination in a very emotional outburst pointing to me in the courtroom:

"Q. Is there anything you wish to add as to why you didn't send a memo or have you said your piece on that particular issue?

That's a two part answer. One, they never respond to your memos, anyhow. I don't know how many memos I did write, not many. I never got a response from any of them. Secondly, we're all going to face it here, everybody that knows us knows John is the fighter of the two of us, John McLaughlin. He must have wrote memos every day.

MR. DORFMAN: Excuse me, Your Honor, I object. He's talking about Mr. McLaughlin writing memos.

THE COURT: Overruled.

THE WITNESS: I saw his memos. He writes them almost every day, complaining, yelling we're being picked on, or this, that.

BY MR. STRETTON:

Q. That's enough.

MR. STRETTON: I have no other questions. Thank you.

THE COURT: Any recross?

MR. DORFMAN: None, Your Honor."

So yes, I was getting on the same page as Tony. We entered back into the courtroom I could see almost all the Jurors stop and look in my direction. I sat down and I decided I knew I could't do anything overt to unduly influencing the Jury however. If they happen to see flashes of my photograph's as I take them out of my briefcase, maybe the images of all the drugs and illegal profits of the traffickers will also make a lasting impression.

The suits on the other side of the room stop us from taking this stuff off of your streets, they want your children to do drugs; you are getting sleepy, sleepy...sleepy....

Sam was still using his number 2 pencils like a light saber cutting and shredding Mappert's responses, to the point he was sitting, now slouched, and with his tie pulled down and gulping a few glasses of water as the sweat seemed to be trickling down his forehead.

The coup de grâce was when Sam hit upon our interrogation by the Internal Affairs unit over the Eric Noonan document:

"Q.   As I understand your testimony then, the lawsuit that is filed on October 14th, 1997 is just routine business, not a problem?

A.   The lawsuit?

Q.   Yes.

A.   Yes, it is irrelevant to any decisions that I made with respect to any of the agents who had these troubles.

Q.   Not even a little -- not even a little mark on your radar screen?

A.   Mr. Stretton, no.

Q.   Don't you remember ordering directly these clients being questioned and warned their McGarrity(sic) rights, that if they didn't answer they'd be fired because they filed this lawsuit, and attached a copy of the Noonan Report?   Do you remember ordering that?

MR. DORFMAN: Objection.

THE COURT: Overruled. You can answer the question.

BY MR. STRETTON:

Q.   Do you remember that, sir?

A.   No. I don't know what you're talking about.

Q.   You know what the McGarrity(SIC) decision says in terms of employees' rights, do you not, that they don't have a right to remain silent if they want to keep their job when they're questioned?

A.   Again, I am familiar with that but I don't know what you're talking about.

Q.   Do you remember ordering that my clients were interviewed as soon as the lawsuit is filed and they are told that –

A.   By whom?

Q.   By you.

A.   No, sir, that's absolutely false. I don't know -- I have no idea what you're talking about.

Q.   Do you remember instructing Mr. Noonan and Mr. McCrey (SIC) to question my clients on reference to the lawsuit?

A.   No.

Q.   Are you aware that they are questioned, after the lawsuit is filed, about the lawsuit and told that their McGarrity(sic) rights are at issue and they had to answer or else they would be discharged immediately?

MR. DORFMAN: I object to the form of the question, Your Honor. That's assuming facts and its assuming statements –

THE COURT: He can answer the question. Overruled.

THE WITNESS: I never ordered anyone to tell your clients anything like that.

BY MR. STRETTON:

Q. You're telling me you aren't aware that they are subject to that interrogation after they filed the lawsuit in October 14th, 1997?

MR. DORFMAN: Same objection.

THE COURT: Overruled.

THE WITNESS: If you're referring to Mr. Noonan -- let me see. Okay, Mr. Noonan is --Mr. Noonan passed away in April of '98, so it would have had to have been before -- I believe April of 1998. It would have had to have been before that. The only thing I can think of that's responsive to your question is that at some point, and I talked about this earlier, at some point after that lawsuit is filed we noticed that at least a draft of Mr. Noonan's report is an exhibit. And Mr. Raquet, the head of our Internal Affairs Division Section, conducted an Internal Affairs inquiry into how a document that is so privileged that neither me nor my predecessor's First Deputy had ever seen it, ended up on a document filed in a courthouse. If that's what you're referring to, I remember that internal investigation, yes, I do.

BY MR. STRETTON:

Q.   And you ordered that internal investigation?

A.   Yes. I asked Mr. Raquet to investigate how that document came to be filed publicly. Yes, I did do that.

Q.   And you ordered that investigation in October of 1997, after this lawsuit is filed, right after it?

A.   I don't remember when, but I have no reason
to doubt your time table. It seems a little quick, but..."
That was the *Butt* heard throughout the courtroom. It's one of those times when you have to instinctively look over at the Jury
and watch them having the same reactions as you did, shaking their heads, and they are looking at each other raising an eyebrow as they do.

One thing that always made me wonder about the Eric Noonan Report. On the copy of the Lawsuit Don Bailey gave me, and I subsequently copied and handed out to my other Agents and Co-Complainants throughout this period and beyond, was page 44 wherein the top of the page has the header like all the rest:

Thomas W. Corbett, Jr.
July 24, 1996
Page 44

However a few spaces down it reads:

EMN/lab
cc: William V. Conley
         Executive Deputy Attorney General
         Criminal Law Division

         Joseph C. Peters
         Assistant Executive Deputy Attorney General
         Organized Crime and Narcotics

         H. Clifford O'Hara
         Director, Office of Investigation
         Criminal Law Division

Louis W. Gentile
Deputy Chief
Bureau of Narcotics Investigation and Drug Control

Now I did not go to law school but based on what was written on this page and all of the testimony of Mappert and all the other Defendants concerning the Eric Noonan report, wouldn't this refute their testimony to the point someone might, well, consider the charge of perjury to be appropriate for some of the defendants?

In the case of the Pennsylvania Attorney General's executive office and the powers to be, I assume 1 plus 1 = "look the other way."

***

Chapter 33

"Justice Day 3 & 4"

"The Big Red 'S' is also for Sam Stretton ..."

Bruce Badinov who looked a lot like Snidley Whiplash[©] with his dyed black hair and never a touch of grey in his mustache, also found himself looking for verbal Kryptonite as our attorney smacked him around on the stand.

I am not a tall person standing at 5'9", but Bruce looked like he was in a high chair as he fumbled through testimony making him appear to be the unprofessional we have all come to loathe. Exceptional was this excerpt from the transcript on the third day:

BY MR. STRETTON:

"Q. Let's look under Subsection C. It says, Generally, employees should not be in a travel status more than 60 days in any 90 consecutive day period at a given site, except as outlined herein. The controller shall review travel vouchers and recommend changes in headquarters, in instances where it appears that a change in headquarters is appropriate. Did I read that correctly?

MR. DORFMAN: Excuse me, Your Honor, but, again, the witness has said this might have been in effect; it might not have been in effect. Then Mr. Stretton starts with, well, with regard to this, what is the policy, and then he's trying to impeach him on the basis of something that nobody can testify is in effect. I think it's improper.

THE COURT: Is that an objection?

MR. DORFMAN: Yes, it is, Your Honor.

THE COURT: Overruled.

BY MR. STRETTON:

Q. Having read that language, is it your understanding that, that is the procedure or policy in effect, back in 1997 or 1998?

A. The policy and practice in effect is that employees can be on TDY more than 60 days. Mr. McLaughlin sent a memo to the Director of Management Service or to the Controller raising this issue, and he is given an answer saying his situation is not applicable, that it is already approved, it is approved through the chain of command, and it is permitted for him to be on an extended TDY for 60 days.

Q.   Precisely, that Mr. McLaughlin is told by the highest authority in the Attorney General's Office that his situation is approved to be different from the regulation that is in place, am I correct, sir?

A.   He's not the only one that has exceeded this 60 days, other employees have, also.

Q.   I understand that, but my point -- I'm not trying to make more of it than it is, and forgive me if I'm doing that. My only point is, as of '97 and '98, there is a policy, which similar, if not the exact language that I read, but in Mr. McLaughlin's case, the controller and others in the Attorney General's Office said that they are approving the procedure for Mr. McLaughlin that is different from the regulation, correct, in other words, they made an exception?

A.   It says, generally. I don't think it is an exception; it's common that employees are on a TDY beyond 60 days. It is not -- the contract, we get forty-five cents an hour, when it exceeds the 60 days, so it isn't a big exception.

Q.   I'm not trying to make more of it than I am. All I'm saying is that it is an exception of sorts. It is an exception to the black letter language and your understanding of the policy back then, yes or no?

A.   Do you want to repeat that, please?

Q.   I tried to put it back in the corner, that's what I tried to do.

A.   You're trying to put me in a corner.

Q.   But Mr. McLaughlin's -- the approval for what Mr. McLaughlin's situation is, is an exception to the policy, as you understood it, back in 1997, early 1998, is that a fair statement?

A.   I'm not sure it's fair to say it is an exception. I mean, it is -- it's common beyond 60 days, that's why we have it in the contract. In negotiation, it is brought out that this is common that

...

Q. Well, didn't your office, through John Adams, have to make a separate column on Mr. McLaughlin's travel vouchers, because of the exception, which is contrary to the written language?

A. I'm not certain.

MR. STRETTON: Thank you. Your witness."

Super Sam struck again. It is just poetic how Sam left Bruce looking smaller and smaller as a professional of human resources. I should know as I have an arsenal of information to back me up, being married to the Demon Princess who holds a Master's Degree in Organizational Management out of the University of Pennsylvania. When Bruce would do something heinous, Jo would start spewing HR related topics out my ears so I know where to look for the weaknesses in the Attorney General's office.

In one swift swoop using Chief Qatar as his hook for reeling in the Fish, the line of questioning went this way:

"And as I understand, you told -- your recollection of that meeting is that you told Mr. McGinnis that you couldn't do that, because the U.S. Attorney didn't want my client or my clients in that particular Office on Essington Avenue?

A. I don't believe I told that to Mr. McGinnis. The reason why we didn't want Mr. McLaughlin there, that is part of that decision, yes.

Q. Are you here yesterday when Judge Stiles testified that, in August of 1998, early Fall of 1998, he said he had no Objection to these agents being present?

A. No, he didn't say that. At the time –

Q. But you are here when Judge Stiles testified.

A. Yes, but I don't think he said that yesterday, either. I recall there are arguments between you and Mr. Dorfman over Mr. Stiles' testimony.

Q. I understand that. But you recall the bottom line testimony, sir, where he said -- and I read his testimony from his prior -- do you want me to read it again so –

A. No.

Q. -- where he states -- where he said he did not object?

A. I recall that.

Q. But that's not your understanding, now, as you sit here?

A. My understanding of what Mr. Stiles is referring to, back in 1998, is quite different.

Q. You agree with Mr. Fisher's testimony, where he also contradicted Mr. Stiles on that particular issue, don't you?

A. Yes, I do.

Q. And Mr. Fisher, obviously, is the person who hired you and brought you into this position, correct?

A. Yes, sir."

Damn, we had them didn't we? I mean we have a former US Attorney saying a sitting Pennsylvania Attorney General, soon to be a nominee for the Supreme Court was telling a *Fish Story*, and a whopper of one. Shouldn't one of these guys be under investigation by the Feds?

I was beside myself, I wanted to run right out and kiss Sam's ring, he was my new god. I kept looking over at the Jury.

However; I didn't feel good regarding the end of the trial. One juror, closest to me, she was evil or at least was giving me the evil eye.

***

Chapter 34

"We have a Verdict..."

"Walking the Marble ..."

Sam's closing was like tying a big red bow you see in one of those new car commercials on TV where the car is waiting for you outside on Christmas Day.

However Christmas just passed and this afternoon when the sun went down and the Jury retired for deliberations the only people left, was our team, and the defense attorney and his secretary. The defendants, the people from the Attorney General's office, all left the building. I guess they assumed they had it in the bag. Mr. Dorfman said at one deposition he wouldn't give us *One Red Cent* on behalf of the Attorney General.

To be perfectly honest; if we won big I just wanted enough money to get out of this hellhole as it was intolerable. I cannot stand a place where the employees were treated so poorly and this was when we were innocent. I could only imagine what would happen if we did something wrong.

Well minutes rolled into hours. Flash helped Mr. Dorfman's secretary out to her vehicle with her files as she was dropping them all over, and Mr. Dorfman had his feet up on a bench with his shoes off, lounging. I ran out the door to help Flash and the secretary and she was frazzled but thankful. Flash let out a couple of one-liners in reference to her boss and like a good secretary who needs her job, she said nary a word, but we both heard what we thought was a chuckle as we carefully made our way up the icy steps.

With no livestock running around, Don opted to call for pizza delivery and was munching in a side room. Both Flash and I couldn't eat. We both walked the marble floors; Flash was doing East and West and I headed North and South.

We had entertainment for a while when a mouse appeared out of one of the courtrooms and was scurrying along Flash's corridor. Flash wanted to feed him but we couldn't get to the pizza in time. The *Chickenman* and company devoured the contents of the now empty boxes and left them in the corner.

The word finally came. The court clerk peered out of the courtroom door fixing his tie and said,
"We have a verdict."
It was 9:27 p.m., February 6th, 2003.
As the Jury came in we all rose and again remained standing for Judge Caputo. Flash and I never sat back down. Although we were the plaintiffs, we sure felt like defendants. There were four of us on our side of the room and I couldn't count the number on the other side at one point in the trial; but now it was just Bob Dorfman and his secretary.
The crier handed the judge the verdict and the jury foreman was asked to read verdict at the same time.
"We find in favor of the plaintiffs."
I felt my legs buckle. Flash grabbed me by the arms, put me in a bear hug and kept saying:
"You did this, you did this, this is all you"
I responded
"It's finally over."
We did not even hear what we won; we did not care; we beat them. The stoic Sam Stretton leaning back on the plaintiff's chair looked at us through his glasses, which were now down at the tip of his nose:
"Do you realize how much you were awarded?"
"No."
It was the only appropriate response. He was still adding, and Don piped in:
"$1.5 Million, those bastards will remember this day for the rest of their lives."
Those *bastards*; how appropriate.
They were at a Republican fund raiser. Apparently they thought they scored a *slam dunk* as their attorney Bob Dorfman put it. He had said to us, we wouldn't get "one red cent."
Flash didn't let him forget it either.
"You're right Mr. Dorfman, you can keep the pennies, and I'll take the Greenbacks."

For one night, one dark, cold freezing night in the dead of winter, "we were the hottest thing on ice."

The tears of joy started running down my face and I remember hugging Sam as he calmly spoke:

"Maybe we can go out some time and have a cocktail and talk this case over." I laughed because this is Sam, ever so quiet, Super-Sam. I tried to hug the *Chickenman* and when I could not get my arms around him I opted for the half a hug handshake.

Sam told us to get out into the hallway and thank the jurors as they left.

"We're allowed to speak to them?" I wasn't going to screw anything up.

"Sure it's over, you won, and you can do whatever you want."

"I looked back, yeah I wish. I knew it wasn't over but this was a major victory."

No one and I mean no one, thought we ever had a chance and I thanked God I had the forethought and the guidance from Mr. Schraeder so many years ago to document and memorialize everything I did when I was in a sensitive investigation.

I woke the Demon Princess who was *cachin'* some Z's as it was way past her bedtime.

"Jo."

"Satan."

"We won."

"Really?"

"No Shit."

"And?"

"1.5 Million, half and half."

"You're right; you said you could do it. "

"Now if I can only make it home in one piece in this ice and snow."

"I'll get my Mom to put *Mary Queen of the Highways* on Alert."

"Go back to sleep; this was all a dream."

"OK."

***

Epilogue

The War on Drugs

This chapter covers the aftermath of our case. The ruling should have given us justice, but it didn't. The defendants appeal the verdict, keeping it tied up in court indefinitely.

Three months later Fisher was appointed to a federal judgeship on the 3rd District Court of Appeals, which has jurisdiction over several lower courts, including the Middle District in Pennsylvania where our case appeal was being heard.

**Statement of Senator Patrick Leahy,
Ranking Member, Senate Judiciary Committee
Judicial Nominations Hearing
October 15, 2003**

"Over the course of this year in the Judiciary Committee, we have seen a number of firsts. At the first nominations hearing of the year, for the first time ever, Republicans unilaterally scheduled three controversial circuit court nominees at one hearing contrary to a long-established agreement and practices of the Committee. Then we saw Republicans declare that the longstanding Committee rules protecting the rights of the minority would be broken when Rule IV is violated. A rule that is adopted 25 years ago -- in order to balance the need to protect the minority Members of the Committee with the desire of the majority to proceed -- is unilaterally reinterpreted to override the rights of the minority for the first time in our history. For the first time ever this year Republicans insisted on proceeding on nominations that the Committee had previously voted upon and rejected after full and fair hearings and debate. Of course that followed the first ever resubmission by a President of the names of defeated nominees for appointment to those same judgeships.

Several other practices are reversed from when a Democratic President is making nominations in light of the

Republican affiliation of the current President. This Committee has proceeded on nominations that did not have the approval of both home-state Senators. Moreover, this Committee altered its prior practice and overrode the objections of home-state Senators to vote on the nominations of Carolyn Kuhl in spite of the opposition of both home-state Senators. Then, in connection with a nomination to the circuit court from Michigan, this Committee for the first time proceeded with a hearing in spite of the opposition of both home-state Senators.

The hearing on the nomination of Michael Fisher to the U.S. Court of Appeals for the Third Circuit is also unprecedented. Never before to my knowledge has a President nominated to a lifetime position on a federal circuit court or this Committee held a hearing on a judicial nominee with an outstanding jury verdict naming him as personally liable for civil rights violations. In February 2003, a federal jury in the U.S. District Court for the Middle District of Pennsylvania found that Mr. Fisher and other high level officials of the Pennsylvania Office of the Attorney General violated the civil rights of two plaintiffs, former narcotics agents with the Bureau of Narcotics Investigation (BNI) in Philadelphia. Never before in the history of federal judicial nominees of which I am aware, has a nominee ever come before this Committee with an outstanding judgment against him for so serious a claim.

The jury verdict is so recent that the trial transcript has only been delivered to the parties within the last several weeks, and so complex that even Mr. Fisher and his lawyers have asked for extensions of time in order to complete their post-trial motions. Soon a federal district court trial judge will be called upon to review the verdict against a person the President has nominated to the Court of Appeals that review all appeals from that trial judge's court. In addition, if the jury verdict is sustained by the trial court, an appeal would lie to the very court to which Mr. Fisher has been nominated. These, too, appear to be unique circumstances.

Accordingly, this is a most unusual proceeding. As the Administration and Republican majority have abandoned traditional practices and standards we are being confronted with more and more difficulties. The few judicial nominations on which the Senate has withheld a final vote this year have each presented extraordinary circumstances or nominees with extreme positions. During the years in which President Clinton is in the White House, Republicans attempted a number of filibusters and, when they are in the majority, successfully prevented votes on more than 60 judicial nominees, including a number of nominees to the federal courts in Pennsylvania.

I begin this hearing without having reached a determination about this nomination. I am troubled by the jury verdict. I have heard from a number of supporters of Mr. Fisher whose opinions I value that they believe him qualified to serve as a judge of the Third Circuit nonetheless." http://www.judiciary.senate.gov/hearings/testimony.cfm?id=4f 1e0899533f7680e78d03281ff1b702&wit_id=4f1e0899533f7680e 78d03281ff1b702-0-2

In October, we received an invitation by Arlen Specter to go to Washington to testify before the Senate Judiciary Committee concerning Fisher's complicity in actions against us, but we were not permitted to appear. Instead, we found ourselves in a closed door session with a tape recorder pushed in front of our faces and only allowed to answer specific questions posed to us; nothing more. I got upset at Don because he did not let me speak. He did not let me comment on the fact that the Attorney General or the US attorney lied under oath and no charges were initiated.

In December, 2003 the Senate confirmed Judge D. Michael Fisher unanimously. The first sitting third circuit federal judge with a first amendment civil rights freedom of speech violation where he is adjudicated guilty, by a jury of his peers, is now a sitting federal judge on the circuit, who will hear the appeal in his own case. Can you say the 'fix' is in?

We continue by looking at the state of Politics and the drug wars today. Dominican nationals connected to the narcotics trade still make significant donations to political campaigns, including Hillary Clinton's 2008 presidential campaign. The same money launderer Pablo Espinal who gave to Al Gore in 1996 and Hillary throughout the years has again been ignored while the confirmation hearings for the Secretary of State confirm that nothing changes. He was listed in 1996 as a PRD Executive Commission Zone President and at the same time had a DEA NADDIS# 12898597342   File# ZL-79-00176342378 listing him as a Money Launderer.

Espinal, Pablo Brooklyn, NY 11225 Jesadan Meat Corporation Inc/Busine	CLINTON, HILLARY RODHAM (D) President HILLARY CLINTON FOR PRESIDENT	1,000 primary	3/31/08
Espinal, Pablo Brooklyn, NY 11225 Jesadan Meat Corporation Inc/Busine	CLINTON, HILLARY RODHAM (D) President HILLARY CLINTON FOR PRESIDENT	1,000 primary	2/31/07
Espinal, Pablo Brooklyn, NY 11225 Jesadan Meat Corp./President	CLINTON, HILLARY RODHAM (D) President HILLARY CLINTON FOR PRESIDENT	250 primary	9/14/07
ESPINAL, PABLO BROOKLYN, NY 11225 JESADAN MEAT CORP./PRESIDENT	CLINTON, HILLARY RODHAM (D) Senate - NY FRIENDS OF HILLARY	500 primary	2/08/05
ESPINAL, PABLO BROOKLYN, NY 11225 JESADAN MANAGEMENT CORP	CLINTON, HILLARY RODHAM (D) Senate - NY HILLARY RODHAM CLINTON FOR US SENATE COMMITTEE INC	1,000 primary	7/18/00
ESPINAL, PABLO BROOKLYN, NY 11225 ASSOCIATED SUPERMARKET	NEW YORK STATE DEMOCRATIC COMMITTEE (D)	3,000 primary	0/21/96
ESPINAL, PABLO BROOKLYN, NY 11225 ASSOCIATED SUPERMARKET	NEW YORK STATE DEMOCRATIC COMMITTEE (D)	2,000 primary	9/19/96

ESPINAL, JUAN FAR ROCKAWAY, NY 11691 LOS PRIMOS MEAT MARKET	CLINTON, HILLARY RODHAM (D) Senate - NY HILLARY RODHAM CLINTON FOR US SENATE COMMITTEE INC	500 primary	8/07/00
ESPINAL, JUAN R FAR ROCKAWAY, NY 11691 LOS BRAMOS MEAT MARKET	NEW YORK STATE DEMOCRATIC COMMITTEE (D)	3,000 primary	0/21/96
ESPINAL, JUAN R FAR ROCKAWAY, NY 11691 LOS PRAMOS MEAT MARKET	NEW YORK STATE DEMOCRATIC COMMITTEE (D)	1,000 primary	9/19/96
DIAZ, SIMON NEW YORK, NY 10033	NEW YORK STATE DEMOCRATIC COMMITTEE (D)	1,000 primary	9/19/96

I cultivated a new informant with direct ties to the Presidential Palace in the Dominican Republic who we would call Teresa for the sake of anonymity. I was told of the Associated Supermarket, which was being used as a front for Dominican traffickers:

Pablo Espinal's Associated Supermarket also known as The Federation of Dominican Businessmen and Industrialists eventually Merge and become known as the National Supermarket Association, which is also known as "The Corporation." It was also known as the Bodega Management Corporation, which was first Incorporated in New York but allegedly finds, people can ascertain who was on the Corporation paperwork and traced them, so they up and dissolve this corporation and incorporate in Nevada where no one can look into the corporation paperwork without filing a lawsuit, which usually fails.

Name/
Status   Corp State   Corp Number Fein

BODEGA MANAGEMENT, INC.

ACTIVE   NV   C18132-2004
BODEGA MANAGEMENT CORP.
191 EAST 161ST STREET, BRONX, NY 10451
DISSOLUTION BY PROCLAMATION   NY
1221773
BODEGA MANAGEMENT CORP.
INACTIVE - DISSOLUTION BY PROCLAMATION
NY   1221773

BODEGA MANAGEMENT, INC.
ACTIVE - 60 DAY LIST OF OFFICERS FILED
NV   2004181320X

NATIONAL SUPERMARKET ASSOCIATION, INC.

NEW YORK Corporate Records
Name: NATIONAL SUPERMARKET ASSOCIATION,
INC.   Type: DOMESTIC NOT FOR PROFIT
Status: ACTIVE - AMENDMENT   Status   Date:
07/31/1998
Date Incorporated: 03/09/1990
Corporation Number: 1429260   FEI Number:

Additional Corporation Names
NATIONAL   SUPERMARKET   ASSOCIATION,   INC.
COMPANY NAME
NATIONAL   SUPERMARKETS   ASSOCIATION,   INC.
COMPANY NAME

Corporation Officers and Registered Agents
Name: S/S THE CORP
Title: PROCESS ADDRESS (REGISTERED AGENT)

Address: 125 EAST 116TH STREET
NEW YORK, NY 10029
Effective Date: 03/09/1990

Name: THE CORPORATION
Title: PROCESS ADDRESS (REGISTERED AGENT)

Address: 17-20 WHITESTONE EXPRESSWAY
SUITE 302
WHITESTONE, NY 11357
Effective Date: 07/31/1998

History Transaction(s):

07/31/1998   980731000375   AMENDMENT
(DOMESTIC   NOT   FOR   PROFIT)   AMENDMENT:
CORPORATION NAME , NATIONAL SUPERMARKETS
ASSOCIATION, INC. , AMENDMENT: COUNTY PRINCIPAL
OFFICE/   QUEENS ,   AMENDMENT: PURPOSE
,AMENDMENT: PROCESS ADDRESS , THE CORPORATION ,
17-20 WHITESTONE EXPRESSWAY , SUITE 302 ,
WHITESTONE, NY 11357

03/09/1990   C116566-6   INCORPORATION
(DOMESTIC NOT FOR PROFIT) ORIGIN : CORPORATION
NAME , NATIONAL SUPERMARKET ASSOCIATION, INC. ,
ORIGIN : COUNTY PRINCIPAL OFFICE/ NEW YORK ,
ORIGIN : DURATION/ PERPETUAL , ORIGIN : NOT-FOR-
PROFIT TYPE/ A ,ORIGIN : PROCESS ADDRESS , S/S THE
CORP , 125 EAST 116TH STREET , NEW YORK,

Rolando Florian Feliz who was living the life of luxury in
an alleged prison in the DR was suddenly killed while being visited
by two girlfriends, by a guard he allegedly tried to stab.

Inmate Shot at Prison in Dominican Republic Dies

SANTO DOMINGO – An inmate serving a 20-year sentence for drug
trafficking died on Sunday, hours after being shot four times by a Police Captain
who he tried to stab at the prison in Najayo, a town in the southern Dominican
Republic, officials said.

Rolando Florian Felix died at a hospital in Santo Domingo, prison
bureau director Manuel de Jesus Perez Sanchez said.

Capt. Lina de Oca Jimenez is being treated at the Police hospital in the capital for a face wound caused by a knife, Perez Sanchez said.

The incident is under investigation and Police re-enforcements have been sent to the maximum-security prison to bolster security, the prison bureau chief said.

The Police captain shot Florian Felix with his service pistol when the inmate got angry and attacked him for ordering a visitor to leave.

Florian Felix is the best-known drug trafficker doing time in the Dominican Republic, having served 14 years of his 20-year sentence for smuggling more than 900 kilos of cocaine into the country.

The drug trafficker had been fighting to win his release in recent years, contending that he is a model prisoner despite trying to escape at least five times.

A court tacked an additional six years onto Florian Felix's sentence after convicting him in a case involving the killing of a former senator's son.

http://www.laht.com/article.asp?ArticleId=335005&CategoryId=14092

I checked the PACER electronic Court system and found Simon Diaz was arrested for "Trading with the Enemy" wherein he made transactions involving Cuba. I checked with the informant to find out if it was the same Simon Diaz who was listed with a NADDIS number and also gave to the fundraiser held at Coogan's restaurant on September 19th, 1996 where the Vice President was caught on film in this photo:

"Yes, it's the same Simon Diaz" I was told. I asked myself:

"Why hasn't this donation been returned, or any of the others? Like the ones the Vice President gave back around the same time, in the China Gate scandal."

Now I was getting direct information fed to me from the Dominican Republic. The current head of the Dominican Revolutionary Party had told his party members he had hired a prominent Washington D.C Attorney to sue Flash and I for defaming Jose Francisco Pena Gomez.

I tracked large loads of cocaine being dropped in the Dominican Republic through a plane allegedly owned by persons connected to the CIA.
http://www.dominicantoday.com/dr/local/2009/6/8/32232/FBI-DEA-probe-2-engine-plane-in-Puerto-Platas-airport

I now tracked the transfers of this plane to the person who did the paperwork, a Paula Maeburn. Her name was on the paperwork as the person who did the transfer of the plane so many times with the funny tail number N1100M Funny how she kept showing up and lived at the same address in Oklahoma City where the title transfers took place and where Casa Aero was HDQT in Florida, which was partnered with NASA. With the budget the way it is today it made one wonder where NASA and SATS now http://www.INSDATS.org got all their money to support their programs. I mean the economy and all you know. However they were involved with a new program in concert with the "Joint Planning and Development Program Office" that just ended the CASA program but moved the SATs program to NASA Research. That link is here:
http://www.nasa.gov/centers/langley/news/factsheets/SATS.html

It was active but the program has shifted gears to the development of the X-48B.
http://www.nasa.gov/centers/langley/multimedia/iotw-x48c.html

This was only the beginning of the nexus from the streets of Philly's Badlands to the possibility of illicit funding of newly designed aircrafts from *not so new* resources.

Of course this is just sheer speculation, from a street Narc and his partners who were ultimately plastered with the pejorative term "Bastard Squad", who just refused to *disappear*.

Stay tuned to this Station; the rats multiply, the tale widens and once again the facts outweigh the innuendo.

***

Appendix

Philadelphia Police Highway Patrol

Bravery Award

Bravery Awards

Bravery Award

Bravery Award

FOP Award

3 Line Squad

Officer dragged by truck

By Thomas J. Gibbons Jr.
Inquirer Staff Writer

A Philadelphia highway patrol officer clung to a stolen pickup truck and was dragged nearly a block yesterday afternoon before squeezing off a shot from his service revolver that wounded the driver and halted the vehicle, detectives said.

Officer John McLaughlin and his partner, William Gallagher, were patrolling in an unmarked car in the 4000 block of North Seventh Street about 2 p.m. when they observed the truck, which had been reported stolen a short time earlier, detectives said.

With Gallagher at the wheel, the officers followed the truck until it halted for a stop sign at Seventh Street and Roosevelt Boulevard in Hunting Park, where they stopped beside it. Leaving the passenger door open, McLaughlin got out and approached the driver of the truck, detectives said.

The man at the wheel of the truck started the vehicle forward, and McLaughlin grabbed the side of the truck. Banging into the open door of his own police cruiser as the truck sped passed, McLaughlin was dragged nearly a block before he fired his gun, wounding the driver in the left hip, detectives said.

The driver of the truck was identified as Michael Hope, 22, of the 3900 block of North Darien Street in Hunting Park. He was admitted to Metropolitan Hospital, Parkview Division, where he was reported in stable condition last night. Hope was charged with aggravated and simple assault, recklessly endangering another person, resisting arrest, theft, receiving stolen property and unauthorized use of a motor vehicle.

McLaughlin, a 12-year Police Department veteran, was treated at the same hospital for a back injury and was released.

Boosted Truck Gives Him 'Lift' By Jack McGuire

Daily News Staff Writer

Highway Patrol Officer John McLaughlin made like a Hollywood stunt man yesterday to collar a suspected truck thief.

McLaughlin was trying to arrest the driver of a stolen truck on 7th Street near Roosevelt Boulevard when the truck suddenly pulled out, with the officer hanging on, Police said.

The officer was slammed against his. parked patrol car, but managed to get his service revolver out. He shot the suspect in the hip, and the truck came to a stop.

McLaughlin, a 12-year veteran of the force, and the suspect , Michael Hope, 19, of Darien Street near Luzerne, were taken to the Parkview Division of Metropolitan Hospital.

Hope was admitted in stable condition. The officer was treated for a back injury and released.

Police said McLaughlin and his partner, William Gallagher, spotted the truck shortly after 2 p.m. on 7th Street near Luzerne. It had just been reported stolen.

The officers pulled the truck over on 7th Street near Roosevelt Boulevard, and McLaughlin went to the driver's side and asked for identification. When the truck pulled out suddenly, McLaughlin was hanging on

Convicted Criminal Michael Hope

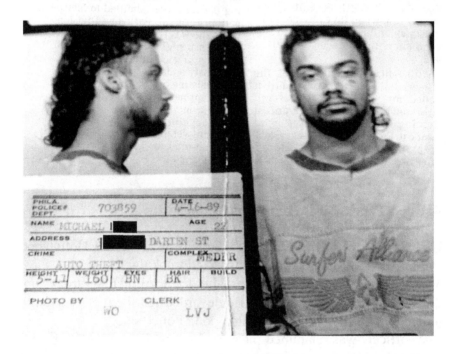

SOG Team

FOP Unit Citation Award

Gun Confiscation from Third St.

Kilo of cocaine and weapons confiscation

Seven kilos of cocaine and two heroin kilos plus thousands in cash

Over 30 weapons confiscation from one house

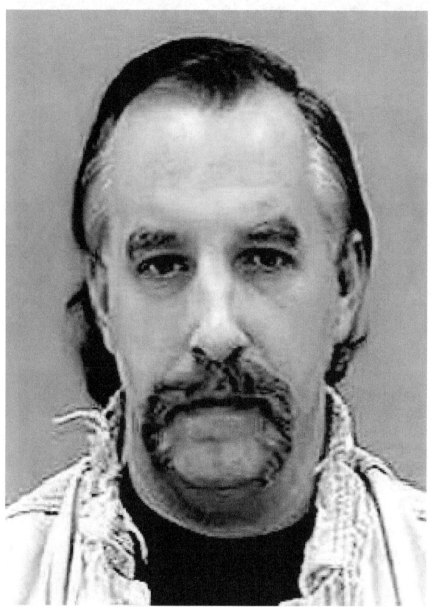

Sparky Plainclothes Circa 1995

Vice-President Al Gore and Drug Smuggler Jorge Cabrera

Credit: Reuters

First Lady Hillary Clinton and Drug Smuggler Jorge Cabrera

Credit: Softwar.net

ORLANDO SENTINEL
LOCAL

Democrats Return $20,000 Donation From Trafficker
October 20, 1996

Already under fire from Republicans for accepting big contributions linked to foreign interests, the Democratic National Committee has returned a $20,000 political contribution from a convicted Miami cocaine smuggler. Democratic National Committee spokeswoman Amy Weiss Tobe said Saturday that the party was unaware until last week that the contributor, Jorge Cabrera, had been arrested after making the donation and is in prison serving a 19-year sentence. 'We never accept money that's been gotten illegally," Tobe said.

Clinton Donor-Drug Smuggler Fingered Castro
by Carl Limbacher

Seldom has an American president behaved as solicitously toward Cuban dictator Fidel Castro as Bill Clinton has during the Elian Gonzalez fiasco. But for Castro, it's not the first time this particular American president has bent over backwards.
"A US drug investigation targeting Fidel Castro's regime was dropped because two sources told prosecutors the key informant orchestrated lies about Cuban government involvement," reported The Miami Herald in November 1996.
The informant? None other than Cuban drug smuggler Jorge Cabrera, who a year before had written a $20,000 check to the Democratic National Committee days after he was tapped for a contribution in Havana. Within a month of his donation Cabrera was dining with Vice President Al Gore in Miami and being feted by Bill and Hillary at the White House.

News of Cabrera's donation came out only after he was put on trial for his coke smuggling. In January 1996, the Clinton supporter was caught in Miami by the DEA, which nabbed him with three tons (yes, tons) of cocaine and 30 boxes of Cuban cigars.

m. 7 of

American Federation of State, County and Municipal Employees • AFL-CIO
4031 Executive Park Drive, Harrisburg, PA 17111-1599
(717) 564-9312 • 1-800-5-AFSCME

November 17, 1997

Bruce Sarteschi, Chief of Personnel
Office of the Attorney General
Personnel Section
14th Floor, Strawberry Square
Harrisburg, PA 17120

Re: John McLaughlin

Dear Mr. Sarteschi:

     This will confirm our telephone discussion of November 17th with regard to John McLaughlin, wherein you advised me that you "stand behind the letter" that was given to Mr. McLaughlin, dated November 17, 1997 from David J. Kwait, advising that Mr. McLaughlin's failure to report to the Greensburg Regional Office by 3:00 p.m. on November 18, 1997 "will constitute insubordination and result in your immediate termination from employment with the Office of the Attorney General." Mr. McLaughlin tells me that he specifically asked his superiors in Philadelphia if that included his use of sick time as a result of his injury and scheduled doctor's appointment. He was advised that it did.

     Mr. McLaughlin has been under physician's care as the result of a November 1996 accident, as you are well aware. Mr. McLaughlin tells me he advised his superiors of his doctor's appointment for tomorrow morning, as well as the fact that his father, who had a heart attack on Saturday, has now been scheduled for surgery on November 18, 1997. In addition, Mr. McLaughlin has been advised by his physician that, under no circumstances, should he drive for five hours straight.

     I advised you of Mr. McLaughlin's health problems and the fact that the collective bargaining agreement allows his use of sick time, and provides for the employer's ability to verify the circumstances surrounding use of that sick time under certain conditions. You agreed. I asked for your confirmation that the Kwait correspondence did not mean that Mr. McLaughlin would be terminated if he called off sick. You said you would not give me that confirmation. You said that the decision was out of your hands.

Edward J. Keller
Executive Director

Harry Pallott
President

Barbara Widner
Secretary

James Byrnes
Treasurer

VICE PRESIDENTS
Timothy McIntyre
DC-83

Randy Rush
DC-84

Kathy Garin
DC-85

Jamaal Husam
DC-86

Ann Marie Krantz
DC-87

Phyllis Wingate
DC-88

Bonnie Marpoe
DC-89

Lenora Wilbon
DC-90

Steven D. Shaffer
State

William Dickson
City

Velma Prather
County

Georgi Galen
School District

Ted Bowers
*Other Political
Sub-Divisions*

As a result of his fear that he will lose his job by taking advantage of his contractual rights, against the advice of his physician, and in spite of his concern that his father may not survive this operation, Mr. McLaughlin has advised me that he will be driving to Greensburg tomorrow as he has been ordered to do. He cannot afford to be without a salary while the wheels of justice slowly turn. These threats and intimidating tactics are flagrant violations of the contract and of the law. I find your attitude and actions toward Mr. McLaughlin outrageous.

Very truly yours,

Karen L. Black
Assistant to the Executive Director

KLB:dme

cc: Michael Fox
       David J. Kwait

Central Intelligence Agency

Washington, D.C. 20505

JUL 07 1999

Mr. John R. McLaughlin
Pa. Office of Attorney General
Regulatory Compliance & Intelligence Section
7801 Essington Avenue
Philadelphia, Pennsylvania 19153

Reference: F-1999-00735

Dear Mr. McLaughlin:

This acknowledges receipt of your 23 March 1999 letter requesting records under the provisions of the Freedom of Information Act (FOIA). Specifically, your request is for records pertaining to:

> **"the investigation into [Jose Francisco] Pena Gomez' and his Party (Revolutionary Dominican Party) illegal narcotics activities."**

For identification purposes we have assigned your request the number referenced above. Please refer to this number in future correspondence.

The CIA can neither confirm nor deny the existence or nonexistence of records responsive to your request. Such information--unless it has been officially acknowledged--would be classified for reasons of national security under Executive Order 12958. The fact of the existence or nonexistence of such records would also relate directly to information concerning intelligence sources and methods. The Director of Central Intelligence has the responsibility and authority to protect such information from unauthorized disclosure in accordance with Subsection 103(c)(6) of the National Security Act of 1947 and Section 6 of the CIA Act of 1949. Therefore, your request is denied under FOIA exemptions (b)(1) and (b)(3); an explanation of these exemptions is enclosed.

Office of the Attorney General

Washington, D.C. 20530

February 11, 1982

Honorable William J. Casey
Director
Central Intelligence Agency
Washington, D.C. 20505

Dear Bill:

Thank you for your letter regarding the procedures governing the reporting and use of information concerning federal crimes. I have reviewed the draft of the procedures that accompanied your letter and, in particular, the minor changes made in the draft that I had previously sent to you. These proposed changes are acceptable and, therefore, I have signed the procedures.

I have been advised that a question arose regarding the need to add narcotics violations to the list of reportable non-employee crimes (Section IV). 21 U.S.C. §874(h) provides that "[w]hen requested by the Attorney General, it shall be the duty of any agency or instrumentality of the Federal Government to furnish assistance to him for carrying out his functions under [the Controlled Substances Act] . . ." Section 1.8(b) of Executive Order 12333 tasks the Central Intelligence Agency to "collect, produce and disseminate intelligence on foreign aspects of narcotics production and trafficking." Moreover, authorization for the dissemination of information concerning narcotics violators to law enforcement agencies, including the Department of Justice, is provided by sections 2.3(c) and (i) and 2.6(b) of the Order. In light of these provisions, and in view of the fine cooperation the Drug Enforcement Administration has received from CIA, no formal requirement regarding the reporting of narcotics violations has been included in these procedures. We look forward to the CIA's continuing cooperation with the Department of Justice in this area.

In view of our agreement regarding the procedures, I have instructed my Counsel for Intelligence Policy to circulate a copy which I have executed to each of the other agencies covered by the procedures in order that they may be signed by the head of each such agency.

Sincerely,

William French Smith
Attorney General

The Director of Central Intelligence

Washington, D.C. 20505

OGC 82-02197

2 March 1982

Honorable William French Smith
Attorney General
Department of Justice
Washington, D.C. 20530

Dear Bill:

Thank you for your letter of 11 February regarding the
procedures on reporting of crimes to the Department of
Justice, which are being adopted under Section 1-7(a) of
Executive Order 12333. I have signed the procedures, and am
returning the original to you for retention at the
Department.

I am pleased that these procedures, which I believe
strike the proper balance between enforcement of the law and
protection of intelligence sources and methods, will now be
forwarded to other agencies covered by them for signing by
the heads of those agencies.

With best regards,

Yours,

William J. Casey

Enclosure

March 23rd, 1999

Drug Enforcement Administration
Freedom of Information Section
John H. Phillips, Chief
FOI Section Room W-6060 LP-2
Washington, D.C. 20537

Dear Sir,

     Pursuant to a lawful investigation, which I initiated on October 20th, 1995, I am requesting under the Freedom of Information Act, any reports, memorandum or any other information regarding the following Drug Enforcement Administration case numbers:

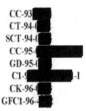

CC-93
CT-94-
SCT-94-
CC-95-
GD-95-
C1-   -I
CK-96-
GFC1-96-

     Thank you in advance for your anticipated cooperation in furtherance of my investigation.

John R McLaughlin

Agent John R. McLaughlin NA II / Intell.
Pennsylvania Office of Attorney General
Bureau of Narcotics Investigation
Regulatory Compliance and Intelligence
7801 Essington Ave.
Phila., Pa. 19153

(215) 937-1300
(215) 937-1342 FAX

U.S. Department of Justice

United States Attorney
Southern District of New York

The Silvio J. Mollo Building
One Saint Andrew's Plaza
New York, New York 10007

March 26, 1996

Carlo ▮▮▮▮
Special Agent In Charge
Drug Enforcement Administration
New York Field Division
99 Tenth Avenue
New York, New York 10011

      Re: Investigation ▮▮▮▮ *DOMINICAN REVOLUTIONARY PARTY*
           (File Name: Bernardo) ▮▮

Dear Mr. ▮▮▮

    This letter will advise you and the DEA Sensitive Activities
Review Committee that Assistant Special-Agent-In-Charge Donald
▮▮▮ and Special Agents Harry ▮▮▮ and Richard ▮▮▮▮ have
briefed us on the status of the above-referenced matter and the
present investigative plan. In addition, we are making
arrangements through Mr. ▮▮▮ promptly to interview certain
material witnesses. As we indicated earlier in the day to Mr.
▮▮▮ by telephone, this Office will support significant
prosecutable federal cases derived from the investigation.

          Very truly yours,

          MARY JO WHITE
          United States Attorney

Att.

cc: Shirah Neiman,
     Deputy United States Attorney
   Guy ▮▮▮
     Chief, Narcotics Unit

COMMONWEALTH OF PENNSYLVANIA
OFFICE OF ATTORNEY GENERAL
June 10, 1997

SUBJECT: Philadelphia Narcotics Agents

would McCaffrey be treated differently?
Did Civil Div. give us a formal opinion

TO: Gerald J. Pappert
First Deputy Attorney General

FROM: Bruce J. Sarteschi
Chief of Personnel

You had asked me to provide options regarding the actions that could be taken under the Collective Bargaining Agreement to address the situation concerning the four Philadelphia Narcotics Agents.

It is highly unlikely that an arbitrator would uphold the termination of these agents because of the information contained in Chief Deputy Attorney General Eric Noonan's memorandum. We also have a timeliness problem since disciplinary actions should be administered within a reasonable time of the knowledge of the event giving rise to the discipline. The allegations against these agents were brought to the attention of OAG officials well over a year ago and no additional information has surfaced. Also, please review the attached copies of the most recent performance evaluations of these agents.

The Collective Bargaining Agreement provides that an inter-city permanent transfer shall be made by agreement between the employee and the employer. Therefore, we cannot unilaterally transfer these agents to other regional offices.

The following are courses of action that are available:

Ryan/Kwait checking

1) Assign the agents to conduct pharmacy inspections. It is my understanding that this is virtually an administrative function that rarely involves any criminal investigative work. If any criminal investigative work is necessary, it could easily be given to another agent. The agents could be reassigned to work out of an office at our 12th Street location and receive their assignments from the Agent-in-Charge of the compliance program in Harrisburg. I have been told that we have a backlog in the pharmacy inspection program.

NO 2) Meet with these agents and the Union and try to negotiate reassignments to the Norristown Office or to another Division in Philadelphia.

3) Reassign these agents to our 12th Street location and have them perform CHRIA assignments. This would necessitate their reclassification to Special Agents. The agents could file grievances alleging that the reassignments were disciplinary actions. Our position could be that since the agents were no longer productive employees, the reassignments were the best course of action for all concerned.

Can we at least arguably fire them - need legal opinion

4) Terminate the employment of these agents. We could argue that the agents are no longer productive employees and their continued employment would create a detrimental effect on the reputation and public image of the Office of Attorney General. However, I do not recommend this course of action.

Attachments
cc: L. Kinch Bowman

① BNI Essington

① Transfers
② Buy-out packages

→ Break up
move to 3 separate offices
Tight leash / supervision
Write up frequently
Tell them their careers as investigators / street
are over

→ CHRIA
Intelligence

Memo to each of the files. CC <u>Union</u>
① Here's why you're being moved
② Here's what we expect going forward from
you

④

∴ If we don't get any workable information, our best option is to break them up and transfer them around.

Talk again to Sam - How much is enough?

✱ Eggles - *Retired* (Disability Retirement) off our
payroll + no longer an employee of OAG ‽

Tuesday, July 29   Change Regions?

GSP   Co   McLaughlin   Macauslei
Lou Rovelli   McKafrey

4 Amigos (3? Eggles been given disability retirement?)

United States Senate
SELECT COMMITTEE ON INTELLIGENCE
WASHINGTON, DC 20510-6475

November 4, 1996

SSCI #96-3847

The Honorable Thomas W. Corbett, Jr.
Attorney General
State of Pennsylvania
16th Floor, Strawberry Square
Harrisburg, Pennsylvania 17120

Dear Mr. Corbett:

I am writing to request that Mr. John R. McLaughlin, a narcotics agent in your office, be permitted to meet with the staff of the Senate Select Committee on Intelligence to discuss the case of the Dominican Revolutionary Party, case number 90021-96. I also request that Mr. McLaughlin be allowed to furnish to the Committee pertinent documentation relating to this case at that time.

Thank you in advance for your cooperation in this matter.

Sincerely,

Charles Battaglia
Staff Director

UNITED STATES OF AMERICA

Congress of the United States

To __John McLaughlin__

__c/o Criminal Law Division, 16th Floor, Strawberry Square__

__Harrisburg, PA 17120__ , Greeting:

Pursuant to lawful authority, YOU ARE HEREBY COMMANDED to appear before the __Select__ Committee on __Intelligence__ of the Senate of the United States, on __December 19__ , 19 __96__ , at __2:00__ o'clock __p.__ m., at their committee room __219 Hart__ __Senate Office Bldg., Washington, D.C. 20510__ , then and there to testify what you may know relative to the subject matters under consideration by said committee,

__and to produce any and all documents and all computer disks__ __containing documents, regardless of format, in your care, custody,__ __or control that refer, reflect, or relate in any manner to the__ __allegations you have presented to the Committee__

Hereof fail not, as you will answer your default under the pains and penalties in such cases made and provided.

To __any agent of the United States Senate__ to serve and return.

Given under my hand, by order of the committee, this __17th__ day of __December__ , in the year of our Lord one thousand nine hundred and __ninety-six__.

_____

Select
Chairman, Committee on __Intelligence__

Tuesday, July 10, 1945   THE STARS AND STRIPES

44th Inf. Div. Set to Sail on The Elizabeth

By Wade Jones
Stars and Stripes Staff Writer

LE HAVRE, July 9 — The 44th Inf Div, which fought from D-Day in Normandy to the war's end in Germany, was on its next-to-last lap home today

Ten percent overstrength, and numbering more than 15,000 men, the division was to set sail soon for America on the Queen Elizabeth from a port in the UK. The 44th was ferried to Southampton last week.

On the high seas already is the 87th Inf Div, which sailed directly from Le Havre Thursday on the West Point, formerly the America. The 34,000-ton West Point had to be loaded from small craft as it lay at anchor in midstream. About 7,600 men of the 343rd, 344th, 345th and 347th Regts of the 87th and Hq companies of the 5th Eng Special Brigade and the Fifth Corps sailed.

The 346th Regt. shipped on another vessel July 4.

Indirect routing of troops scheduled to sail for the U.S. on larger

Navy Experts Learn What Makes Baka Bomb Tick

Experts at the Naval Aircraft Modification Unit at Johnsville, Pa., examine a 20-foot Baka bomb found intact on Okinawa. Left to right: Lt. Comdr. Walter Chewing, Ambler, Pa.; Art 1cl Roger Jackson, Long Beach, Cal. in cockpit; Lt. Wilson Prichett Jr. Haverford, Pa., and Comdr. Charles E. Kirkbridge, Collingswood, N.J. In spite of the nickname Yanks have given the Baka (stupid) bomb, ordnance men assert the Jap piloted suicide plane is one of the most accurate ever developed.

Lt. Wilson Prichett in Cockpit

AGENT JOHN MC LAUGHLIN - 2 - PERFORMANCE EVALUATION PERFORMANCE
PROBATIONARY
02-95/02-96

Agent Mc Lauglin has been assigned to the Region 9 Office since February, 1995. During his probationary period he has demonstrated that he is a highly self-motivated, very dependable, loyal and very competent agent.

Agent Mc Laughlin's initiative has made him one of this Region's most active Narcotic Agent. The quality and quantity of the work he performs is excellent. Since his assignment to Region 9 he has made numerous arrests resulting in the seizures of large quantities of drugs and money.

Agent Mc Laughlin's work habits are excellent. He accepts all assignments given to him willingly and completes them in a professional manner.

Agent Mc Laughlin gets along well with his co-workers and other law enforcement personnel he comes in contact with while performing his duties.

With continued effort on his part, Agent Mc Laughlin will be one of the most productive agents in this Region and for years to come bring credit to himself and the agency as a whole.

Thank you for a job well done.

1-10-96

NARCOTIC AGENT IV

1/10/96

REGIONAL DIRECTOR

1-11-96

AGENT JOHN MC LAUGHLIN
NARCOTIC AGENT II

-2-

JOHN MCLAUGHLIN
PERFORMANCE EVALUATION
FEBRUARY 96/ FEBRUARY 97

As a result of circumstances which are beyond the control of Agent McLaughlin, he was unable to initiate any drug prosecutions during this rating period. Therefore, much of this evaluation is based on past performance.

I have always found Agent McLaughlin to be a dependable, competent employee, whose quality and quantity of work was superior. Agent McLaughlin's initiative in the enforcement of the drug laws has been instrumental to the success of BNI in Philadelphia.

In an effort to properly document this, Agent McLaughlin along with his partner Agent Micewski, in a period of one year, were responsible for confiscating over $3,579,343.00 in narcotics, approximately ½ million dollars in U.S. currency, thirty weapons, numerous cars, and 515 defendants were arrested.

In addition, Agent McLaughlin along with Agent Micewski's relentless and tenacious efforts were responsible for dealing a crushing blow to the Dominican heroin market which flourishes in Philadelphia.

Unfortunately, adverse legal opinions initiated by the District Attorney has been devastating to not only the Attorney General's Office and to the public we serve, but to Agent McLaughlin and his family as well.

Despite these circumstances, agent McLaughlin continues to do his newly assigned duties as Intelligence Officer with much enthusiasm.

The quality of his work, work habits, dependability, initiative and analytical ability, as was his work in narcotic enforcement, is excellent.
As Agent McLaughlin's supervisor, I never doubted his integrity and professionalism as a law enforcement officer.

It is my hope that justice will prevail and the good name of Agent McLaughlin, as well as that of BNI, will once again be restored to the standard of excellence.

3/14/97

Agent John McLaughlin
Narcotic Agent II

3-14-97

Michael Lutz
Asst. Regional Director

3-18-97

Regional Director

Don Bailey,

Enclosed find assorted documents that should be of value to our cause. I am also forwarding you a list (below) of community activist that will back up the work we did and that they want us back.

The statistics below are also what the task force was responsible for until the "powers" shut down our office.

Port Richmond on Patrol—	Mary Bannis	Phone	93
Community of United Neighbors Against Drugs - Mariam Colon		Phone " 22	7
Mantua Against Drugs	Herman Rice	Phone " 22	6
Tackawanna Against Drugs	Peggy Hoch	Phone " 83	8
United Neighbors Against Drugs	Sister Keck	Phone " 426	
United Neighbors Concerned Town Watch	Roseanne Rivera	Phone " 2	
Kensington Interrupting Drug Sales	Eleanor Maenner	Phone "	
Vietnam Vets Against Drugs	Richard Montgomery Phone "	
Tacony Town Watch	Mary Cianci	Phone " 3	
Wadsworth Against Drugs	Greg Wicks	Phone "	

* Mike Lutz (who was our immediate supervisor) was the main contact with these groups

Statistics on Task force until shut down

4,232 Arrests

Confiscated:

      929 Lbs Cocaine
      8,289 lbs Marijuanna
      42 Lbs Methamphetamine
      74 Lbs Crack Cocaine
      32.5 lbs Heroin
      16.5 Gals Hashish Oil
      16 Gal P2P
      7 Methamphetamine Laboratories

      These drugs are estimated at $70,000,000.00 Street value

      400 Weapons
      267 Vehicles
      Just under $5,000,000.00 in Cash
      Millions in Real Estate

COMMONWEALTH OF PENNSYLVANIA
OFFICE OF ATTORNEY GENERAL
November 3, 1992

ERNEST D. PREATE, JR.
ATTORNEY GENERAL

Reply To:

16th Floor, Strawberry Square
Harrisburg, Pennsylvania 17120
(717) 783-2600

John McLaughlin, Patrol Officer
Highway Patrol, Special Patrol Bureau
Office of Attorney General - Region IX
7801 Essington Avenue
Philadelphia, Pennsylvania 19153

Dear John:

I would like to take this opportunity to personally thank you for your informative presentation at our recent Drug Interdiction Training Seminar.

The professional skills, abilities and expertise that you displayed during your lecture on <u>Patrol Investigations</u> will, I am sure, benefit the law enforcement officers that were in attendance.

I am aware of the time it takes to prepare such a thorough presentation, and I want you to know how much I appreciate your efforts.

Thank you.

Sincerely,

David R.
Agent-in-Charge
Drug Interdiction Unit

DRF:pma

Full Name, Mailing Address & Zip Code

		day, year)	Receipt this period
Jose R. Hidalgo P.O Box 1603 West New York, NJ 07093	Occupation Requested	09/19/96	1000.00
Receipt for: [X] Primary [ ] General [ ] Other (specify)	Aggregate Year To Date > $ 1000.00		
Miguel Hierro 70 Haven Aven #2b New York, NY 10032	Occupation Requested	09/19/96	1000.00
Receipt for: [X] Primary [ ] General [ ] Other (specify)	Aggregate Year To Date > $ 1000.00		

Full Name, Mailing Address & Zip Code

	name of employer		day, year)	Receipt this period
Pablo Espinal 975 Nostrand Avenue Brooklyn, NY 11225	Associated Supermarket Occupation President		09/19/96	2000.00
Receipt for: [X] Primary [ ] General [ ] Other (specify)	Aggregate Year To Date > $ 2000.00			
Juan R. Espinal 24100 Ocean Crest Blvd. Far Rockaway, NY 11691	Los Tramos Meat Market Occupation General Manager		09/19/96	1000.00
Receipt for: [X] Primary [ ] General [ ] Other (specify)	Aggregate Year To Date > $ 1000.00			

		day, year)	Receipt this period
Simon Diaz 615 West 186th Street Apt. 2-J New York, NY 10033	Occupation Requested	09/19/96	1000.00
Receipt for: [X] Primary [ ] General [ ] Other (specify)	Aggregate Year To Date > $ 1000.00		
Francisco De La Rosa 149-10 85th St. Howard Beach, NY 11414	Occupation Requested	09/19/96	2000.00
Receipt for: [X] Primary [ ] General [ ] Other (specify)	Aggregate Year To Date > $ 2000.00		
Anselmo Almonte 1838 McGraw Ave. 5 Bronx, NY 10472	Occupation Requested	09/19/96	1000.00
Receipt for: [X] Primary [ ] General [ ] Other (specify)	Aggregate Year To Date > $ 1000.00		
Maximo Perez 149-35 120th Street Ozone Park, NY 11420	Occupation Requested	09/19/96	1000.00
Receipt for: [X] Primary [ ] General [ ] Other (specify)	Aggregate Year To Date > $ 1000.00		

Full Name, Mailing Address & Zip Code

Juan Nunez

, NY

	day, year	Receipt this period
	09/19/96	1000.00

Occupation
Requested

Receipt for: [X] Primary [ ] General
[ ] Other (specify)

Aggregate Year To Date> $ 1000.00

Full Name, Mailing Address & Zip Code

Miguel Hierro
70 Haven Aven   #2b
New York, NY 10032

	day, year	Receipt this period
	09/19/96	1000.00

Occupation
Requested

Receipt for: [X] Primary [ ] General
[ ] Other (specify)

Aggregate Year To Date> $ 1000.00

Jose R. Hidalgo
P.O. Box 1602
West New York, NJ 07083

	day, year	
	09/19/96	1000.00

Occupation
Requested

Receipt for: [X] Primary [ ] General
[ ] Other (specify)

Aggregate Year To Date> $ 1000.00

Full Name, Mailing Address & Zip Code

Oswald Torres

, NY

	day, year	Receipt this period
	09/19/96	1000.00

Occupation
Requested

Receipt for: [X] Primary [ ] General
[ ] Other (specify)

Aggregate Year To Date> $ 1000.00

NAME OF ACTIVITY OR EVENT

Coogan's

| | | 59 | 41 |

ACTIVITY IS: [X] FUNDRAISING [ ] EXEMPT [ ] DIRECT CANDIDATE SUPPORT
CHECK IF THE RATIO IS: [X] NEW [ ] REVISED [ ] SAME AS PREVIOUSLY REPORTED

FULL NAME, ADDRESS, ZIP CODE

Coogan's Restaurant
4015 Broadway
New York, NY

Food & Bevera	@ Coogan's	09/16/96	2000.00
A010			
		1,150.00	82

CATEGORY: ADMINIS/VOTER X FUNDRAISING EXEMPT
EVENT YEAR-TO-DATE: $ 2000.00 DIRECT CAND SUP

FULL NAME, ADDRESS, ~~ZIP CODE~~ ~~PURPOSE/EVENT~~
Melissa Kay Cohen | Photographer | | | |
176 East 71st Street, #5A | | 09/19/96 | 433.09 | 142.92 | 290.1
New York, NY 10021 | A012 | | | |

CATEGORY: X ADMINIS/VOTER   FUNDRAISING   EXEMPT
EVENT YEAR-TO-DATE: $ 694278.16   DIRECT CAND. SUP

FULL NAME, ADDRESS, ZIP CODE | PURPOSE/EVENT | | | |
Coogan's Restaurant | Food & Bevera | | | |
4015 Broadway | ge Coog--s Evnt | 09/19/96 | 72.00 | |
New York, NY | A010 | | 42.48 | 29.

CATEGORY: ADMINIS/VOTER X FUNDRAISING   EXEMPT
EVENT YEAR-TO-DATE: $ 2072.00   DIRECT CAND. SUP

---

		day, year	Receipt this per
Ramon Luis Mart Abreu, M.D., P.C. 454 Washington Avenue New York, NY 10003	*Sp* Occupation *Doctor*	10/21/96	1000.00
Receipt for: |X| Primary		General |	Other (specify)	Aggregate Year To Date> $ 1000.00		

		day, year	Receipt this peri
Jose Contreras , NY	*Requested* Occupation	10/21/96	1000.00
Receipt for: |X| Primary	|X| General |	Other (specify)	Aggregate Year To Date> $ 1000.00		

	Cras Ousquoya	day, year	Receipt this period
Francisco De La Rosa 149-' 0 85th St. Howard Beach, NY 11414	Occupation Co-owner	10/21/96	300.00
Receipt for: |X| Primary		General |	Other (specify)	Aggregate Year To Date> $ 2300.00		

Full Name, Mailing Address & Zip Code	Name of Employer Cras Ousquoya	Date/month day, year	Amount of Each Receipt this period
Francisco De La Rosa 149- 0 85th St. Howard Beach, NY 11414	Occupation Co-owner	10/21/96	300.00
Receipt for: |X| Primary		General |	Other (specify)	Aggregate Year To Date> $ 2600.00		

Full Name, Mailing Address & Zip Code	Name of Employer	Date (month, day, year)	Amount of Each Receipt this por
Pablo Espinal 975 Nostrand Avenue Brooklyn, NY 11225	Associated Supermarket	10/21/96	3000.00
Receipt for: [X] Primary [ ] General [ ] Other (specify)	Occupation President Aggregate Year To Date > $ 5000.00		
Full Name, Mailing Address & Zip Code Juan R. Espinal 24100 Ocean Crest Blvd. Far Rockaway, NY 11591	Name of Employer Los Bremos Meat Market	Date (month, day, year) 10/21/96	Amount of Each Receipt this par 3000.00
Receipt for: [X] Primary [ ] General [ ] Other (specify)	Occupation General Manager Aggregate Year To Date > $ 4000.00		
Full Name, Mailing Address & Zip Code Jose Vazquez 4602 Park Avenue Apt.1 Weehawken, NJ 07087	Requested Occupation	10/21/96	Receipt this 5000.0
Receipt for: [X] Primary [ ] General [ ] Other (specify)	Aggregate Year To Date > $ 5000.00		

The November Group
1400 1ST NW
Washington, DC 20005   1,762.35   70,220.00   70,220.00   1,7

According to court documents, Davis, the part owner of the Washington based consulting firm, The November Group, learned in May or June 1996 about planned Teamsters donations to various Democratic campaigns and began trying to use the money as "a means to induce the DNC to raise money for the Carey campaign."

McAuliffe introduced Davis to his Clinton/Gore '96 finance aide, Hartigan, as a point person who could coordinate labor contributions, according to Senate documents.

http://www.washingtonpost.com/wp-srv/politics/special/campfin/stories/cf100997c.htm

NARCOTICS AGENTS REGIONAL COMMITTEE

Philadelphia, Pennsylvania 19148
215-350-7403

ennsylvar

OᵖLodge #

VICE PRESIDENT (CENTRAL)
▬▬

VICE PRESIDENT (WEST)

VICE PRESIDENT (EAST)
▬▬

CHIEF TRUSTEE
▬▬

REGIONAL TRUSTEES
▬▬

GRIEVANCE COORDINATOR
▬▬

October 6ᵗʰ, 2003

Senator Orrin G. Hatch
United States Senate
Committee on the Judiciary
224 Dirksen Senate Office Building
Washington, DC 20510

Phone: (202) 224-5225
Fax: (202) 224-9102

The Honorable Orrin G. Hatch,

My name is John R. McLaughlin. My partner, Charles A. Micewski, and I are Employed by the Pennsylvania Office of Attorney General as Narcotics Agents currently assigned to the Intelligence Unit. Our attorney, former Congressman Donald A. Bailey filed a Civil Rights First Amendment Retaliation Lawsuit against Pennsylvania Attorney General D. Michael Fisher and his top support Personnel. This action culminated in a Jury Verdict on 2-7-2003 with a $1.5 Million dollar verdict against D. Michael Fisher which included Punitive Damages. As you know, the Federal Judge decides if the facts warrant Punitive Damages and instructs the Jury accordingly.

The appeal is still ongoing and is before the Third Judicial Circuit, amazingly enough this is where D. Michael Fisher is seeking appointment.

On October 3ʳᵈ, 2003 I was contacted by David Brog of Senator Spector's Office and was told that he was making the recommendation that we be called to testify at the upcoming hearing October 14ᵗʰ, 2003. I informed him that we require a Subpoena as the last time I was called to testify before the Senate Select Committee on Intelligence, I was ordered not to go.

We are therefore requesting as per Senator Spector's recommendation, that we be Subpoenaed to testify at the Nomination for D. Michael Fisher. As time is short, I am faxing this request and will follow with the hardcopy. Our Contact information is as follows:

John R. McLaughlin
▬▬

Office Fax : (215) 937-1342

Charles A. Micewski
▬▬

CC: Senator Arlen Spector
        Donald A. Bailey, Esq.

Again the same references by the Phila. First Assistant District Attorney and another Assistant District Attorney : On December 9th, 1996 in Phila Criminal Justice Center Courtroom 902 before the Honorable Myrna Field, Phila. First Assistant District Attorney Arnold Gordon is forever memorialized on the record as saying *"I want to make one further point with regard to McLaughlin and McKeefery since their names have been mentioned on a number of occasions, in fairness to them. Neither of those two officers have been convicted of any crime. Neither of them has , to my understanding, admitted that they purposely lied in either of the two search warrants. In fact, it has come to me indirectly that their explanation was that they didn't, that it was a mistake."*

In the same proceeding Arnold Gordon further states: *"What I'm saying is that the problem I forsee is that, although I've taken this action—I may be wrong and they may be right. In other words, I don't know that those officers lied in a search warrant. In fact, I may be unfairly stigmatizing them by the actions I've taken in these cases. I understand that. I made it on my best prosecutorial judgement."*
(Attachment 1 marked as Plaintiff Exb. 1)

Again, another Phila. Assistant District Attorney, Norman Gross, was in front of the Honorable Gary S. Glazer on September 16th, 1996 in Courtroom 1008 and stated on the record: *"Your Honor, if your question is, does the District Attorney's Office believe or have information to believe that Officer McLaughlin committed perjury, provable perjury in <u>any</u> of these cases, the answer is no."* He further states in the same hearing: *"If we have to explain every time we took action in a particular case, obviously the defense could completely stymie any <u>POLITICAL</u> — Any viable prosecution by forcing us to get up there and explain our tactical decisions."*
(Attachment 2 marked as Plaintiff Exb. 2)

O

272

PHILADELPHIA POLICE DEPARTMENT
COMPLAINT OR INCIDENT REPORT

YEAR	DIST./OCC.	D.C. NO.	SECT.	DIST.	VEH. NO.	REPORT DATE
1926	12817		6	613		3-10-98

CRIME OR INCIDENT CLASSIFICATION: Burglary 0507   TIME OUT 83   TIME IN

LOCATION OF OCCURRENCE: 1314 Chestnut St   ☐ IN ☐ OUT   TYPE OF PREM.

DATE OF OCCUR. 3-9-98   DAY CODE 1   TIME OF OCCUR. 8:45 P   NATURE OF INJURY

	AGE	RACE	SEX	PHONE (HOME)

314 Chestnut S.

FOUNDED: ☐Yes ☐No   REPORT TO FOLLOW: ☐Yes ☐No ☐Close Out   CODE   INV. CONT NO.

WITNESS: ☐Yes ☐No   TRACEABLE PROP.: ☐Yes ☐No   UNIQUE DESCRIPTION OF OFFENDER: ☐Yes ☐No   OTHER EVIDENCE: ☐Yes ☐No

DESCRIPTION OF INCIDENT:
Re Baig Report
Owner of Bldg

PROPERTY DESCRIPTION | PROP. CODE | INSURED ☐Yes ☐No | STOLEN VALUE $

location - Spt 6-A
PPc #613   (or location)
C.O. Notify + D. Sgt Motto
(Scene Held)

VEHICLE 1 — OWNERS NAME | VEHICLE 2 — OWNERS NAME
VEHICLE 1 — OPERATORS NAME | VEHICLE 2 — OPERATORS NAME

REPORT PREPARED BY   NO. 9733   DIST./UNIT 6   TOTAL PAGES 2   PAGE

U.S. Department of Justice

Michael R. Stiles
United States Attorney
Eastern District of Pennsylvania

615 Chestnut Street · Suite 1250
Philadelphia, Pennsylvania 19106-4476
(215) 451-5200

February 18, 1999

Michael R. Stiles, United States Attorney for the Eastern District of Pennsylvania, today announced that his office has closed its investigation of the conduct of agents of the Philadelphia office (Region IX) of the Pennsylvania Bureau of Narcotics Investigation (BNI). The matter was closed without the filing of criminal charges against any person. The investigation, which covered a period prior to 1996, has occasionally been the subject of news reports.

Because of recent inquiries from the media about the status of the investigation, the United States Attorney determined that a public announcement that the investigation had concluded was appropriate. Since the investigation did not result in the filing of criminal charges, no further comment about it is permissible under Justice Department standards.

Posted on Tue, Feb. 11, 2003

2 ex-narcs, transferred by Pa. after whistle-blowing, awarded $1.5M

By JIM SMITH
smithjm@phillynews.com

Two state narcotics agents who claimed they had been improperly transferred after complaining that the feds had allowed a CIA-backed drug dealer slip away have finally cleared their names.

In a big way.

A civil has awarded the agents, John R. "Sparky" Mc-Laughlin and Charles Micewski - both former Philly cops - a total of $1.5 million in damages.

The verdict, by a U.S. District Court jury in Wilkes-Barre on Friday, was based on claims filed against Pennsylvania Attorney General Mike Fisher and other state officials.

The agents, who were assigned to the state narcotics bureau's Philadelphia office, claimed the forced transfers - far from Phialdelphia - came after they complained that federal and state authorities had allowed a political candidate from the Dominican Republic, one the CIA was backing, to leave the United States in 1995 with about $500,000 in alleged drug profits disguised as political contributions.

After they complained of the CIA connection, federal and city authorities stopped prosecuting the agents' drug cases, and began investigating the agents for alleged misconduct.

"These guys weren't allowed to clear their names. Their investigations were scuttled. An investigation totally exonerated them...There was never a scintilla of evidence that they ever did anything wrong," said one of their attorneys, Don Bailey, of Harrisburg.

Fisher and the other defendants "essentially destroyed my clients' careers," in law enforcement, said the agents' trial lawyer, Samuel C. Stretton, of West Chester.

"All I want is my name...My father died not knowing that I got cleared," said McLaughlin, a Philadelphia cop for 17 ½ years who became a state drug-enforcement officer in 1995.

Fisher, along with his first deputy, Gerald J. Pappert, and his chief of investigations, David J. Kwait, a former FBI agent, were found liable for $1 million in "punitive" damages and for $425,000 in "actual" damages.

Another $75,000 in actual damages was assessed against two codefendants, James Caggiano, who heads the Bureau of Narcotics Investigations, and Bruce Sarteschi, BNI's human-resources director.

The defendants will appeal, a state spokesman said.

http://www.philly.com/mld/dailynews/news/local/5153281.htm?temp.../printstory.js 02/11/2003

Coming from an Irish-Catholic, blue collar family in southwest Philadelphia, I joined the Philadelphia Police Department in 1977, made the K-9 unit three years later,then the Philadelphia Highway Patrol Line Squad four years after that. I moved to the Office of the Attorney General's Bureau of Narcotics Investigations Task Force in 1992 while still with the PD, and finally putting my foot though the door in 1995 as a Narc. I was in their employ throughout the period covered in "Damned from Memory."

Made in the USA
Middletown, DE
20 August 2020